Portland Community College Library

WITHDRAWN

D0686601

Faith in the Market

Faith in the Market

Religion and the Rise of Urban Commercial Culture

Edited by
John M. Giggie and Diane Winston

Rutgers University Press

New Brunswick, New Jersey, and London

Library of Congress Cataloging-in-Publication Data
Faith in the market : religion and the rise of urban commercial culture /
edited by John M. Giggie and Diane Winston
p. cm.
Includes bibliographical referencs and index.
ISBN 0-8135-3098-9 (cloth : alk. paper) — ISBN 0-8135-3099-7 (pbk. : alk.
paper)
1. United States—Religion—19th century.   2. United States—
Commerce—History—19th century.   3. City and town life—United
States—History—19th century.   4. Cities and towns—Religious aspects—
History—19th century.   5. United States—Religion—20th century.
6. United States—Commerce—History—20th century.   7. City and town
life—United States—History—19th century.   8. Cities and towns—
Religious aspects—History—20th century.   I. Giggie, John Michael,
1965–   II. Winston, Diane H.
BX2505 .F35 2002
291.1'7'0973—dc21   2001058695

British Cataloging-in-Publication information is available from the British
Library.

This collection copyright © 2002 by Rutgers, The State University
For copyrights to individual pieces please see the Acknowledgments.
All rights reserved
No part of this book may be reproduced or utilized in any form or by any
means, electronic or mechanical, or by any information storage and retrieval
system, without written permission from the publisher. Please contact Rutgers University Press, 100 Joyce Kilmer Avenue, Piscataway, NJ 08854–8099.
The only exception to this prohibition is "fair use" as defined by U.S. copyright law.

Manufactured in the United States of America

For our families:
Marisa, Julia, Christian, and Alexandra
Chris, Sara, Erin, and Isabelle

Contents

Acknowledgments

Like so many successful ventures, this book has a complex and colorful back story. The direct inspiration for the volume was an invitation from David Goldfield, editor of the *Journal of Urban History*, to guest edit a special issue on religion and the city. Only a few years earlier, this charge would have been enough by itself for a groundbreaking collection, but several recent books had begun to explore this territory. Accordingly, we decided to complicate the directive by adding commercial culture to the mix and concentrating on life since the explosive growth of modern industrial capitalism in North America. Focusing on the interaction among religion, urbanization, and commercialization seemed to be a logical next step in understanding American culture and society. Our interest in commercial culture, as well as our decision to solicit participation from an interdisciplinary team of scholars, was a direct result of our work with Robert Wuthnow and our longtime association with the Center for the Study of Religion at Princeton University.

As we solicited essays for the journal, we quickly discovered we had hit pay dirt. This was a rich but just-beginning-to-be-explored topic that had attracted the attention of historians, religionists, Americanists, and sociologists also working in material culture, commodification, performance, and gender studies. Our next step, then, was to pursue a book project subsequent to the journal and to find a publisher that shared our vision. We were fortunate to find the requisite commitment from David Myers and Suzanne Kellam at Rutgers University Press.

In the process of assembling contributors and editing manuscripts for the book, we received help and encouragement from several key people. We would like to thank Robert Wuthnow, Leigh Schmidt, Jonathan Sarna, Don Miller, David Morgan, James Lewis, Jon Butler, Harry Stout, John McGreevey, Albert Raboteau, David Wills, Sean Wilentz, and James McPherson for their support. We are particularly grateful to the volume's contributors. Each one worked hard to make his or her essay a small gem and graciously acceded to suggestions, recommendations, and revisions. Finally, we would like to thank our families for the love and encouragement that made work on this collection possible.

The editors would like to thank the following publishers for permission to reprint material that appeared previously:

Diane Winston, "Living in the Material World: Salvation Army Lassies and Urban Commercial Culture, 1880–1918," and Roberto Lint Sagarena, "Building California's Past: Mission Revival Architecture and Regional Identity" appear in the *Journal of Urban History* 28, no. 4 (May 2002). Reprinted by permission of Sage Publications, Inc.

Fran Grace, "The Best Show in Town: Carry Nation and the Selling of Temperance in the Urban Northwest," draws on material in her *Carry Nation: Retelling a Life* (Bloomington: Indian University Press, 2001).

Judith Weisenfeld, "'Saturday Sinners and Sunday Saints': The Nightclub as Moral Menace in 1940s Race Movies," appears in modified form in *Through a Glass Darkly: On Religion, Race, and Gender in American Film, 1929–1950* (Berkeley and Los Angeles: University of California Press, 2002).

Melani McAlister, "Faith in the Nation: Black Islam and African American Cultural Politics, 1955–1970," appears in modified form in *Epic Encounters: Culture, Media, and U.S. Interests in the Middle East, 1945–2000* (Berkeley and Los Angeles: University of California Press, 2001). The epigraph to McAlister's essay, an excerpt from Amiri Baraka's "It's Nation Time," from *The LeRoi Jones/Amiri Baraka Reader* by Amiri Baraka (Copyright © 2000 by Amiri Baraka), is quoted by permission of the publisher, Thunder's Mouth Press.

Etan Diamond, "Beyond Borscht: The Kosher Lifestyle and the Religious Consumerism of Suburban Orthodox Jews," appears in modified form in *And I Will Dwell in Their Midst: Orthodox Jews in Suburbia* (Chapel Hill: University of North Carolina Press, 2000).

Faith in the Market

Introduction

John M. Giggie and Diane Winston

Hidden in Plain Sight

Religion and Urban Commercial Culture in Modern North America

For anyone curious about the development of urban religion during the past century, a walking tour of the downtown of any North American city might prove an important starting point. The simple task of physically locating a church, synagogue, or mosque would reveal how often they are nestled within a grocery store or above a clothing outlet, set in a bustling commercial strip, or housed in a refurbished theater. But religion's entanglement with commercial culture does not end there. It would not be unusual to see the faithful, acting with the full blessing of their leaders, purchase clothing that telegraphed their beliefs, buy household objects embodying their devotion, advertise their brand of salvation in newspapers, or use the airwaves to publicize their unique revelation. The lesson learned from this tour of the city would be plain: in urban areas, sacred life and commercial life are deeply intertwined.

This collection of essays explores the interplay of religion, commercial culture, and urbanization in North American cities since the 1880s. Drawing on a range of methodologies and sources, contributors study how members of urban houses of worship invented fresh expressions of religiosity and piety by incorporating consumer goods, popular entertainment, and techniques of advertising and marketing into their spiritual life. Others consider the ways in which society and culture drew on religious imagery for commercial purposes. The authors collectively argue that the rapid advance of industrial capitalism in North American cities from the late nineteenth century onward did not fuel a declension in religious devotion and practice, as many historians suggest, but rather a profound transformation, even flowering, of it. Key to revising the older scholarship and to reimagining the character of modern urban religions is the authors' shared conviction that commercial culture acts as a mediating space wherein men and women can confront the ambiguities of city life. Thus religion thrives not by avoiding the hallmarks of urban capitalism but by selectively appropriating aspects of it and nurturing a range of new spiritual identities ranging from Salvation Army "slum angels" to Orthodox Jewish suburbanites and from Christian Scientist captains of industry to Black Muslim artists.

Stated this boldly, our seminal claim sounds sensible but hardly radical. Yet it overturns long-held popular and scholarly assumptions about cities, religions, and commercialization. Cities, in contradistinction from the countryside, were sites of danger and excitement, where vice (a subjective designation for commercial culture) vanquished religion. Godly people, unable to compete against the lures of the flesh and snares of the soul, gave up physical and imaginative ground to atheists, secularists, and heathens. But while compelling and even dominant for more than a century, this narrative does not represent the lived experience of many city dwellers. It does, however, express the fears and frustrations of many white mainline Protestants who experienced both urbanization and the influx of Catholics, Jews, African Americans, and activist women as a rude jolt to what they perceived as the established social order.

Historically, Christians who enjoyed the greatest degree of power in cities tried to categorize and contain the changing urban landscape by labeling it immoral and irreligious. In their view, the city itself became suspect as newcomers and new commercial institutions multiplied and spread their contagion in the form of saloons, brothels, and the evils inherent to such establishments. "True" religion in the city became a contradiction in terms, and commercial culture was seen as the devil's playground. The case may not be stated so starkly today, but cities are still viewed as sites for worldly experience rather than as seedbeds for religious innovation. We contend that this view of the interaction between religion and the city really represents the reification of an older white Protestant perspective and obscures a vibrant urban religiosity that developed out of the give-and-take between faith commitments and commercial culture.

The notion that commercial culture is important to the study of religion and cities is, of course, not entirely novel. Ever since Max Weber, scholars have commented on the acquisitive behavior of America's religious groups, and it is difficult to find any historian who treats the rise of modern urban environments without paying attention to the role of consumption. But this volume of scholarship is distinctive in two significant ways. First, it insists that commercial culture lies at the heart of the evolution of both urban religion and of urbanization for people of different faiths. And, second, it argues that to examine religion and urban commercial culture apart from one another is to risk losing insight into the historical development of religious traditions and cosmopolitan cities.

Our challenge, then, is to change the way that people generally think about the relationship between religion, urbanization, and commercial culture. In the past, scholars have typically studied these in ways that divide each from the other two. Urban religion, for example, has been seen as epiphenomenal to the growth of cities—as a discrete category of analysis that supposedly had little direct bearing on how city dwellers lived their daily lives. Or religion and urban commercial culture have been viewed as opposing cultural forces, with religion functioning as a sanctuary and place of healing from the corrupting and degenerating influence of mammon.

During the last decade, continued interest in social history and concurrent explorations of urbanism and commercial culture have made it increasingly difficult for scholars working in these areas to ignore religion, a key factor for the production of meaning and identity. As a result, in addition to studies about the growth of urban commercial culture,[1] a wealth of work has illumined the role of religion in the city[2] and the nexus of religion and commercial culture.[3] Nevertheless, few works have focused on the intersection of all three.[4] This oversight is all the more striking since several new collections have focused either on religion in the city[5] or promised fresh understandings of religion in America by stressing novel categories of analysis, such as the lived practices of daily religion.[6]

The absence of significant scholarship on religion and urban commercial culture stems from several sources, not least of all an academic indifference, reflecting the twentieth century's fascination with material progress and scientific technology, to faith-based ideas and institutions. Religion was relegated to the province of backwater hicks and Bible-thumpers whose contribution to the world of ideas was to clarify what the intelligentsia rejected (thus there is plenty of scholarship on the Scopes trial, televangelism, and the Religious Right). Urban religion, however, seemed an oxymoron. From Weber's dicta on secularization to Harvey Cox's celebration of the secular city, the century's leading academics pronounced religion's passing, especially in the cosmopolitan centers. Many also accepted at face value the testimonies of nineteenth-century urban observers who recorded religion's demise without questioning the narrative stance of these earlier interlocutors. A look back at Thomas Dixon Jr.'s 1896 bestseller, *The Failure of Protestantism in New York and Its Causes*, is illustrative. Dixon, a moderate Social Gospel minister, offered a gloomy portrait of the mainline churches' failure to meet the spiritual and material needs of Manhattan's poor. Contemporaries echoed this assessment, and their writings colored subsequent scholarly appraisals.[7] The tone of these tomes, both primary sources and secondary accounts, suggested there was little to learn by studying the dismal plight of metropolitan congregations, which in ignoring poverty impoverished themselves.

Well, yes and no. While the trajectory of mainline Protestantism in American cities could be told as a cautionary tale, this declension is not the whole story of urban religion. The case was not exactly the same for evangelicals, Catholics, Jews, African Americans, and others. Both Robert Orsi and Tony Carnes mine stories of these groups in their new collections through (mostly) contemporary ethnographies that illustrate religion's range in city life. Happily, both collections reveal what previously had been hidden in plain sight: amid the urban cacophony, believers transform cityscapes into religious vistas. That their prayers and pilgrimages escaped notice for so long says more about the assumptions of those who missed this panoply of religious vitality than those who practiced it.

While the writers in the Orsi and Carnes collections document the extent, texture, and vibrancy of urban religion, few include an analysis of the influence of commercial culture on beliefs and behaviors. While scholars cannot be expected to cover all interpretative bases, overlooking the impact of commercialization—the processes through which everyday entertainment, consumer goods, leisure activities, branding, marketing, and advertising affect culture and society—is problematic in studies of the city, where it is a defining feature. Still, if explorations of urban religion are relatively new, studies of religion and commercial culture have an even shorter history, with the mid-1990s pioneering work of Laurence Moore and Leigh Schmidt serving as landmarks.[8] One explanation for the dearth of work may be a disinclination to entwine the two. Recollections of Jesus upbraiding the moneylenders leaves even the most biblically illiterate with the sense that Christianity, America's preeminent faith tradition, is not supposed to be of this world. The idea of religion in the marketplace, marketing itself or being marketed, is disquieting despite Moore's argument that religion and commerce have been commingled throughout much of human history and increasingly so in a democratic society where, once disestablished, religion needed to "sell" itself to survive.[9]

Accordingly, the study of religion and commercial culture is helpful for understanding American history in which disestablishment, urbanization, and the growth of the market are key features. And overcoming the queasiness about religion in the marketplace enables an appreciation of how a range of groups in different times and places used aspects of commercial culture to express varying degrees of discontent or delight with society and to stamp their own identity on the cityscape. The authors included in this volume, while representing various disciplines and drawing on distinctive methodologies, are united in the proposition that religion is an integral and necessary part of the story of how cities develop in North America. That story, moreover, is not one in which religion and commercial culture are pitted against each other but rather placed together in a sometimes volatile but surprisingly consistent embrace.

The essays that constitute this book are organized into three broad categories—evangelical experimentation, Protestant transformation, and minority adaptation—and arranged in rough chronological order within each group. The three sections, when viewed as a whole, are not intended to represent an exhaustive investigation into the topic but instead to serve as a series of bright spotlights illuminating little-noticed aspects of the historical relationship between commercial culture and city life. Each represents a series of methodologies and claims that underscore our commitment to study anew the contours of urban religion. First, the success of evangelical Christianity in founding and growing urban religious movements is directly related to the creative ability of its leaders to develop spiritual practices based on popular entertainment and to challenge traditional gender roles. Second, different groups of Protestants have long attempted to secure power and popularity among other urban denizens by borrowing new codes of architecture, personal adornment, and habits of reading straight from the everyday world of city commerce. And third, black Protestants, Black Muslims, Catholics, and Jews often negotiated their place and cultural identities in urban America by making use of the specific cultural tools provided by commercial culture, whether through film, fashion, architecture, or advertisement.

Part I. Evangelical Experimentation

During the 1880s and 1890s, Salvation Army "lassies," the popular sobriquet for female members of this evangelical movement, piqued public interest by regularly parading down New York City's streets. At other times, intent on saving souls, they bravely invaded even the most dangerous commercial enterprises. Protected by their plain blue uniforms, lassies presented themselves as desexualized beings, thus avoiding social proscriptions that limited what "proper" women could and could not do. In the opening essay, Diane Winston shows how the Salvation Army used the uniform to brand its workers and at the same time promote new possibilities for its female members. Forgoing fashion's dictates for respectable women, Salvationists slipped the bonds of conventional domesticity and gained access to "male" activities and urban spaces.

Like Winston, David Morgan is interested in shifting notions of gender and evangelical culture during the Progressive Era, but he focuses on male spiritual leaders who made use of an expanding commercial industry, namely the rise of mass-produced religious images, to make Christianity more masculine. In an age that was just discovering the widespread uses of advertising, urban evangelicals invested great hope in the power of inexpensive lithographs, engravings, postcards, and photographs to help them reinvigorate Christianity.

Morgan argues that urban revivalists, such as the hugely popular Billy Sunday, feared that industrialization limited men's ability to enjoy productive physical work and enticed them with effeminizing fantasies of rich clothes and luxurious fineries. Evangelical leaders strove to make religion more manly and appealing by inventing a visual culture in which they (and Jesus) were depicted as vigorous, virile, and aggressive. Thus Billy Sunday sold images of himself preaching in dramatic poses, published autobiographies that stressed his heroism, and, building on his baseball career, marketed himself as a celebrity sports hero.

Offering another perspective on the juncture of religion, gender, and urban commercial culture during the Progressive Era, Fran Grace turns to the urban Midwest and Northeast for her analysis of Carry Nation, the popular temperance leader and evangelical preacher. Grace suggests that Nation's transformation from a rural Kansas grandmother into a national crusader for the gospel of prohibition was due to her success at imitating the theatrics of vaudeville performers and tapping into a growing urban consumer market for religious primitivism. Effortlessly moving between religious and commercial stages, Nation delighted audiences by lamenting the sins of alcohol and then taking her hatchet to the nearest saloon. Her aggressive style invigorated urbanites yearning for a robust, rousing, and physical Christianity.

Rounding out this section is Terry Todd's study of the fundamentalist leader John Straton's attempt to save New York City from the sins of Jazz Age commercialism. Todd argues that, for Straton, modern commercial culture was an incubator of urban evil, found in ample abundance at dance halls, speakeasies, and amusement centers. But that same commercial culture also furnished Straton with tools for cleansing the city and boosting the popular appeal of fundamentalism. Straton dedicated the last years of his life, in the 1920s and early 1930s, to publicizing the message of fundamentalism through some of the most visible emblems of urban commercial culture. He used his automobile as a moving pulpit from which he preached to sidewalk crowds, he founded his own religious radio station, and he helped design a skyscraper church to symbolize evangelicalism's soaring urban presence. While Straton's ultimate success at establishing a fundamentalist beachhead in Manhattan is debatable, his effort to incorporate modern commercial culture into a religious crusade prefigured the work of later evangelicals.

Part II. Protestant Transformation

In the early twentieth century, some urban Protestants used commercial culture to create a sense of historical memory, others employed it to demonstrate their own significance as a religious group. Roberto Lint Sagarena offers an example of this process in the construction of the regional identity of southern California beginning in the late 1920s. After a devastating earthquake destroyed much of Santa Barbara, California, some residents saw a silver lining in the tragedy. Here was a chance to reconceive the city's built environment. Lint Sagarena shows that what evolved was a largely successful effort by white Protestants to create a city based on an imagined history of harmonious ecumenism and a romanticized dream of the state's Catholic Spanish past. By establishing public rituals that celebrated a peaceful and safe history of interracial contact, on the one hand, and by standardizing near-uniform codes of highly stylized Mission and Spanish Revival architecture, on the other hand, Protestant leaders implemented a vision of the past that consolidated their benevolent role and minimized earlier instances of racial conflict.

Paul Ivey also explores the central importance of commercial culture and urban architecture by focusing on the growth of Christian Science in the early twentieth century. Ivey contends that key to understanding why Christian Science congregations expanded so rapidly was their use of established classical revival architecture. This architectural style physically concretized elements of Christian Science and correlated with urban reform movements prized by the bourgeoisie. Through the design of their houses of worship, Christian Scientists effectively communicated their core beliefs and integrated them with the social aspirations of middle-class urban reformers and leaders.

Paul Kemeny, in his study of the demise of Boston's Watch and Ward Society during the 1920s, demonstrates that urban religious groups who thought they could easily control the new commercial culture were mistaken. Founded by Boston's most powerful white Protestants to monitor and uplift society's morals, this voluntary organization focused on curtailing the rash of new urban magazines, newspapers, and books that featured "vice-ridden" stories. Ignoring accusations by social critics such as H. L. Mencken that it was unconscionably regulating the public's freedoms, the Society turned to the police, courts, and established newspapers to aid in its crusade to check the flow of "obscene" literature flying off the city's small presses and into the public's all too willing hands. The Society's failure to regulate the production and dissemination of the inexpensive printed materials signaled the steep price to be paid when religious elites tried to peremptorily control the growth of urban commercial culture's new products.

Part III. Minority Adaptation

For members of minority communities living in North American cities, commercial culture has been a crucial resource for publicly expressing and sustaining their religion as well as for challenging the dominant culture's norms and stereotypes. Judith Weisenfeld treats the "race" movies of the 1940s as a rich source of insight into the tensions that many blacks felt about the impact of urbanization and commercial culture upon their spiritual lives. The films depict African American anxieties over the ministry as the primary vehicle for producing urban leadership, the lessening of the church's social influence as it competed with commercial entertainments, and the growing feminization of many congregations.

Similarly, Catholics turned to commercial culture both to express social tensions and to adapt to urban life. In the years after World War II, Catholic girls negotiated the demands of their faith with the dictates of contemporary fashion by participating in modesty crusades. As Kathryn Jay illustrates, between 1947 and 1963 thousands of urban Catholic girls joined Supply the Demand for the Supply (SDS), an organization that encouraged them to pressure clothing stores to stock and sell modest but stylish clothing. The goal of SDS was twofold: to remake a corner of the youth fashion industry with an eye cast toward standards of Catholic decency and to provide young Catholic women an opportunity to participate safely in the world of urban commercial culture. As Jay argues, SDS enabled Catholic adolescents to be both fashionable and faithful.

In her essay on black Islam in northern cities from 1955 to 1970, Melani McAlister contends that its rise in popularity was due to its creative appropriation of urban forms of popular culture, specifically music, art, and writing. In particular, she argues that the Nation of Islam's flowerings influenced the emergence of the Black Arts movement, and in turn these forms of urban religion and art excited an anticolonial radicalism among young African Americans living in northern cities. What made possible the free-flowing connections of religion, art, and politics in modern cities was the migration of southern blacks to places like New York, St. Louis, and Chicago and the subsequent formation of communities less attached to traditional religious institutions than those left behind.

In the concluding essay, Etan Diamond demonstrates how Orthodox Jews in the post–World War II era built a sense of religious identity in the outlying regions of cities by adapting to modern patterns of consumption. Focusing on Orthodox Jews who moved to suburbs that sat just outside the city limits of Toronto, Canada, Diamond offers a case study of how the dynamic between religion and urban commercial culture is experienced at the peripheries of a major city. Enjoying fine wines and luxury foods while still conforming to strict religious customs, Orthodox Jews found that commercial culture held out the promise of incorporating them into the quotidian pleasures of modern life without forcing them to give up their spiritual traditions. Thus Toronto's Orthodox Jewish community fashioned a "kosher lifestyle" based on their participation in an infrastructure of upscale kosher grocers, butchers, bakers, and restaurants that stretched from the inner city to the suburbs.

This collection does not intend to ask and answer every question about the historical relationship between religion and urban commercial culture in modern America. As becomes evident upon reviewing the essays, many religious groups remain to be studied, including New Age spirituality, Afro-Caribbean traditions, and the range of Eastern religions. Likewise, this book may be subject to cavils that it neglected to cover some vital areas of analysis. That, too, is true, as there are many other forms of commercial culture and their impact on urban religion that need to be investigated. However, our primary objective is to provide a range of rigorous case studies that clearly demonstrate the importance of commercial culture to the experience and expression of spiritual life among residents of American cities since the 1880s. Indeed, it is the authors' hope that this collection might inspire a critical reappraisal of how urban religion is taught and studied and ultimately lead to a richer understanding of the subject.

Notes

1. For example, see Timothy J. Gilfoyle, *City of Eros: New York, Prostitution, and the Commercialization of Sex* (New York: W. W. Norton, 1992); William Leach, *Land of Desire: Merchants, Power and the Rise of a New American Culture* (New York: Pantheon Books, 1993); T. J. Jackson Lears, *Fables of Abundance: A Cultural History of Advertising in America* (New York: Basic Books, 1994); David Nasaw, *Going Out: The Rise and Fall of Public Amusements* (New York: Basic Books, 1993); William R. Taylor, *In Pursuit of Gotham: The Commerce and Culture of New York* (New York: Oxford University Press, 1992).
2. For example, see Gerald Gamm, *Urban Exodus: Why the Jews Left Boston and the Catholics Stayed* (Cambridge: Harvard University Press, 1999); David G. Hackett, *The Rude Hand of Innovation: Religion and Social Order in Albany, New York, 1652–1836* (New York: Oxford University Press, 1991); Paula Kane, *Separatism and Subculture: Boston Catholicism, 1900–1920* (Chapel Hill: University of North Carolina Press, 1994); James W. Lewis, *The Protestant Experience in Gary, Indiana, 1906–1975: At Home in the City* (Knoxville: University of Tennessee Press, 1992); John McGreevey, *Parish Boundaries: The Catholic Encounter with Race in the Twentieth Century Urban North* (Chicago: University of Chicago Press, 1996); Gary Wray McDonogh, *Black and Catholic in Savannah, Georgia* (Knoxville: University of Tennessee Press, 1993); Deborah Dash Moore, *To the Golden Cities: Pursuing the American Dream in Miami and Los Angeles* (New York: Free Press, 1994); Clarence Taylor, *The Black Churches of Brooklyn* (New York: Columbia University Press, 1994); Thomas Tweed, *Our Lady of the Exile: Diasporic Religion at a Cuban Catholic Shrine in Miami* (New York: Oxford University Press, 1997); Judith Weisenfeld, *African American Women and Christian Activism: New York's Black YWCA, 1905–1945* (Cambridge: Harvard University Press, 1997).

3. For example, see Susan Curtis, *A Consuming Faith: The Social Gospel and Modern American Culture* (Baltimore: Johns Hopkins University Press, 1991); Andrew Heinze, *Adapting to Abundance: Jewish Immigrants, Mass Consumption and the Search for American Identity* (New York: Columbia University Press, 1990); Jenna Weissman Joselit, *The Wonders of America: Reinventing American Jewish Culture, 1880–1950* (New York: Hill and Wang, 1994); Eugene McCarraher, *Christian Critics: Religion and the Impasse in Modern American Social Thought* (Ithaca, N.Y.: Cornell University Press, 2000); R. Laurence Moore, *Selling God: American Religion in the Marketplace of Culture* (New York: Oxford University Press, 1994); Kathryn J. Oberdeck, *The Evangelist and the Impresario: Religion, Entertainment and Cultural Politics in America, 1884–1914* (Baltimore: Johns Hopkins University Press, 1999); Leigh Eric Schmidt, *Consumer Rites: The Buying and Selling of American Holidays* (Princeton, N.J.: Princeton University Press, 1995), Harry Stout, *The Divine Dramatist: George Whitefield and the Rise of Modern Evangelicalism* (Grand Rapids, Mich.: Eerdmans, 1994).

4. Etan Diamond, *And I Will Dwell in their Midst: Orthodox Jews in Suburbia* (Chapel Hill: University of North Carolina Press, 2000); Troy Messenger, *Holy Leisure: Recreation and Religion in God's Square Mile* (Minneapolis: University of Minnesota Press, 1999); Diane Winston, *Red-Hot and Righteous: The Urban Religion of The Salvation Army* (Cambridge: Harvard University Press. 1999).

5. Tony Carnes, ed., *New York Glory* (New York: New York University Press, 2001); Robert A. Orsi, ed., *Gods of the City: Religion and the American Urban Landscape* (Bloomington: Indiana University Press, 1999).

6. Walter H. Conser Jr. and Sumner B. Twiss, eds., *Religious Diversity and American Religious History: Studies in Traditions and Culture* (Athens: University of Georgia Press, 1997); David J. Hall, ed., *Lived Religion in America* (Princeton, N.J.: Princeton University Press, 1997); Harry S. Stout and D. G. Hart, eds. *New Directions in American Religious History* (New York: Oxford University Press, 1997); Thomas Tweed, ed., *Retelling U.S. Religious History* (Berkeley and Los Angeles: University of California Press, 1997).

7. For example, see Aaron Abell, *The Urban Impact of American Protestantism, 1865–1900* (London: Archon, 1962); Robert D. Cross, ed., *The Church and the City* (New York: Bobbs and Merrill, 1967); Samuel Lane Loomis, *Modern Cities and Their Problems* (New York: Baker and Taylor, 1887); Henry F. May, *Protestant Churches and Industrial America* (New York: Harper, 1949); Arthur M. Schlesinger, *The Rise of the City, 1878–1898* (New York: Macmillan, 1933); Charles Stelzle, *Christianity's Storm Centre* (New York: Fleming H. Revell, 1907); Josiah Strong, *Our Country: Its Possible Future and Present Crisis* (New York: Baker and Taylor, 1885); Josiah Strong, *The Challenge of the City* (New York: Missionary and Education Movement of the United States and Canada, 1911).

8. For example, commercial culture is not used as an interpretative lens in recent collections of "new" models and themes for American religious history by Conser and Twiss, Hall, Stout and Hart, or Tweed.

9. Moore, *Selling God*, 2–11.

Part I
Evangelical Experimentation

One

Diane Winston

Living in the Material World

*Salvation Army Lassies and Urban
Commercial Culture, 1880–1918*

After graduating from Vassar College in the early 1880s, Elizabeth Swift and her sister, Suzie, embarked on a European tour. While visiting England, these privileged daughters of a New York state banker encountered the newly formed Salvation Army, an evangelical movement intent on saving the heathen masses. Many of their contemporaries derided the Army's sensationalism, evidenced when uniformed soldiers paraded on city streets with brass instruments and bass drums, but the Swift sisters saw the army as an opportunity for service, spirituality, and community.[1] For the two young women from Poughkeepsie, the ragtag crusade was a very potent package.

But there was a hitch, one that would have frustrated any fashion-conscious young women of the age. When Elizabeth enrolled in the London Training School for officers—the Army equivalent of clergy—she was given a plain, dark blue uniform. She wore it dutifully until, when it was "stretched with wearing," she asked for permission to "go over to Paris and have a uniform fitted properly." Advised instead to have her outfit made locally, Elizabeth found a "fashionable tailor" in the West End. She brought him an expensive piece of broadcloth, which she had done up in a "princesse gown" with a "modest pannier" (the wire framework used to puff out a skirt at the hips) and "silk ruching" (pleated trimming) at the neck and sleeves.[2]

When an officer at the school asked Elizabeth why she wore silk ruching instead of the standard linen collar, the young American staunchly defended her choice. But a few days later, "the spirit of God put the questions to me and I had to answer straight." Convinced that God had instructed her to stop spending "His money" on frivolities, she stripped the trim off her uniform and afterward stuck to plain skirts and narrow sleeves.

Swift's words seem to imply that following God meant turning away from the markers of the emerging commodity culture. In the late nineteenth century, as mass production made a range of fashion options widely available to the middle and working classes, Swift's elegant, handmade clothes telegraphed her upper-class social status. Wearing the plain Army uniform provided no such worldly signposts; in fact, its drab aspect signified a rejection of fashion's role in nego-tiating social position. Yet an alternate reading is to consider what Swift gained by giving up her modest pannier and silk ruching. Donning the dark suit gave Swift and her female colleagues a new degree of access to urban commercial culture. Defined by their uniforms, lassies—as Salvationist women were fre-quently called—participated in aspects of city life that were closed to re-spectable women. Thus branded by their military blues, lassies engaged in activities, such as commanding troops and administering corps, that exceeded the bounds of acceptable feminine behavior. Likewise, they could "invade" pub-lic spaces—saloons, dives, and brothels—considered outside the realm of fem-inine propriety.

This essay argues that Army women enjoyed greater social mobility, per-sonal autonomy, and professional opportunity than most of their female con-temporaries between 1880 and 1918 because their religious identity desexualized them, allowing them to participate in male-identified activities in the expanding urban marketplace. Specifically, Army women took leadership roles in the pub-lic sphere, and they engaged in spiritual warfare at commercial establishments. The historical record allows a close look at how three Army women commin-gled spiritual themes, gendered discourse, and urban realities to wield their command and expand their personal and professional territory as Salvationist leaders in New York City, the Army's national headquarters. Equally intriguing is the possibility, which can only be inferred from the extant records, that rank-and-file Salvationists also saw the same benefits to exchanging linen and lace for a plain blue suit.

Secularized Religion

The Salvation Army began in London 1865 as the Christian Mission, a religious outreach run by William Booth, an independent evangelist deter-mined to reach the unchurched urban masses. Booth, supported by his wife, Catherine, an early proponent of women's right to preach, tried to save souls wherever poor and working-class people could be found by giving a cheerful gloss to the gospel message. In 1878, when Booth changed the name of his organization to the Salvation Army, he was already called "the General," and his new "army" rapidly adopted a military look and language. Their weekly news-paper was the "*War Cry*," ministers were "officers," and members were "sol-diers." Salvationists wore plain dark clothes that varied from soldier to soldier until Booth standardized a simple blue uniform.[3]

To capture the attention of the "heathen masses," early Salvationists adopted flamboyant tactics. Reaching the unchurched public on its own territory seven days a week meant that the secular marketplace and its entertainments—rather than the churches—were the main competition. Thus Salvationists borrowed liberally from popular culture ("Why should the devil have all the good tunes?" Booth allegedly asked), and they also developed a self-consciously dramatic flair. When the Army's official landing party disembarked in New York City's Battery Park, George Scott Railton, the commanding officer, and seven "Hallelujah lassies" knelt in prayer, planted the Blood-and-Fire flag, and claimed America for God. Reporters ballyhooed the "sensation" that the Army made marching through lower Manhattan singing hymns to familiar tunes like "Sewanee River."[4] The curiosity and interest stirred by the Army is evident in Figure 1.

The Army easily mediated between the sacred and profane because its theology, woven from Holiness, revivalist, and postmillennialist strands, sought to "secularize religion, or rather [to] religionize secular things."[5] The Holiness movement taught that all life was under God's rule and all creation should glorify Him. Thus Salvationists turned theaters and saloons into sacred spaces, made vaudeville and pageantry spiritual entertainment, and used clothing, kettles, and collection boxes as religious objects. In an increasingly materialistic world, Salvationists espoused a theology that hallowed the daily stuff of life. The Army set up its own Trade Department, reasoning that a religious person would prefer honestly marketed products made with an extra special something. The department carried items ranging from clothes to postcards, wall mottoes to musical instruments. Most important, its products had added value; the tea wasn't just tea, it was a salvation blend.

Thus, in its bid to compete with secular culture, Army leaders used popular products, lively music, and dramatic testimonies to express themes of love and salvation. Yet the Army's underlying aim was more than just saving individual sinners. Fired by a postmillennial fervor that was itself the legacy of American revivalism, Salvationist leaders planned to spiritualize the world and, in the process, to "sanctify the commonplace."[6] Their crusade to hallow the city—its buildings, streets, and public squares—was part of their attempt to establish the Kingdom of God. An 1896 editorial in the *War Cry* explained:

> The genius of the Army has been from the first that it has secularized religion, or rather that it has religionized secular things. . . . On the one hand it has brought religion out of the clouds into everyday life, and has taught the world that we may and ought to be as religious about our eatings and drinkings and dressing as we are about our prayings. On other hand it has

THE DAILY GRAPHIC: NEW YORK, SATURDAY, MARCH 13, 1880—TEN PAGES.

MISSIONARIES TO MANHATTAN

Seven Women And One Man Come From England In The Uniform Of "Salvation Army"

(In "The New York Tribune," March 11, 1880)

NEW YORK, N. Y.—Among the immigrants who arrived by the steamship "Australia" from London yesterday were eight persons—one man and seven women—dressed in a peculiar uniform, with red bands around their hats and an inscription in gilt letters, "The Salvation Army." They carried two silk

Figure 1

The Salvation Army's uniforms attracted attention when the landing party disembarked in lower Manhattan. Note the women's plain hats, which later evolved into bonnets. *Salvation Army Archives.*

taught that there is no religion in a place or in an attitude. A house or a store or factory can be just as holy a place as a church.[7]

Postmillennial perfectionists in the first half of the nineteenth century held similar notions, but their zeal had waned. Their triumphalist dreams had fallen on the blood-soaked fields of Gettysburg and Antietam, while new currents in biblical scholarship, natural science, and the social sciences questioned the primacy of religious truth. Adjusting to a smaller portion of the broader social discourse, many religious leaders fortified their bailiwicks, focusing their attention on ever bigger steeples and large-scale building programs. The commercial culture of advanced industrial capitalism filled the breach with its own normative set of meanings, signs, and symbols. The new commercial aesthetic made possible by the rise of mass production reshaped culture and society in the century's final quarter. Animating this culture was a set of beliefs antithetical to republican political philosophy, traditional Christian values, and the economic axioms of an earlier producer-oriented era. The new beliefs hallowed acquisition as the key to happiness, the new as superior to the old, and money as the measure of all value. It predicated a society where democracy did not mean equal opportunities for owning land or for wielding political power but rather for desiring and obtaining commodities and goods. And of all places in the New World, none epitomized these trends as much as New York City.[8]

The Salvation Army, whose postmillennial theology held that all aspects of everyday life could be sacralized, reflected a surprising resemblance to the *zeitgeist*. The Holiness aim to sacralize everyday life wed a materialist sensibility to an expansive spirit not dissimilar from that of the commercial culture of advanced industrial capitalism.[9] Both sought to saturate public space and control public discourse with a vision of individual transformation that would lead to a corporate utopia. The Army's means was the internal experience of salvation, while the commercial culture offered fulfillment through external experiences mediated by money. Each directed its message to the individual, yet both had important consequences for urban, social, and moral space.[10]

Whether marching through the alleys of Little Italy or testifying in Chinatown, Salvationist soldiers aimed their message at spectators who normally eschewed religion. In order to attract the unchurched, they mimicked the era's popular entertainments. The brass bands, colorful flags, and lively singing could have been advertisements for the latest minstrel or variety show.[11] Only when bystanders stopped to listen did they discover that the familiar forms had a different content. Parades and popular music initially conveyed a straightforward evangelical message: a call to repentance and salvation. But over time the forms grew more sophisticated, and the content did likewise. Pageants proceeded from parades, and lectures turned into dramatic presentations with slides and living tableaux. By World War I, the Army had extended its message to film, too.

Slaves of Fashion

William Booth's use of the uniform, like many of his stratagems, exemplified a knack for marketing. Their "peculiar" uniforms set Salvationists apart from the rest of society—a theme that echoed in many of the *War Cry*'s articles. "It separates one not only from the world but from the old self," wrote Suzie Swift, Elizabeth's younger sister.[12] Like a religious habit, the uniform signified the wearer's commitment to God. For many recruits, this new identity was approached warily. The uniform bestowed spiritual authority, yet it also signaled a repudiation of conventional mores. That repudiation was due, in large part, to the public's initially negative perception of the Army. For nearly a decade, many opinion-makers characterized the group as vulgar, sensationalist, and crude. Its noisy spectacles appeared antithetical to Christianity; its preaching women and boisterous parades were deemed scandalous.[13] Barbs were not limited to print. Mobs attacked Salvationists, and the police arrested Army members. When Suzie Swift wrote her mother of an intended visit home, the reply was unequivocal. "Do not come back to me in attire which, however fit it may be for the London slums, is suitable nowhere else. Spare me that pain."[14]

While Mrs. Swift saw the Army uniform as a badge of shame, that identification changed over time as Salvationists became known as godly soldiers dedicated to humanitarian service. Army lassies traveled freely from the dregs of the Bowery to the heights of Fifth Avenue because they were immediately identifiable as religious workers. Their uniforms were a source of power and a protective shield. Yet fashion's potent hold remained—obvious in numerous *War Cry* articles decrying it as antithetical to authentic Christianity. In one piece, a Mrs. Captain Gally recalled how she struggled to put on the uniform because she "had become such a slave to fashion although I had been a professing Christian for years."[15] In another screed, George Watson railed against soldiers enslaved to the "God of Fashion:" "Fashion is Satan's royal weapon for the achievement of his purpose in the damnation of souls. . . . Holiness and fashion are two opposites. It is impossible to possess a clean heart and live a consecrated life and yet be a devotee of fashion."[16]

Fashion, celebrating consumption and individual autonomy, embodied a set of values contrary to the Army's. Its lure was so strong that fashion was among the few facets of secular culture that Salvationists could not redeem. Wearing the uniform required women to renounce the trappings that society deemed essential for a sexualized female identity, in effect compelling reflection on one's relationship to God, self, and society. These very fundamental relationships—especially between self and society—appeared highly negotiable in the late-nineteenth-century city. Urban anonymity permitted individuals to reinvent themselves in ways that would have been impossible in smaller, tightly knit communities. Clothing facilitated reinvention, obscuring class and regional markers. Shop girls wore copies of haute couture, matrons donned rags to go slumming, and former farm boys traded overalls for a crisp shirt and tie. Salvationists reinvented themselves, too, casting off old identities to be "born again." Clothes made the man or woman, but the uniform made a soldier.

Nevertheless, fashion's devotees devised little ways to make the uniform more distinctive or to avoid it entirely. Cognizant of the problem, Maud Booth, who shared command of the American Army with her husband, Ballington, from 1887 to 1896, wrote Salvationist women, "I know that the wearing of the uniform has always been, and will always be, to a certain extent, a cross." But, she continued, since the Army's good intentions were now widely recognized, its official attire was, at least, no longer an object of ridicule and persecution. If all Army women would wear the uniform, "what a mighty power should we, as women, become."[17] But wearing a version of the uniform was not sufficient. Clothing had to conform to regulations because, Maud explained, "it is absurd on the face of it to have the brass 'S' of a Salvationist stuck on the collar of a velvet waist, or to see the Army bonnet worn above bangs."[18]

The message finally got through to the ranks. After the late 1890s, the *War Cry* ran only occasional articles about the uniform. The Army was well established in the larger society, and its distinctive clothing telegraphed its role as a religiously based provider of philanthropic service. In fact, the uniform was so ensconced in Army culture that officials perceived its utility as a marketable commodity in and out of their ranks. The Army's Trade Department advertised its "perfect fitting, well-made garments" at "most attractive prices." Army commanders posted uniformed lassies beside Christmas kettles to spur donations and permitted both Junior Leaguers and chorus girls to wear the outfit when helping to raise funds. The uniform's religious purpose—to maintain simplicity and avoid display—became its greatest asset. Ironically, the blue outfit called attention to itself, providing a "label" for the Army's "brand name."

Women Warriors

Unlike many of her contemporaries, author Agnes Maule Machar tried to find the good in the Salvation Army. Writing in 1884, she applauded the Army's use of noise and spectacle as a strategy for snaring young men whose "fondness for social pleasure" would otherwise lead them astray. But she could not condone the "unhealthy passions" aroused during Salvationist meetings.[19]

She was particularly worried about the effects such passions had on young women who routinely experienced hysterical fits during services. And she was also concerned by newspaper reports alleging that Salvationists lived in mixed-sex barracks where male recruits frequently seduced their female colleagues.

As Machar's criticism indicates, the Army's deployment of its female members—allowing them to lead services, sending them to dens of vice and drink, and dispatching them across the country to start up "corps" (churches)—shocked contemporaries. While Salvationist publications redefined what "modesty" and "respectability" meant in God's service, secular writers alleged that young girls who joined the movement had neither. Steeped in Victorian cultural assumptions, both Christian and secular critics viewed "religion" and "lady-like" as terms incompatible with the Army's—and its lassies'—radical behavior.

Salvationists were aware of popular prejudices against the lassies and countered with their own constructions of Army womanhood. Thus, even if the *New York Times* declared "whoever joins the Salvation Army from the nature of the case bids good-bye to respectability as much as if he went on the stage of a variety show," the example set by Maud Booth suggested otherwise.[20] Booth's words and deeds, her very persona, challenged the notion that joining the Army spelled an end to a woman's respectability. By projecting a refined demeanor in her public appearances, she modeled behavior that was simultaneously feminine and activist, religious and secular. Writing in the *War Cry*, she countered secular stereotypes by arguing that the desire to save sinners bestowed the "power to rise above" one's circumstances. "I do not think for a moment that God wants his women to be anything else but modest but I cannot see that they in any way endanger their modesty by entering a saloon as God's messenger. That would be Christ's mission were He on earth today."[21]

In 1887, when William Booth sent his son and daughter-in-law to lead the American Army, the young couple was already skilled at a variety of outreach strategies. Maud had helped Booth's daughter, Kate, "open fire" in France and Switzerland, while Ballington had headed up Army forces in Australia. Among Maud's preferred modes of presenting her message were the by-invitation-only parlor meeting and the Chautauqua-style lecture, both popular with the era's well-to-do. Chautauqua, a summer retreat in Westchester, New York, provided Protestant laity with a happy compromise between religion and commercial entertainment.

For the Salvation Army, seeking to widen its outreach to the middle and upper classes, the Chautauqua format was an opportunity to speak in a cultural vernacular that mitigated its use of the streets. Army critics deemed its outdoors evangelizing vulgar and sensational, and Army women—who preached publicly and fraternized with their male counterparts—were considered coarse and morally lax. Accordingly, Maud Booth's use of a class-identified mode of communication was as important as her message. Her persona was significant, too. The seemingly wayward daughter of a proper Anglican rector, Booth's "angelic" face and dignified mien surprised the movement's detractors.

Thus, when Booth announced a lecture on "The New Woman," the auditorium at the Army's national headquarters in New York attracted a standing-room-only crowd. The audience, assembled for a religious critique of this controversial creature, was greeted by an all-female platform of officers, band members, cadets, and soldiers. Booth's plummy tones may have blunted the edge of an arguably feminist thrust, but for those with ears to hear, the message was straightforward. "This is a woman's meeting," she began. "The women are going to do everything here tonight." She proceeded to explicate a model of womanhood that, while explicitly condemning the media caricature of the "mannish" female, implicitly affirmed many of the New Woman's aims. Booth enthusiastically supported women's right to education, athletic exercise, and work—but she called her ideal the "advanced woman" and affirmed her devotion to family, home, and religion.

Booth believed that Salvationist women needed to augment their feminine nature with some masculine qualities. The result was the "Woman Warrior," a term coined within the Army as opposed to the "Hallelujah lass," a demeaning epithet hurled by detractors until Salvationists adopted it as their own. The Woman Warrior wed "tender, gentle, loving attributes" to "courage, strength, action, sacrifice, and loyalty." While some scholars have suggested that groups such as the Army used religion to instill middle-class notions of respectability among the poor and working classes, Booth's pronouncements on women warriors complicate this conclusion. Booth did not always hold herself or her female followers to conventional standards; rather, a spiritual mission often conflicted with society's notions of ladylike behavior. Not content simply to challenge the notion of separate spheres, Booth also contested concomitant class assumptions. "I presume all officers have had the good sense to discard gloves altogether in this hot weather," she wrote in a column. "I have always looked upon this as one of the emancipations the Salvation Army has brought to women. The opinion of the world on what is ladylike dressing does not enter into Salvation Army dressing."[22] Salvationists, savvy about the uniform's utility in the battle for souls, used it strategically. In Figure 2, the lassies are evangelizing at a fancy dress ball to guests who initially mistook their outfits for clever costumes.

How could the Army be a vehicle for embourgoisement when its leader preferred the word "woman" to "lady"? Booth clearly believed that the Army's concept of female behavior was not dictated by social convention or class expectations but by religious instrumentality. "Woman, I think, is a beautiful

_____ *Figure 2* _____

An Army uniform enabled a woman to enter places that a respectable female otherwise eschewed. Here two officers try to sell *War Cry*s to revelers at an infamous costume ball. Many of the partygoers likely wondered whether the women were in costume.
Salvation Army Archives.

name. I cannot bear to hear an Army warrior called a 'lady.' It always seems to me to be so out-of-place, such a come-down from the holy, natural, unaffected name of woman, and besides that it savors always to me of the world."[23]

Maud may have sensed that new opportunities for women, tied to the expanding urban market, were among the factors necessitating a class of women warriors. Long-standing beliefs about women's separate (and domestic) sphere were challenged by the increased presence of females as pedestrians, customers, patrons, and employees. Commercial culture changed women's lives in myriad ways. Shop girls jostled society matrons at department stores where both went to inspect the latest seasonal styles. Poor and working-class women found that new openings in retail, offices, department stores, and manufacturing were better than jobs as domestics, in the needle trades, and in sweatshops. Wealthy women who worked outside the home as friendly visitors and volunteers discovered new pastimes. Young women went off to college while their mothers and older sisters browsed in department stores, lunched at elegant hotels, and attended "ladies'" matinees. Leavening this life of leisure were a growing number of women's clubs focused on fellowship and benevolent activities.

Such changes did not go unnoticed. The New Woman personified the growing public discourse on women's roles, serving as a popular foil for the cultural anxiety provoked by newly available alternatives to traditional feminine behavior. For the right kind of woman, one who was both religious and adventuresome, the Salvation Army was an exciting prospect. Stories in Army publications indicated that most female officers came from small towns where career choices were limited.[24] These recruits tended to be from farming families or from the petite bourgeoisie rather than from the wealthier classes. When a daughter of the upper class did fall sway to the Army, the event was news, as in 1892 when Emma Van Norden, the offspring of an old New York banking family, became a Salvationist.[25] For months afterward, reporters followed the young recruit, even to an Army encampment in Staten Island.

The Army appealed to Van Norden and other members of the "upper tendom," a popular term for the privileged, because it took advantage of the historical moment, a time when middle- and upper-class women sought meaningful work. Expectations of women's capacities were changing, yet few professional options, as opposed to wage-earning jobs, were available. For the wealthy woman who was not content just to be a friendly visitor, a proto–social worker who visited the poor, yet who was more religiously inclined than a settlement house worker, the Army held appeal. Moreover, female Salvationists flourished. Educated women rose rapidly through the ranks. Some were promoted to ensure the visibility of respectable women, others succeeded because their education and background prepared them for leadership. Such women, when confronted by hostile characterizations in the media, ardently defended themselves or, as Maud Booth did, turned the criticism on its head—embracing the very qualities that were derided. Thus, in Booth's ears, the term "lady" rang jarring and worldly while "woman" sounded unaffected and holy.

Well-to-do women who joined the Army tended to be the daughters of professional men from large towns and cities. Most had strong religious feelings that were untapped by the churches they attended. Alice Terrell, a New Yorker of "Puritan-Knickerbocker" descent, discovered the Army when it took over the downtown church that her congregation had abandoned. "Little Alice" became a soldier in 1882 and served with corps in New York, New Jersey, and Pennsylvania.[26] When the Swift sisters joined the Army, Suzie became the first female editor of an Army publication, and Elizabeth, after marrying Samuel Brengle, the Army's leading Holiness writer, became an author in her own right.[27] Carrie Judd Montgomery, a best-selling author of books on faith healing, joined the Army when she and her millionaire husband became convinced that its missions were the most effective way to reach the unchurched.[28]

More typically, however, women warriors came from modest backgrounds. Actual profiles as well as the stories in Salvationist periodicals indicate that many grew up in small towns. In fictional accounts, a worldly young woman realizes the emptiness of her life when she sees the Army in action. The story's tension arises when the protagonist's attachment to the world, especially its things (such as dress and fashion) and its conventions (regarding women's roles), conflicts with her desire for a service-filled, God-centered life. In some stories, the heroine dies before she is saved and, with her last breath, regrets her ill-spent years.[29] In other examples, she successfully flees the constraints of small town life and, through the Army, finds meaningful service in the city.

Real-life stories were less dramatic. Recruits were the daughters of farmers or owners of small businesses. They had been baptized in a church, usually Methodist or Episcopal, but had either fallen away or found their religious practice cold and formal. Although the 1880s and 1890s were a time of expanding opportunities for women, these late teens and young adults were not part of the tide. Few careers were open to them unless they left home. But absent the press of financial need, many lacked the impetus to strike out on their own.[30] With the Army's appearance came a whiff of wider possibilities. A young woman attended a Salvationist meeting where, amid the red jerseys and poke bonnets, she found radiant faces testifying to a vital faith. If she joined the Army and her family disowned her, she had little time to grieve. Officers were sent to "open" new corps every few months. Most were posted to cities much larger, and more exciting, than the farms and small towns they left behind. Lassies would move to a posting with few resources and be expected to build a corps quickly and make it self-sufficient. Within a few months, there would be a new assignment.

Writing about her own "eventful life," Captain A. Y. Dixon began, "my birth occurred in Western Pennsylvania where also I was reared—a farmer's daughter." Dixon said she was willful and selfish until, at age eighteen, she lost both her husband and mother. Seeking forgiveness for past sins, Dixon found salvation and joined the Army. She served corps in her home state, in Connecticut, and in Massachusetts, where she was attacked and imprisoned. Sentenced for the crime of marching in the streets, Dixon spent sixty days in a state workhouse toiling at "arduous" labor and surviving in "loathsome" conditions. She nevertheless did not lose sight of her mission: "Notwithstanding the fact that the soft soap ate the skin off our hands and our 'inner man' fairly revolted at the sight of the prison food, the peace of God filled our hearts and we found exceeding great recompense of reward talking to the poor, sinful, despairing creatures."[31]

Like A. Y. Dixon, many women who joined the Army were young, idealistic, and ready to be mobile. When Minnie Myers first saw Salvationists in her hometown of Alpena, Michigan, she disliked them, "but underneath it all I loved them because their lives were so pure." She became a soldier and was sent to Detroit where she was horsewhipped and battered by persecutors.[32] May Harris grew up in the Connecticut hills, the daughter of a Danbury furrier. Although her father was not religious, he took the family to an Army meeting, at which Harris was converted. After enlisting, she was stationed in a small town where an angry mob burned down the corps' building and threatened to throw her into the fire, too.[33]

Lassies such as A. Y. Dixon, Minnie Myers, and May Harris met Maud Booth's expectations for women warriors. Unlike their more privileged Salvationist sisters who held administrative and editorial positions, these women did frontline work that often elicited local resistance. While officers serving in New York slum posts were rarely attacked after the early 1880s, lassies working in small towns experienced physical violence throughout the decade. Such attacks indicate that, in many communities, female Salvationists were not considered respectable women. That men felt no compunction about horsewhipping or beating them indicates the lassies' role as public religious figures exceeded the limits of acceptable female behavior outside urban centers.

Despite their hard work opening corps, women warriors received the most coverage when they were persecuted. In general, the public seemed to prefer reading about the Army's "slum angels," lassies who lived among the urban poor and tended to their domestic needs—cooking, cleaning, nursing, and childcare. Slum angels were conflated with the "True Woman" while woman warriors were representative of the New Woman—de-sexed, aggressive, and active in the public sphere. This was not Booth's intention, yet at a time when women's roles and behavior were increasingly contested, the notion of women warriors, as well as the reality of women taking public roles as religious leaders, was too unsettling for mass appeal. After Booth's resignation, the term "Woman Warrior" was heard no more. Rather, Booth's female successors, sisters-in-law Emma Booth-Tucker and Evangeline Booth, accepted the Army's stated goal of equality for women as well as the limitations imposed on it by contemporary society.

Slum Angels

In contrast to her sister-in-law, Maud, Emma Booth-Tucker projected a more subdued style of female leadership. While Maud had grown up in a conventional Victorian household and embraced the Army as a form of rebellion, Emma may not have felt the same need to differentiate herself from her upbringing. Catherine Booth provided a ready exemplar of a working mother, and Emma slipped easily into her role. During her six years in the United States, she shared command with her husband, Frederick Booth-Tucker; experienced six pregnancies; and oversaw the care of their seven children.[34] When Emma, whose Army appellation was "the Consul," addressed female Salvationists, she focused less on their public roles and responsibilities than on the difficulties of balancing work and family.[35] Constantly in the public eye, Emma traveled as much as, and often independently of, her husband. But wherever she was and whatever she did, she projected a "mother's heart"—a nurturing image resonant with the cult of domesticity.

In fact, Emma Booth-Tucker came to represent the epitome of the "womanly woman," a favorite construct of the era and a foil for the more provocative New Women. Unlike that aggressive, self-centered creature, the womanly woman embodied the domestic, feminine traits of wife, mother, and helpmeet. Her moral authority assured her place on the public stage, so there was no need for her to be aggressive or confrontational. Frances Willard, head of the Woman's Christian Temperance Union and a longtime supporter of the Salvation Army, exemplified the type. Both she and Booth-Tucker legitimated their public roles with an explicit and active commitment to their faith. When the Consul was killed in 1903, the secular press eulogized her example: "The subject in which Mrs. Booth-Tucker took the least interest was, perhaps, the great feminist movements of her generation. . . . She never talked women's rights. She took them. . . . With a temperament emphatically masterful and militant, she did the things that other women talk about."[36]

Emma commanded an army, but she was less interested in women warriors than in the slum sisters, Army women who lived and worked among the poor.

Maud Booth pioneered the American slum brigades, borrowing Emma Booth-Tucker's strategy from their London days, and it was during Booth-Tucker's watch that slum missions and rescue work, another female ministry, flourished. Though both endeavors were well-established religious and volunteer efforts for nineteenth-century women, the Army took them several steps further. Typically, friendly visitors were volunteers who went into slums to educate residents and to evaluate them as charitable prospects. The slum sisters, on the other hand, lived among those whom they sought to help, providing domestic services as they were needed. Similarly, the slum brigades' forays to saloons and brothels had been pioneered by earlier reformers, but the lassies' visits were more consistent and oftentimes more insistent.

An 1891 article in the *War Cry* saluted ten cadets who visited 1,025 saloons in one week. The reporter described the range of reactions elicited by the lassies, including a dousing of warm liquor and cold beer.[37] More often, articles recounted the life-changing experiences that Salvationists spurred among the denizens of demimonde. A description from an 1892 article portrayed a typical night. The group started out at a dance hall, where patrons wept when the women "dealt earnestly and tenderly with them about their souls and salvation." Next, the women visited a brothel, where lewd songs, violent brawls, and pervasive profanity approximated Salvationist notions of hell. But no sooner did the lassies begin a hymn than they were surrounded by listeners who, falling to their knees, joined in "Room for Jesus."[38]

Women reporters, in particular, fell sway to the slum workers' mystique, portraying them as "slum angels" who toiled selflessly amid the urban squalor. Such accounts often began with the journalist "disguising" herself in a plain frock and patched apron so she, too, could pass unnoticed in the city's bleakest streets. In an article for the *New York World*, Julia Hayes Percy began her night of revelation ("revelations of such misery, depravity, and degradation that, having been gazed upon, life can never be quite the same afterward") by sharing tea and plum cake at the Army's Brooklyn barracks with "Maud" and "Em." The women took a ferry to Manhattan where Hayes, overwhelmed by the "vile stench," breathlessly compared the "dirt and garbage" with the Salvationists' abode of warmth and cleanliness.[39] In another *World* piece, "Em," Captain Emma Bown—the head of the slum work—appeared as a modern, metropolitan saint. "She is tall, slender, and clad in coarse brown gown, mended with patches. A big gingham apron, artistically rent in several places, is tied about her waist. She wears an old plaid woolen shawl and an ancient brown straw hat. Her dress indicates extreme poverty; her face denotes perfect peace."[40]

Even more rhapsodic was G. A. Davis's description of Bown in *Frank Leslie's Weekly*. "In the fourteenth century, this dark-eyed, mobile-featured Englishwoman would have been a rapturous ascetic, seeing visions and dreaming dreams; here in the nineteenth, she brings to practical uses the same spirit of self-abnegation and takes the slums and the alleys for her cloister and her cell."[41]

Unlike women warriors, slum sisters pushed women's roles only a little further than secular society would have liked. Slum sisters had more autonomy and mobility than many late-nineteenth-century women, but their work was defined by the domestic sphere—cooking, cleaning, nursing, and childcare. Even as Emma Booth-Tucker extolled and promoted this feminine model in her own life, she appropriated more of the masculine role for herself.

The Army's slum work never expanded to the degree that its other endeavors did. The slum sisters did not have the same appeal, especially for members of the upper tendom, as did the more expansive model of women warriors or their successors (such as rescue workers, editors, and administrators). Weekly notices in the *War Cry* advertised for "good, devoted girls" willing "to sacrifice everything and go and live among the poor," but few answered the call.[42] Slum work was among the most grueling of the Army's activities, and women attracted by the Salvationists' promise of gender equality found few opportunities for public ministry and leadership in the tenements. Those who chose slum work were primarily single women whose simplicity and deep faith made such toil and privation possible. Yet the very characteristics that drew workers to the field were the cause of its shortcomings, according to an early observer of the Army's social work. In 1906, Columbia University student Edwin Lamb completed a doctoral dissertation on the Army's social programs. Lamb argued that the slum work's lack of growth was the result of the intellectual limits of its workers.

> The slum officers are imbued with the idea that personal salvation according to the doctrines of the Army is the all-essential need. They would not be engaged in this work themselves were it not for the hold these doctrines have upon them. . . . But, in a community almost entirely Catholic or Jewish, such aggressive evangelism is not likely to increase the influence of its advocates. Many settlements have learned with grief, this very same lesson. Another reason for the lack of success is the mental caliber of those engaged in the work.[43]

Other critics condemned the commercial aspect of the slum brigade: the lassies sold copies of the *War Cry* to saloon-goers—a practice that the woman themselves saw as consistent with evangelical mission but that struck some outsiders as improper. In a study of life on the Bowery, I. N. Nascher noted: "The women of The Salvation Army enter these places not to do evangelical work by the distribution of *War Crys* as tracts, but they come as news vendors to sell their wares. Their religious garments save them from abuse. They are engaged in a purely business enterprise."[44]

Nascher's observation underscores the subversive dimension of even the slum sisters' work. While their ministrations seemed circumscribed by the traditional female role, they also pushed the boundary by using their religious (and unworldly) identity as a foil for participating in the commercial (and worldly) sector: selling *War Crys*, invading brothels, and storming saloons. While critics such as Nascher noted the incongruity of religious women engaged in the commercial world, the Army dismissed such distinctions, citing their Holiness theology as a mandate to redeem all aspects of society. By the 1920s, as the Army became more identified with social service than evangelical witness, its links to the market economy continued to grow. In fact, the Army was increasingly identified with aspects of the urban commercial culture—holding Christmas collections outside department stores, recycling upper-class commodities for lower-class use, and opening thrift shops for the poor.

The Commander in Rags

When Emma Booth-Tucker's younger sister, Evangeline Booth, took command of the American Salvation Army in 1904, her first priority was to strengthen the organization. Working on two fronts, Booth built up the Army's infrastructure while bolstering its external image. To accomplish the former, she and her staff (an inner circle of dedicated and savvy men) utilized the regnant business principles of organization, efficiency, and systemization in a process parallel to historian Ben Primer's description of denominational rationalization.[45] Yet Booth diverged from the leaders of most other Protestant groups: rather than create a faceless bureaucracy, she gave the Army a persona—her own. The formal portrait of Booth in Figure 3 was taken in her later years, and it reflects her sense of purpose and command.

Fueled by ambition and what she perceived as the righteousness of her crusade, Booth sought funds to make her dreams a reality. During her thirty-year tenure, the Salvation Army grew in size, stature, and scope. Its property value rose from $1.5 million to $48 million, its reputation as an effective social service provider was secured, and its welfare services expanded nationwide. Before the advent of federal aid to victims of the Great Depression, the Army served more than 20 percent of the country's needy population.

Taught since childhood to command, Evangeline Booth was forthright and decisive. The Salvation Army was a family business; moreover, it was a public arena in which strength and power were paramount. Its inspiration may have been religious, but maintaining the organization—supplying bricks and mortar,

_____ *Figure 3* _____

Evangeline Booth in dress uniform. Note the trim on her jacket and the modified style of bonnet.

Salvation Army Archives.

recruiting soldiers and sponsors—required the secular skills of institution building. These Booth mastered: among her greatest accomplishments were raising
money and acquiring real estate. Yet while her command reflected her ease with
masculine notions of leadership style and authority, her rhetoric reflected a feminine sensibility. Booth's speeches drew on images of love, nature, and family.
Even when she adopted the masculine discourse of social progress, she
inflected her message with the female language of reform. In "The Salvation
Army Appraises Prohibition," Booth noted that the best argument for the liquor
ban was "the vital statistics of insurance companies."[46] But her remarks concluded with reasons that would have resonated with Frances Willard.

> The women of America do not tolerate an inebriated manhood. It is no
> mere coincidence that the Eighteenth Amendment, prohibiting liquor,
> should have been historically simultaneous with the Nineteenth Amend-
> ment, giving the vote to women, and should have preceded by a few years
> only the proposed Twentieth Amendment, drafted to abolish child labor.
> These legislative enactments and proposals are, all of them, parts of a gen-
> eral movement toward the defense of domestic life against the destroying
> menace of selfishness in the environment.[47]

In many ways, Evangeline, even more than her sister, Emma, adopted masculine behavior while espousing feminine ideals. Evangeline identified more
with her father, William Booth, than with her mother, Catherine. Choosing not
to marry when William advised against it, Evangeline assembled a nontraditional household made up of several informally adopted children and two long-
standing relationships.[48] Even when she paid homage to women's traditional
homemaking role, Evangeline cast it in a broader context, "We women have
made many homes in the world. But we have now the task of changing the
world into a home."[49]

Throughout the nineteenth century, the dominant gender discourse had
delineated a "woman's sphere," which considered women's responsibility to
home, family, and religion to be a moral duty. By the end of the century, however, that traditional definition of womanhood was increasingly contested. Many
middle-class clubwomen, reformers, and religious workers used the older rhetoric of domesticity to justify "moral housekeeping" in the civic arena. Seeking
to inscribe the bonds of home and family onto society at large, they touted
women's ability to transform their poor and working-class sisters into religious
paragons and proper homemakers through the power of "motherly" love and
"sisterly" compassion. Moreover, they aimed to instill the recipients of their
benevolence with the belief that women's moral superiority was grounded in
feminine virtues such as modesty, chastity, and piety.

But reformers were hard-pressed to appeal to young women giddy with new possibilities. They tried offering entertaining alternatives to commercial amusements. The Army, for example, sponsored a ten-day summer vacation for working girls, and other reform and religious groups opened reading rooms and social clubs.[50] But such events held limited appeal. More exciting was the potential for social and financial independence that accompanied expanded employment opportunities. In 1900 nearly a third of New York's 343,000 female wage earners were between sixteen and twenty years old; four-fifths of these women were single, and a majority were either immigrants or the daughters of foreign-born parents.[51]

Evangeline Booth sought to capitalize on women's greater independence while also upholding their primary role as nurturers. A supporter of women's suffrage, she extolled new opportunities for women, yet she also advocated traditional notions of female moral and religious superiority. In the pamphlet "Woman," Booth acknowledged the spread of the women's movement worldwide and celebrated the possibilities it offered, including the right to choose a fulfilling career over a feckless marriage. But she also urged women not to abandon their most precious legacy: safeguarding and fostering religious faith. In language updating Maud Booth's argument that the real "New Woman" was one reborn through Jesus Christ, Evangeline offered her description of Christian feminism:

> For what we call the women's movement is not social merely, not political merely, not economic merely. It is the direct fulfillment of the gospel of the Redeemer. It was Jesus who taught the world the full lesson of what is meant by chivalry to women. It was He Who, at the well of Samaria, talked with the oft-divorced woman and told her of a God Whom she could worship in spirit and in truth. . . . Happy, then, is the woman who realizes, even in these days of enfranchisement, that her life, however abundant it may be, is still hidden in the Christ of God.[52]

Booth's vision of Army womanhood found its fullest expression during World War I. At the same time, her plan to deploy female Salvationists to the front lines pushed against conventional expectations of women's roles by using religious identity to infiltrate the public arena. What had succeeded in American cities now was put to the test at the front lines of a real battle. Booth's advisers ascertained that while other religious and social welfare agencies offered a range of services to Americans soldiers, the Army could bring them a little bit of home. Deciding her "girls" could "mother" the troops, Evangeline put out a call for young, single, female officers and soldier-volunteers whose moral rectitude and Christian commitment were unshakable. (Several married and widowed

Salvationists also served abroad.) Of the approximately 250 Salvationists who served in France, women were a small minority. Yet it was these Sallies—the popular nickname for Army women during the First World War—who made the deepest impression on the doughboys and whose presence distinguished the Army from other welfare agencies.

The Sallies combined the adventuresome spirit of women warriors with the domestic duties of slum sisters. Drawn from a mix of backgrounds, they braved mud, rain, artillery shells, and mustard gas. They slept in old barns, bathed intermittently, and spent most of their days toiling behind primitive stoves readying endless supplies of doughnuts and coffee. The women's diaries rarely describe their actions in religious terms or provide ruminations on their spiritual direction. Occasionally, a writer asked God for strength or recounted a religious exchange with a soldier. But their religiosity was expressed most clearly by their actions, and the message was evident to those who observed them. Walter S. Ball, a reporter for the *Providence Journal*, noted that the Sallies' religion was part of everything they did: "They let the work of their hands do most of the preaching without ever for an instant forgetting that there's a big idea somewhere that inspires them."[53]

Evangeline Booth used the Sallies, as she had used herself—and as her predecessors used the image of slum sisters and woman warriors—both to embody the Salvationist mission and to expand the franchise. Religious commitment enabled the women to serve where few of their sex would ever go—in this case, a makeshift hut at the front lines of the era's most gruesome fighting. Even as the Sallies insinuated themselves into formerly masculine territory, however, they asserted their female identity—cooking pies and doughnuts, darning socks and sewing on buttons, offering prayers and a mother's love.

The Salvationist religion, represented by the lassies' wholesome womanhood and expressed as reverence for God, home, and country, appealed to a nation where the undertones of Protestant evangelicalism slipped easily into the secular thrust of Progressivism. Evangeline Booth found an accurate formulation when she called for a religion of action. She honed the concept further when she told capitalists that it was their patriotic duty to support the Army. Yet she herself could only take the message so far. Her performances and public relations efforts reached many, but the Sallies brought the significance of a religious commitment to life. Even though their numbers were few, the authenticity of their work made a deep impression on the public.

The Army's World War I success was riddled with ironies. Never again did Salvationists have to worry about financial survival; their war service moved them to the front ranks of American philanthropies. The public perception of the

Army had been transformed. As one soldier wrote: "We always thought of The S.A. as an organization made up of well-meaning people who collected money on the streets with a tambourine for the purpose of feeding the poor at Thanksgiving or Christmas. . . . We were wrong, dead wrong."[54] Rather, the new view was that the Army was a religiously based movement providing social services that reflected Americans' most cherished ideals: God, home, and country.

The Army's success sprang from its acceptance of a secular trinity—a modern credo for a pluralist urban culture that hallowed society's core values. Not surprisingly, the Army's sectarian religious message had become diffuse. Thrift shops, kettles, and collection boxes were part of the cityscape—elements that enriched society but did not sacralize it. In fact, the city's commercial culture had proved stronger and more resilient than expected. The Army, which had appropriated worldly strategies in order to subvert their meaning, was itself changed in the process. Likewise, Army women who had pioneered public roles found their subversive stance mediated by their identification as mothers, sisters, and caregivers. As the Army increasingly identified with the culture it wished to redeem, its female followers found themselves further from the center of action. The uniform, initially a sign of daring and a badge of distinction, came to represent an old-time religion that seemed increasingly out of place in the city.

Notes

1. William Clark, ed., *Dearest Lily* (London: International Headquarters of the Salvation Army, 1986), vi. Elizabeth Swift married Samuel Brengle, one of the Army's foremost evangelists and Holiness teachers.
2. *War Cry*, August 5, 1893, 10.
3. For histories of the Salvation Army, see Edward McKinley, *Marching to Glory: The History of the Salvation Army in the United States, 1880–1980* (San Francisco: Harper and Row, 1980); Norman Murdoch, *Origins of The Salvation Army* (Knoxville: University of Tennessee Press, 1994); Pamela Walker, *Pulling the Devil's Kingdom Down: The Salvation Army in Victorian England* (Berkeley and Los Angeles: University of California Press, 2001).
4. *New York Times*, March 11, 1880, 5.
5. *War Cry*, September 23, 1896, 8.
6. William Booth, "The Millennium: or The Ultimate Triumph of Salvation Army Principles," *All the World* 7 (August 1890), 337–343; *War Cry*, July 31, 1909, 2.
7. *War Cry*, September 23, 1896, 8.
8. William Leach, *Land of Desire: Merchants, Power, and the Rise of a New American Culture* (New York: Pantheon Books, 1993), 3–12.
9. See David Carrasco, "The Sacrifice of Tezcatlipoca: To Change Place," in *To Change Place: Aztec Ceremonial Landscapes*, ed. David Carrasco (Boulder: University Press of Colorado, 1991).

10. The Army's loud music and comic antics were aspects of a charivari. Some spectators, familiar with the English tradition of "rough music," may have intuited the subversive quality of the Army's performances. See Natalie Davis, "Charivari, Honor, and Community in Seventeenth-Century Lyon and Geneva," in *Rite, Drama, Festival, Spectacle*, ed. John MacAloon (Philadelphia: Institute for the Study of Human Issues, 1984), 42–57.

11. *War Cry*, July 25, 1885, 1; May 28, 1887, 7; June 9, 1888, 4.

12. *War Cry*, September 18, 1886, 1. The article is actually bylined SFS. Suzie F. Swift wrote for the *War Cry* and edited another Army publication, *All the World*.

13. For example, the *New York Times*, July 16, 1885, 5, called the Army "a miserable failure" and suggested that "positive injury has been done to the young girls who have donned the fantastic garb of the 'army' and taken part in its hysterical services."

14. *War Cry*, September 18, 1886, 1.

15. *War Cry*, October 11, 1890, 15.

16. *War Cry*, April 6, 1889, 13.

17. *War Cry*, October 10, 1891, 9.

18. Ibid.

19. Agnes Maule Machar, "Red Cross Knights: A Nineteenth Century Crusade," *Andover Review* (August 1884): 206–207.

20. *New York Times*, February 2, 1892, 4.

21. *War Cry*, September 24, 1887, 8.

22. *War Cry*, August 4, 1894, 9.

23. *War Cry*, August 19, 1893, 8.

24. *War Cry*, February 22, 1890, 1–2; *Conqueror*, February 1895, 61–65; *Conqueror*, January 1896, 18–20; *War Cry*, March 21, 1903, 3.

25. *New York Times*, December 10, 1892, 8.

26. *War Cry*, March 21, 1903, 3.

27. *New York Times*, December 10, 1892, 8; *New York Times*, July 31, 1893, 2.

28. *War Cry*, June 11, 1892, 1, 4.

29. Mrs. F. M. Howard "The Reevers' New Year," *Conqueror*, January 1896, 18–20; *War Cry*, March 24, 1888, 1, 12; October 27, 1888, 1–2.

30. For example, see *War Cry*, March 26, 1887, 1; May 12, 1888, 4; February 16, 1889, 1; March 8, 1889, 1; May 11, 1889, 1; August 24, 1889, 9; July 8, 1893, 4; August 17, 1895, 13; December 12, 1895, 10; November 21, 1903, 3.

31. *War Cry*, February 22, 1890, 1, 2.

32. *War Cry*, October 4, 1890, 10.

33. *Conqueror*, February 1895, 61–65; Salvation Army Archives, Alexandria, Va., clippings from file on Wallace Winchell.

34. Emma and Frederick had two children who accompanied them to the United States. She subsequently had six more children, two of whom died as infants. She also adopted an orphan.

35. *Conqueror*, June 1896, 277–278.

36. *New York Tribune*, November 11, 1903, sect II, 4.

37. *War Cry*, May 9, 1891, 6.

38. *War Cry*, February 20, 1892, 10.

39. *War Cry*, March 1, 1890, 1.

40. *War Cry*, February 22, 1890, 8.

41. G. A. Davis, "Under the Blood-Red Banner-IV," *Frank Leslie's Weekly*, December 21, 1893, 420.
42. *War Cry*, November 30, 1889, 5.
43. Edwin G. Lamb, "The Social Work of the Salvation Army" (Ph.D. diss., Columbia University, 1909), 120.
44. L. L. Nascher, *The Wretches of Povertyville: A Sociological Study of the Bowery* (Chicago: Joseph J. Lanzit, 1909), 257.
45. Ben Primer, *Protestants and American Business Methods* (Ann Arbor, Mich.: UMI Research Press, 1979).
46. Evangeline Booth, *The Salvation Army Appraises Prohibition* (New York: Salvation Army National Headquarters, n.d.), 5.
47. Ibid., 10.
48. Booth's household consisted of Lieutenant Richard Griffiths, her personal secretary, and Major Mary Welch, who oversaw domestic arrangements.
49. Evangeline Booth, *Woman* (New York: Fleming H. Revell, 1930), 33.
50. *War Cry*, October 6. 1906, 13.
51. Kathy Peiss, *Cheap Amusements: Working Women and Leisure in Turn-of-the-Century New York* (Philadelphia: Temple University Press, 1986), 34.
52. Booth, *Woman*, 16.
53. *War Cry*, August 17, 1918, 2.
54. *War Cry*, October 18, 1918, 12.

Two

David Morgan

Protestant Visual Culture and the Challenges of Urban America during the Progressive Era

In the years before World War I, the baseball evangelist Billy Sunday swept through cities from Davenport, Iowa, to New York on a mission to renew American spiritual life. Bristling at the heart of his message was a passionate concern for American masculinity. "Come on, boys, you've got a chance to show your manhood," he urged the hundreds and thousands of men who attended the special meetings for business- and working men in all of his campaigns.[1] Showing manhood was very much what Sunday's revivals were about, as the many postcards picturing the evangelist himself make clear. Damning booze in brusquely physical terms, Sunday promised he'd "fight till hell freezes over" and had the phrase inscribed on a postcard showing him about to hammer a fist into his imagined foe (Fig. 4).

Over the course of the nineteenth century, Protestant moral reform and religious revival exhibited a range of attitudes toward the city. In antebellum America, evangelical reform movements often regarded the city as a brood of temptations and vices. By midcentury, however, the city could be seen as something more positive, if no less in need of Christian influence, and by the end of the century the enterprise of Christianizing urban America had secured a privileged spot on the agendas of evangelical and liberal Protestants alike. A generally overlooked aspect of this history is the ambitious use of visual culture among Protestants of different stripes to wage their moral campaigns and to lead the errant to spiritual renewal. This essay examines the varied roles that mass-produced images assumed during the Progressive Era. In an age that was discovering the potential of advertising, American Protestants invested great hope in the mass-produced image as an aspect of urban commercial culture that

_____ *Figure 4* _____

C. V. Williams, photographer, Billy Sunday preaching, "I'll fight till hell freezes over," post-card, 1908.
Courtesy Billy Graham Center Museum.

could assist religious campaigns and spiritual formation by visualizing and disseminating a reinvigorated, muscular Christianity. Protestants had long applied illustrated tracts, almanacs, and instructional materials to moral and social reforms such as immigrant assimilation, temperance, and abolition. But in the second half of the nineteenth century, growing numbers of evangelical and liberal Protestants made use of engravings, lithographs, and postcards as they designed pedagogies and mission strategies for work in American cities. If the problem was a flagging masculinity in urban America, images of a renewed, reclaimed Christian heroism were to attract the unconverted and to galvanize the indolent and the backslider by celebrating the charisma of Jesus and his virile representatives. Indeed, inexpensive, mass-produced images were thought to command a special power in fostering and disseminating charisma among boys and men.

Nineteenth-century city planners and landscape architects like Frederick Law Olmsted, who designed New York's Central Park and the landscape plan for Chicago's Columbian Exposition, championed a hopeful belief in the redemptive power of the properly designed city.[2] But if Olmsted contended that Central Park would help redeem New Yorkers from the confusion and materialism of their city, some Protestant reformers insisted that the real threat of urban life was a sapping of masculine vigor. Popular voices such as Billy Sunday called for Christ and religion to be more "manly," and this was the purpose to which such postcards as Figure 4 answered. The search for a masculine Jesus was a visual one that responded to what many Protestants believed was the menacing role that the city played in the moral decline of the nation. New reproductive technologies such as half-tone engraving and photography represented powerful means of disseminating influence and signaled an important shift in visual production, since they allowed for the inexpensive and far-flung distribution of works of art. In the hands of Protestants as different as G. Stanley Hall and Billy Sunday, who were both vitally concerned to reverse what they believed was an epidemic emasculation of American men, urban commercial culture was baptized for use in moral campaigns and evangelical revival.

Popular depictions of religious revivals that took place throughout the Southeast and Northeast during the opening decades of the nineteenth century often pictured calm and orderly gatherings in the woods.[3] But by the midcentury revival of 1857–1858 the pastoral locale for revival was anachronistic. In contrast to the broad pattern of rural revival meetings earlier in the century, the revival of the late 1850s and national revival campaigns thereafter focused on cities and were conducted by such evangelists as Dwight Moody, Reuben Torrey, and J. Wilbur Chapman, who made careers of tending to America's major cities. Dedicating large efforts to Boston, Baltimore, Brooklyn, Manhattan, Pittsburgh,

Philadelphia, and Chicago, these evangelists depended heavily on such inner-city organizations as the Young Man's Christian Association (YMCA) to help gather large urban audiences.[4] If earlier representations of the city had stressed its corrupt ways and the necessity of persevering in it for the sake of one's salvation, by midcentury the city was seen as a special opportunity for delivering the message to large crowds and achieving correspondingly large results. Prominent northern cities were the engines of American industry and commercial well-being, but for both evangelists and pious industrialists, cities required the virtues and piety of Protestantism in order to tame and assimilate their laboring masses.[5]

An illustration from an 1862 issue of the *Well-Spring* (Fig. 5), a Boston-based Sabbath school newspaper, compares the early formation of three young boys in a rural scene of Sabbath school on the left with the same three on the right, now grown up in the city and thriving as an "honored minister," a "successful physician," and a "wealthy merchant." Having started out as "rude-looking" boys in the "street school," Peter, James, and John (the names were doubtless meant to evoke the three most important disciples of Jesus) were transformed in Sabbath school, where "the word of God had got into them, . . . sowing the good seed of piety, industry, and virtue in their hearts."[6] The message of the image was clear: the discipline of a religious formation in youth would yield productive, respectable, and prosperous adult lives. What was sown in the humble setting of the country church would bloom in the urban world as accomplished Christian gentlemen. It was a familiar trajectory among the pious, self-made magnates, the legendary rugged individualists such as John D. Rockefeller Sr. or John Wanamaker, who grew from modest origins to spectacular wealth, often migrating from country to city. Figure 5 emends the antebellum judgment against the city by celebrating urban respectability as the proper outcome of a Christian formation of boys. If, as historian Dell Upton has written, the urban landscape of the early Republic was viewed moralistically as a "competitive material world [that] seemed to promote the loosening of traditional standards of personal discipline," then Figure 5 advertised a solution that regarded the city in a more positive light.[7] Commerce and the professions were held up as appropriate callings for urban Christians whose roots were sunk in the evangelical ethos of rural America.

Liberal Protestantism and the Urban
Context of the Progressive Era

The appeal to youth was crucial since at midcentury 43 percent of the American white population was under sixteen years of age, and evangelicals found that converting children was far easier than converting their parents.[8] In

_____ *Figure 5* _____
Eli Whitney, engraver, "Sabbath School and Sabbath School Graduates," *Well-Spring* 19, no. 48 (November 28, 1862), cover.
Courtesy Billy Graham Center Museum.

fact, historian Anne Boylan cited a missionary of the American Sunday School Union who claimed in 1859 that "most, if not all, the Churches of the West of recent formation, have grown out of Sunday-schools previously existing."[9] Illustrated materials worked very well as rewards for Sunday school attendance among children and youth and to induce desired behavior such as attention and punctuality. Children, in turn, brought their parents and siblings to church. The market for illustrated children's literature was catered to by such mammoth publishers of religious materials as the American Tract Society (New York) and the American Sunday School Union (Philadelphia), both of which were pioneers in illustrating their mass-produced publications.[10]

The concern for youth was not limited to conservative Protestants in the antebellum period. The formation of young people also occupied liberal Protestants in the second half of the century, particularly those who applied the postmillennial optimism of mainstream American Protestantism to a progressive view of national development. These reformers believed the key was education. While antebellum reform initiatives often focused on individual conversion, reformers in the Progressive Era directed their efforts toward much broader, institutional change.

Since the 1840s, a theology of nurture articulated by the Congregationalist minister Horace Bushnell had pressed for an organic unfolding of the personality over time and the long-term influence of environment on the development of the child. Bushnell rejected the older Calvinist view that children were incapable of significant religious formation until they achieved higher rational powers. He also dismissed the evangelical quest for instant conversion as occurred in revival meetings. The human person was to be molded or shaped over time from birth or even before. And this was to happen in the home. Bushnell worried about the distractions and temptations of the city, those "haunts of vice." He strongly urged parents living in "large towns," as an "absolute rule, having no exceptions," never to allow their children to be away from home during the evening. It was the duty of parents, and particularly of the mother, Bushnell claimed, to make the home "a place of attraction" to children, which meant providing books, pictures, games, diversions, and plays to keep children engaged at home rather than wandering unprotected among the dangers of the city.[11] This caution is reflected in the profusion of nineteenth-century engravings of children in the home, praying or reading scripture with mother or father. But as the century ended, more Americans were living in cities than ever before, and the hopes for domestic Christianity had to be replaced with a new strategy. If children were to be Christianized, Americanized, and saved from urban vice, the institutions of public and religious education would need to be applied to the task.

The legacy of Bushnell's organic conception of character formation is evident in the psychology of childhood and adolescence that emerged by the end of the century. The work of Harvard-trained researchers Edwin Starbuck and G. Stanley Hall was foundational in stressing the importance of youth in the formation of the religious sensibilities of adults. A Chicago-based organization, the Religious Education Association (REA), founded in 1903 by William Rainy Harper, president of the University of Chicago, applied the scientific approach to the study of children and adolescents to the tasks of religious education. Harper and the host of liberal Protestants who belonged to the REA and contributed to its scholarly journal, *Religious Education*, believed that the attempts at educating young people in the American Sunday school had failed. Spearheaded by Chicago businessman Benjamin Jacobs at an interdenominational national convention of Sunday school educators in 1872, the "Uniform Lesson Plan" was an attempt to standardize Sunday school curriculum to be used by mainstream Protestants throughout the nation as well as around the world. A generation later, however, many Protestants found the benefits of the plan promised by Jacobs and his supporters to be lacking. Members of the REA insisted that the reason for failure was the inability of the Uniform Plan to accommodate the different ages of students. Harper and his colleagues argued for a graded or age-specific curriculum that would be keyed to the particular level of psychological development of the learner. This "child-centered" pedagogy was a hallmark of progressive educational reform at the turn of the century, and the REA sought to apply it to religious education with great zeal.

At the first convention of the REA, a department on religious art was established in order to gather ideas and materials to enhance worship. *Religious Education* published many articles advocating the use of art and film in the religious classroom and worship space. Fine art, or more accurately, reproductions of fine art, asserted Congregationalist clergyman from Oak Park, Illinois, William Barton, exerted a humanizing power that American Protestants should refuse to do without. Failing to learn the moderating influence of beauty, "our commercialism will swamp us," Barton warned. "We need the love of art," he maintained, "not as a veneer on the surface of a swift-grown and possibly decaying prosperity, but as an evolution of life through industry toward the ideal."[12] Thus Barton counseled Protestant churches to stock their libraries with useful books on religious art. Another Chicagoan and contributor to *Religious Education*, Frederica Beard, developed a detailed curriculum of religious fine art for the Sunday school. Beard believed that pictures could induce pious feeling as well as positive behavior, and she saw special application for them among the challenging children of America's immigrants. She cited the harmonious effect of a tastefully decorated public schoolroom on an otherwise unmanageable group of "sixth grade Poles and Bohemians" and pointed out that pictures on the wall of a Sunday school classroom helped create a "pleasant homelike room" that attracted people such as "foreigners, especially Italians, [who] are interested in pictures."[13] Beard provided long lists of inexpensive reproductions of paintings of biblical subjects that she considered suitable for particular age groups of boys and girls. Certain subjects and artistic styles were keyed to age and gender as most effective for assisting with religious instruction. The idealized imagery of Renaissance and baroque art was considered more fitting for younger children, while the sharper realism of nineteenth-century religious art worked better with older students. Pictures showing Christ engaged in outdoor activities and associated with men were appropriate for boys; images portraying moments from the life of Jesus when he was with his mother, other women, or blessing children were best for female students. Among Beard's favorite artists was the late-nineteenth-century German painter Bernhard Plockhorst, whose *Christ Blessing the Children* (Fig. 6) she reproduced in her book, *Pictures in Religious Education* (1920), and placed on her list of images "peculiarly fitting for girls."[14]

Among the most prolific and widely read psychologists of the "child-study" movement was G. Stanley Hall, founder and president of Clark University in

———— *Figure 6* ————

Bernhard Plockhorst, *Christ Blessing the Children*, 1885, from Abram P. Elder, ed., *The Light of the World; or, Our Saviour in Art* (Chicago: Elder, 1896), plate 99.

Worcester, Massachusetts, as well as a Sunday school teacher and one-time seminary student. Hall directed his attention to the role of Christian art in his study *Jesus, the Christ, in the Light of Psychology* (1917). There he assigned to literature and the visual arts of his day an immense task: "to reincarnate the risen Lord in the modern world."[15] Whereas the critical methods of modern historical analysis had placed in doubt the unquestioned authority of biblical texts, Hall sought to base the legitimacy of Christ as a hero for the modern psyche on the power of the imagination to evoke what modern humanity required. He spoke of the "psychological Jesus Christ" as more important than the "historical Jesus" and insisted that the "true Christ is present in human hearts to-day and not merely in the ancient and very imperfect annals of incompetent recorders" (viii). True religion was not a projection of God into a heavenly realm, the conjuring of an afterlife, or reliance on miracles, but a psychologization of all such needs: "there must be no craven, supine or neurotic flight from present now and here reality" (xiv). There is only the temporal formation of the self. Even the church threatened the vitality and this-worldliness of the modern soul: "The church is a cult and no longer stands for the highest culture. It has become an idolater of its symbols, and lost the holy passion to penetrate ever deeper into their significance. It has lost control of, and often all vital touch with the leaders of mankind, and makes only a falsetto, sporadic appeal to educated youth" (xvi). Hall called for "nothing less than a new Christianity," which is how he had ended the second volume of *Adolescence*, which appeared in 1916. Psychology was to provide this new religion by demonstrating how Jesus, the heroic symbol of the world's highest religion, encompassed within his life the ideal formation of the self and offered a heroic model that could be used to transform the ancient creeds of Christianity into the symbolic confessions of today's "educated youth" (ever the concern of Hall). The "falsetto appeal," which was all the church could muster, signifies the great threat it posed: a feminization of the virile, passionate strength that adolescent boys and young men especially needed in the shaping of their souls. Hall lamented the corresponding state of much recent art: "Most pictures of Jesus during the last century give him a distinctly feminine look. The brow, cheek, and nose, if all below were covered, would generally be taken for those of a refined and superior woman" (22). Particularly telling in the physiognomy of Christ's emasculation in nineteenth-century art was the meagerness of his beard, which was often portrayed by artists as "light, exposing the upper part of the chin, and its scantiness, with the usually copious hair of the scalp and the feminine features, sometimes almost suggest[ing] a bearded lady" (23).

Hall feared that "the personality of Jesus is in some danger of paling into ineffectiveness" (28). He therefore stressed the importance of an artistic treatment that would infuse the image of Christ with "beauty, power, and sublimity." Hall was convinced of the power of mythic imagery to speak to the soul. Artists offered modern Christianity the ability to inspire the imagination rather than to constrain reason with uncompelling articles of belief. Inspired by Nietzsche's concept of a heroic Übermensch to lead humanity beyond itself, Hall yearned for "a normative Jesus figure" and warned, "Without it man lacks orientation for the direction of growth and progress" (32).

Gail Bederman has argued that Hall "feared overcivilization was endangering American manhood."[16] Overcivilization consisted of the increased organization of life, the growth of cities and the concentration of life within them, prolonged education, and the decrease of outdoor, physical activities. The result was neurasthenia, or the debilitation of vital forces in the body. A principal manifestation of this excess of refinement was effeminacy. The older fear of the city was coupled with rising anxieties about threats to American masculinity. The solution urged by Hall and many others was the fostering of what Hall called in a lecture to the YMCA in 1901 "rational muscle culture" in the education of boys and young men.[17] On another occasion, as Bederman has pointed out, Hall encouraged teachers to indulge under certain conditions boys' need for savagery or primitive conduct such as fighting and listening to violent stories.[18]

The need for a hero dominated Hall's thinking about the formation of boys and young men, a hero with charisma or vital force that would be communicated to young males in the formative stages of their personalities as an ideal in which to invest the energy that modern civilization and urban life threatened to sap and misdirect. Hall considered the need for a compelling Jesus figure to depend on deploying the hero archetype in the costume and relevance of modernity: "Could we not have Jesus as an athletic champion, illustrating perhaps the ideal of doing the prodigies that athletes so admire? Could Jesus be knight priest, banker, sailor, landed proprietor, society man, manufacturer, actor, professor, editor, etc.? and if so, how? and if not, why not?"[19] Although the heroic possibilities of the college professor seem clear enough, Christ as "landed proprietor," "society man," or "manufacturer" is surprising, that is, until one realizes they comport with the perceived need to reclaim Christianity, or its charismatic founder, for modern urban, industrial society.

A similar set of concerns animated the advertising mogul and pioneer of public relations Bruce Barton, another liberal Protestant who blamed the lack of interest among American boys and young men in the church on the excessive influence of women.[20] Like Hall, Barton was convinced that American men did not have available to them the real Jesus, who ought to be the heroic figure of a male cult of youth, an active young man who rightly inspired admiration and imitation. Barton faulted artists for creating feeble visual portrayals of Christ, and he longed for a fitting picture of the Christ he knew. In his 1914 manifesto on Christian virility, *A Young Man's Jesus*, Barton excoriated painters who portrayed Christ as "soft-faced and effeminate." Speaking to his audience of like-minded young men and presaging the male bonding that became a mark of later versions of bear-hugging, stadium-filled muscular Christianity, Barton proclaimed: "We are His age: we know Him: He is ours."[21] Presaging his momentous career as one of the nation's most influential admen, Barton proffered in a frontispiece to his book a proper image of Jesus that seems calculated to have met Hall's criteria—at least insofar as evident masculinity and density of facial hair were concerned. Poised like a billboard, seeking out the viewer with a penetrating gaze, Darius Cobb's *The Master* (Fig. 7) displays a copious beard and mustache and sports a heavy brow that recalls the "primitive" energies that Hall endorsed as the antidote to overcivilization. This Neanderthal Jesus was clearly immune to the emasculating neurasthenia and other nervous disorders that plagued modern men; judging from his hirsute visage and intense glare, he would also appear to be a candidate for the heroic ideal of a modern "superman" that Hall called on artists to contribute to the revitalizing of Christianity.

Hall's invocation of a modern Jesus anticipated Barton's characterization of Christ as business executive extraordinaire in his best-selling book, *The Man Nobody Knows* (1924). There Jesus was said to have radiated charismatic effulgence and exerted boundless influence over others not by virtue of miracles or supernatural intervention but by sheer personal magnetism, the same vital force that captains of industry and corporate America commanded in their day-to-day ministries of executive influence. The importance of heroism and charisma occupied both Hall and Barton, as well as many others. Conducting a psychological analysis of heroes and gods, Hall had enumerated four inferences regarding Christ's "personal impressiveness." Jesus must have been large, strong, and beautiful, and he must have exhibited bearing and presence or personal magnetism.[22] Barton's evocation of the man nobody knew conformed entirely to this image.

Urban Revivalism and the Iconography of Charisma

Liberal Protestants like Hall and Barton were not alone in harnessing the hope of Christian faith in modern America to the charisma of the hero. At the opposite end of the theological spectrum, revivalist preacher Billy Sunday was renowned during the years before and during the First World War for his masculinist rhetoric and jingoistic oratorical acrobatics, all of which projected a carefully cultivated image of the revivalist as a heroic athlete for Jesus. Sunday's revival meetings gathered millions before his platform, from which he delivered rousing homilies calculated to bring audiences to their feet. A former

_____ *Figure 7* _____
Darius Cobb, *The Master*, from Bruce Barton, *A Young Man's Jesus* (Boston: Pilgrim's Press, 1914), frontispiece.

professional baseball player, Sunday built on the importance of masculinity in American urban revivalism since Moody's day as a special attraction to male audiences. No other evangelist, Bruce Barton claimed in a flattering essay on Sunday, "can number a larger proportion of men than women on his convert rolls."[23] No doubt that was due to Sunday's insistence that Jesus "was no dough-faced, lick-spittle proposition . . . [but] the greatest scrapper that ever lived."[24] Signaling his allegiance to the conservative, nationalistic politics of his friend, former president Theodore Roosevelt, Sunday fashioned an American middle-class Christianity with a militant, masculine appeal to American self-interest: "Moral welfare makes a man hard. Superficial peace makes a man mushy. . . . The prophets all carried the Big Stick."[25]

In his insightful biography of Sunday, historian William McLoughlin argues that Sunday's success during the early years of the twentieth century depended on the evangelist's effective appeal to middle-class whites. Beleaguered by labor unrest, urban poverty, depressions and panics, and political corruption, whites longed for the social arrangements and ideology of the pre-entrepre-neurial capitalism of an earlier day, an age when most Americans lived in the countryside or the small town, industry was not the economic powerhouse it had become, and immigration was an economic threat confined for most rural whites to distant urban areas. Such urban blights as child labor, slums, prosti-tution, and unemployment were the product of rampant industrialization and unbridled capitalization. Most evangelical Christians were inclined to associate urban problems with the lack of personal virtue and the consequence of bad choices of individuals. Evangelists such as Billy Sunday, McLoughlin main-tains, helped many pious Americans deny the need for meaningful social and economic reform since the problem, as they desired to understand it, was per-sonal sin and lack of faith, not exploitation by the class of entrepreneurs and industrialists (many of whom supported Sunday, for example, J. P. Morgan, W. E. Dodge, Cyrus McCormick, Louis Swift, Philip Armour, Andrew Carnegie, John D. Rockefeller Jr., Henry Clay Frick, H. J. Heinz, and Henry Leland).[26] The religious conversion that Sunday promoted was to be achieved by a turn toward individual virtue, not by addressing the economic conditions underlying poverty. This appealed to the entrepreneurial class, since nondrinking workers were more productive and reliable. As one sympathetic mainline denomina-tional writer commented of Sunday's Pittsburgh campaign (1913), local busi-nessmen generously supported the evangelist's meetings because they "regarded the total expenditure as more than returned in mills, factories, shops, and in every department of commercial life in Pittsburgh and the surrounding country in a single week."[27]

So it is little surprise that many of the leading capitalists of the day under-wrote Sunday's revivals and welcomed his ambitious urban campaigns. He preached an ideal "American way" and "old-time religion," visions of a simpler, more honest, more decent nation in which disruption or adulteration of the sta-tus quo was not tolerated. "You walk the streets of New York or Philadelphia or

Chicago," Sunday complained, "and not one out of every three faces will have in them the strains of pure Americanism."[28] His audiences, who believed with Sunday that crime and other urban problems were properly attributed to immigrants who gathered in urban enclaves and refused to assimilate to the "American way," shared his unease with urban immigrants. Accepting Christ as one's personal savior meant conducting one's life in a particular way, that is, being a decent American, which meant being a Christian American or more especially an evangelical Protestant American. What this meant was quite apparent from Sunday's sermons: don't drink; don't smoke; don't swear; don't indulge in gambling, card-playing, theater-going, novel-reading, or excessive displays of fashion; and observe the evangelical understanding of gender roles. It also meant endorsing American capitalism, patriotism, and conservative nationalist politics. Decent Americans played by this system or set of rules governing everyday life, all of which amounted to a neat economy of belief: "Keep your account straight so when the Great Bookkeeper calls for a statement, your account will show a balance in your favor."[29]

Sunday continued an American evangelical tradition of pushing Arminianism to extremes, conflating free will in accepting the personally directed salvation of Jesus with the optimism of American rugged individualism. Personal success became the index of God's favor. Although one did not earn salvation, one did earn God's blessing. By rejecting sin and calling on Christ's forgiveness, Christians opened themselves to God's plan for their lives, which, for many American evangelicals in Sunday's audiences, meant success and wealth. Humans participated in a significant way in achieving the reward of a blessed lifestyle: "Let's get cleaned up for God, and see if the Lord won't do great things. He will not send the wind to drive our ships unless we have faith to lift our sails."[30] American masculine self-determination intermingled with providence to the point of becoming virtually indistinguishable: "Why don't you be a man? Why don't you show a man's courage, and take up the cross of the Son of God? Why don't you rise up to what you might be? We were all meant for better things."[31]

According to one of Sunday's biographers, William T. Ellis, "The oldest problem of the Christian church, and the latest problem of democracy, is how to reach the great mass of people." Ellis believed that Sunday's revivals solved this problem. For Ellis, there was "no question that [Sunday] stirs a city as not even the fiercest political campaign stirs it."[32] Other sympathetic observers agreed. Writing in a Protestant Episcopal publication about Sunday's Pittsburgh campaign of 1913 (the first city of over half a million inhabitants to host a Sunday crusade), one contemporary was struck by the citywide impact of the event: "City politicians came forward at the meetings and asked for prayer. The daily newspapers gave more space to salvation than they did to scandal, not for one day, but day after day and week after week. As a mere spectacle of a whole modern city enthralled by the Gospel it was astonishing, unbelievable, unprecedented, prodigious."[33] The secret to this successful mass communication, according to Sunday, was a carefully controlled procedure. In order to achieve maximum impact for his campaigns, Sunday enthusiastically practiced "business methods" in religion, rigorously organizing each revival and commencing on-site planning as much as one year in advance. He made deliberate use of media and many forms of advertising. And at each revival he made a point of endorsing such "business methods" and encouraged his audience of businessmen to do the same in their congregations. Understanding his job as selling the ideal of the self-made man, Sunday cast the task of evangelism in terms of salesmanship and advertising. Although he was often criticized for the theatricality of his diction and gesticulation, dismissed by some as "offer[ing] himself as a substitute for a vaudeville show," Sunday and his publicity machine were careful to underscore (and often inflate) the numerical results of his flamboyant style of preaching.[34]

If the many remarks in the press as well as the caricatures both fond and spiteful are any indication, people recognized Sunday's vernacular manner of preaching as his trademark. Sunday capitalized on this "brand recognition" by using photographs and postcards to model the life of evangelical belief. For years at revival meetings, Sunday's personal secretary, Fred Seibert, sold tracts, Sunday's authorized biography, and postcards with images of Sunday striking the dramatic gestures and poses that animated his sermons. Typically, the postcards visualized an athletic figure hurling invective or grasping a chair, which he might fling across the stage in the next instant (Fig. 8). This image carried a quotation from a Sunday sermon: "Break Away from the Old Bunch or Be Damned." In the sermon, Sunday challenged his listeners to repentance. Several of the postcards reproduced in the Ellis biography capture a pivotal homiletic moment, as when the orator removed his coat to rumble with the "liquor business," or in another prepares to deal its deathblow (see Fig. 4), in which the preacher raises his fist and utters, "I'll fight till hell freezes over." Some of the most histrionic images show the evangelist standing on a chair with arms flailing or curled over his lectern in the manner of a grappler, manhandling his audience into submission. Still others present a well-dressed and eloquent speaker, snapshots of the self-made man, the fellow who started out in a slovenly wooden shed (also reproduced in a photograph in the Ellis biography) in small town Iowa but made it big. As accoutrements of fame and celebrity status, the postcards documented and broadcast the truth about pulling oneself up by the bootstraps. They were visual sermons preaching the evangelical doctrine of Arminianism applied to American life.

_____ *Figure 8* _____

C. V. Williams, photographer, Billy Sunday with chair, "Break Away from the Old Bunch or Be Damned," postcard, 1908.
Courtesy Billy Graham Center Museum.

The biography of Sunday sold at the meetings was written by Sunday's friend and assistant, the preacher Elijah P. Brown, and entitled *The Real Billy Sunday* (1914). The book included numerous photographs of the evangelist as well as family members, including one page of six images with the caption "As He Appears at Home, Between Meetings." The photographs are portraits of the ideal Christian family man, posing with his children, his dog, in his yard, and seated in the porch swing of his house.[35] Not only did these images visualize the fruits of Sunday's call to conversion to the American lifestyle, they testified to the fact that Sunday exemplified the "Americanism" that he preached. By selling the book and postcards at the meetings, Sunday fostered a cult of personality in which religious charisma was converted into popular celebrity. Longing for righteousness became desire for the American way. As a kind of evangelical baseball card, photographs of Sunday's aggressive preaching style offered his admirers icons of Christian heroism.

While Max Weber contended that charisma was replaced in modern, secular society by rational bureaucratization, Sunday proved the contrary.[36] His operation subtly blended routine and method with personal magic in the attempt to maximize and to sustain his appeal. People flocked to watch him perform his message, and they gladly took home the mass-produced visual records of the preacher's charisma. Alternately seen in the grip of inspiration and righteous rage, Sunday was glorified in postcard images as a hero doing battle for the American soul. Engaged in a lively, entertaining, and manly struggle against vice and sinfulness, Sunday looked toward a triumph that promised a fuller realization of America as the object of God's providential mission and favor. In effect, the postcards acted as visual tracts that spoke directly to the viewer and encoded in images without text the evangelist's message of a manly American Christianity. The athleticism of the speaker appealed to Sunday's audience because it suggested an untrammeled and compelling style. Sunday delighted in lampooning a sniffling, fastidious clergy as well as the "social club" (another version of the "old bunch" scorned in Figure 8) that he believed many congregations had become, having lost "the old-time fire and the old-time spirit" that his preaching sought to reignite.[37] While institutional Christianity was failing to respond, Sunday believed, his parachurch organization, infused with and at the service of his personal charisma, thrived on an aggressive use of visual and print media to magnify and broadcast his charm and appeal among urban Americans.[38] The renewal of genuine religion, according to Sunday, centered on the charismatic figure who performed it. Postcards of the evangelist were souvenirs of having been present at his charismatic performance.

Despite their considerable theological differences, Sunday, on the one hand, and Hall and Barton, on the other, shared a belief that traditional institutional Christianity in America had failed to capture the allegiance of many Americans, so they each offered as a solution their own understandings of a charismatic revival in which images played a central role. Hall believed that the heroism of the mythic leader, evoked by the artist, would ignite the fervor and dedication of youth and therefore called on artists to produce a new image of Jesus Christ. Barton considered the matter a problem in public relations and promoted a new campaign in which Christ was remasculinized in order to be made attractive to American men. Sunday presented himself as the embodiment of charisma, the fetching leader for urban masses who were atrophying in the pews of uninspired churches. The postcards sold at his revivals commodified his aura or presence into material forms that admirers took home with them as mementos of the charismatic leader. The personalized commodities that audiences purchased on site were calculated to promote and circulate his charisma. "Charisma not only disrupts social order," one student of Weber has stressed, "it also maintains or conserves it."[39] Weber's inclination to contrast charisma and the process of secular institutionalization may reflect his view that the modern world was disenchanted. Sunday's evangelical efforts in the modern American city might be seen as an attempt to reverse this secularization by injecting religious institutions with a reviving power of charisma. Similarly, Hall and Barton sought to revitalize an emasculated modern culture by invoking the charisma of a manly Christ reclaimed from anachronism and feminine influence. It was a mass-culture invention of icons of male heroism that could be cheaply manufactured and easily distributed to the city-bound populations of American men. If antebellum views of the city were often pessimistic, by century's end a new understanding had emerged: the city was a challenge that a deft configuration of commerce, charisma, and faith could answer.

Notes

1. Quoted in Bruce Barton, "Billy Sunday—Baseball Evangelist," *Collier's* 51 (July 26, 1913), 7.
2. On the history of American urbanism and city planning, see Giorgio Ciucci, Francesco Dal Co, Mario Manieri-Elia, and Manfredo Tafuri, *The American City: From the Civil War to the New Deal*, trans. Barbara Luigia La Penta (Cambridge: MIT Press, 1979).
3. See, for instance, the bucolic scene of a camp meeting in the woods that appeared in the *Family Christian Almanac for 1858* (New York: American Tract Society, 1857), doubtless intended to promote the current evangelical revival in the United States. Another instance is found in James H. Hutson, *Religion and the Founding of the American Republic* (Washington, D.C.: Library of Congress, 1998), 101.
4. For important studies of urban revivalism in the United States, see Kathryn Teresa Long, *The Revival of 1857–58: Interpreting an American Religious Awakening* (New York: Oxford University Press, 1998); Daniel M. Robertson, *The Chicago Revival, 1876: Society and Revivalism in a Nineteenth-Century City*, Studies in Evangelicalism, no. 9 (Metuchen, N.J.: Scarecrow Press, 1989); and William G. McLoughlin, *Revivals, Awakenings, and Reform: An Essay on Religion and Social Change in America, 1607–1977* (Chicago: University of Chicago Press, 1978), 141–153. Revivals in urban areas during the antebellum period are of course well known, beginning with George Whitefield in the eighteenth century. By the second half of the nineteenth century, however, major cities became the singular focus of numerous influential evangelists as the great hope for reviving the nation.

5. For full-scale studies of the social control that evangelicalism was believed to provide, even if, in fact, it often did not, see Paul Johnson, *A Shopkeeper's Millennium: Society and Revivals in Rochester, New York, 1815–1837* (New York: Hill and Wang, 1978); and Paul Boyer, *Urban Masses and Moral Order in America, 1820–1920* (Cambridge: Harvard University Press, 1978).

6. "The Sabbath School and its Graduates," *Well-Spring* 19, no. 48 (November 28, 1862), 1.

7. Dell Upton, "Another City: The Urban Cultural Landscape in the Early Republic," in *Everyday Life in the Early Republic*, ed. Catherine E. Hutchins (Winterthur, Del.: Henry Francis du Pont Winterthur Museum, 1994), 105.

8. United States Bureau of the Census, *A Century of Population Growth from the First Census of the United Sates to the Twelfth 1790–1900* (Washington, D.C.: Government Printing Office, 1909), 103.

9. Anne M. Boylan, *Sunday School: The Formation of an American Institution 1790–1880* (New Haven, Conn.: Yale University Press, 1988), 34.

10. For a discussion of antebellum mass-produced Protestant imagery, see David Morgan, *Protestants and Pictures: Religion, Visual Culture, and the Age of American Mass Production* (New York: Oxford University Press, 1999).

11. Horace Bushnell, *Christian Nurture*, introduction by John M. Mulder (Grand Rapids, Mich.: Baker Book House, 1979), 344.

12. William E. Barton, "The Library as a Minister in the Field of Religious Art," *Religious Education* 4, no. 6 (February 1910): 595.

13. Frederica Beard, *Pictures in Religious Education* (New York: George H. Doran, 1920), 32, 81. Discussion in this section draws on Morgan, *Protestants and Pictures*.

14. Beard, *Pictures*, 110, 67. Beard mistakenly indicated that Heinrich Hofmann painted the image.

15. G. Stanley Hall, *Jesus, the Christ, in the Light of Psychology*, 2 vols. (Garden City, N.Y.: Doubleday, 1917), vol. 1, viii. All page references in the text hereafter are to volume 1 of this publication.

16. Gail Bederman, *Manliness & Civilization: A Cultural History of Gender and Race in the United States, 1880–1917* (Chicago: University of Chicago Press, 1995), 77.

17. G. Stanley Hall, "Christianity and Physical Culture," *Pedagogical Seminary* 9 (September 1902), reprinted in *Health, Growth, and Heredity*, ed. Charles E. Strickland and Charles Burgess, Classics in Education, no. 23 (New York: Teachers College Press, Columbia University, 1965), 157.

18. Bederman, *Manliness & Civilization*, 98.

19. Hall, *Jesus*, 34–35.

20. For insightful studies of Barton, see Warren Susman, "Piety, Profits, and Play: The 1920s," in *Men, Women, and Issues in American History*, vol. 2, rev. ed., ed. Howard H. Quint and Milton Cantor (Homewood, Ill.: Dorsey Press, 1980), 202–227; and T. J. Jackson Lears, "From Salvation to Self-Realization: Advertising and the Therapeutic Roots of the Consumer Culture, 1880–1930," in *The Culture of Consumption: Critical Essays in American History, 1880–1980*, ed. Richard Wightman Fox and T. J. Jackson Lears (New York: Pantheon Books, 1983), 1–38.

21. Bruce Barton, *A Young Man's Jesus* (Boston: Pilgrim Press, 1914), xvii.

22. Ibid., 35–38.

23. Barton, "Billy Sunday," 8.

24. Quoted in William G. McLoughlin Jr., *Billy Sunday Was His Real Name* (Chicago: University of Chicago Press, 1955), 179. Long has discussed revivalism and masculinity in *The Revival*, 68–92. For a helpful study of masculinity and Protestant revivalism in Sunday's day, see Gail Bederman, "'The Women Have Had Charge of the Church Work Long Enough': The Men and Religion Forward Movement of 1911–1912 and the Masculinization of Middle-Class Protestantism," *American Quarterly* 41 (1989): 432–465. This movement attracted the support of Protestant intellectuals and mainline churchmen, such as Washington Gladden, who sneered at Sunday's revivalism. Bederman notes that increase in male membership occurred in the Episcopal Church as well as the Congregationalist (454), both of which included many clergy who castigated Sunday in the press.

Different as Bruce Barton's liberal Protestant faith was from Sunday's fundamentalism, both men stressed personality and its power of persuasion in their representation of belief. Barton's celebratory article on Sunday's style, "Billy Sunday—Baseball Evangelist," reproduced more than half a dozen of Sunday's postcards, including Figures 4 and 8 illustrated here. Not surprisingly, Barton also found G. Stanley Hall a source of wisdom. Bruce Barton, "How You Can Do More and Be More: An Interview with G. Stanley Hall," *American Magazine* 96 (November 1923): 14–15, 90.

25. McLoughlin, *Billy Sunday*, 141.

26. Ibid., 136, 39, 58.

27. Quoted from the *Lutheran Observer*, in "Billy Sunday in Big Cities," *Literary Digest* 48 (April 4, 1914): 761.

28. Quoted in McLoughlin, *Billy Sunday*, 148.

29. Quoted in ibid., 21–22.

30. Sunday sermon, "The Three Groups," printed in Elijah P. Brown, *The Real Billy Sunday* (New York: Fleming H. Revell, 1914), 252.

31. Sunday sermon, "Under the Sun," in Brown, *Billy Sunday*, 263.

32. William T. Ellis, *Billy Sunday: The Man and His Message* (Philadelphia: John C. Winston Company, 1914), 299.

33. Quoted in "Billy Sunday in Big Cities," 761.

34. Quoted in ibid.

35. Brown, *Billy Sunday*, facing p. 174.

36. Max Weber, *On Charisma and Institution Building: Selected Papers*, ed. S. N. Eisenstadt (Chicago: University of Chicago, 1968).

37. Sunday, "Three Groups," 242.

38. Sunday was not, of course, the inventor of what might be called "mass-mediated charisma." Harry Stout has shown this to have been George Whitefield's genius. Whitefield's innovations were not lost on later generations of American revivalists from Charles Finney to Billy Graham; see Harry S. Stout, "Religion, Communications, and the Career of George Whitefield," in *Communication and Change in American Religious History*, ed. Leonard I. Sweet (Grand Rapids, Mich.: Eerdmans, 1993), 108–125. See also Harry S. Stout, *The Divine Dramatist: George Whitehead and the Rise of Modern Evangelicalism* (Grand Rapids, Mich.: Eerdmans, 1991).

39. Edward Shils, "Charisma, Order, and Status," *American Sociological Review* 30, no. 2 (April 1965): 203. The following observation is Shils's.

Three

Fran Grace

The Best Show in Town

Carry Nation and the Selling of Temperance in the Urban Northeast

In the hundred years since Carry Nation led a citizens' army against saloons in Topeka, Kansas, the rowdy escapades of the Kansas grandmother have slipped from public awareness. Yet a century previous, prohibition was "in" and, with it, an array of things for sale: jewelry, performances, books, songs, etchings, and stoves—all of which helped to promote the "gospel of prohibition." Carry Nation and her hatchet came onto the scene of temperance politics just in time. In the early years of the temperance movement (1800–1860), evangelical leaders could rely on a Protestant-dominated culture to promote their anti-alcohol values via the spoken and printed word, a method modeled on the promotional tactics of the tract and missionary societies. Temperance literature hit the print market as popular authors like Timothy Shay Arthur, Louisa May Alcott, E.D.E.N. Southworth, and others gave the country heroes and heroines who eschewed booze or courageously recovered from it. Arthur's *Ten Nights in a Bar-Room* (1854) sold millions of copies and was a Broadway blockbuster even in the early 1900s when Carry Nation performed in it. In this pathos-packed story, Joe Morgan's life is ruined because evil saloonkeeper Simon Slade gets him hooked on booze. Joe finally turns his life around after Slade accidentally kills Joe's daughter, little Mary Morgan, in a saloon brawl. There were visual images as well: *Drunkard's Progress* (1846) by Nathaniel Currier etched into people's minds the steps of degeneration from "first glass to drunkard's grave." The well-dressed man sips a glass of whiskey with a friend in the first frame, and, by the last frame, he has suffered jail (for robbery and rioting), disease, unemployment, humiliation of his family, loss of friends, poverty, and suicide.

But as the twentieth century dawned, temperance-turned-prohibition activists needed a more sophisticated marketing strategy that would appeal to a culture less and less supportive of Protestant religious and moral values. They had to remake their prohibition crusade to appeal to a more religiously diverse, commercially competitive, and consumer-oriented market. Carry Nation came to the rescue—with her hatchet. Although Nation died in 1911 just as the national prohibition movement was gaining state and local strides, her savvy about how to use commercial culture to promote religious values in urban settings revived the beleaguered prohibition movement at a crucial juncture between 1900 and 1910. After her death, the Anti-Saloon League (founded and headed by evangelical ministers) eventually developed a political and marketing strategy successful with middle-class and upper-class citizen-consumers. But it was Nation who took the selling of Protestant temperance sensibilities to a new level.

This essay argues that Carry Nation used commercial culture in the urban Northeast to spread her gospel of prohibition. Specifically, it analyzes her sacralization of secular entertainment stages and her selling of crusade "relics" and suggests that, ultimately, her strategy was successful because she exploited northeastern urban consumer-culture's fascination with the religious primitivism of the American West. She packaged herself, her public ideas of temperance, and her "relics" to hook consumers yearning for the symbols and mythology of muscular Christianity. She very pragmatically assumed that both religion and commercial culture were necessary in convincing skeptical northeastern urbanites to join the cause of prohibition. Moreover, this essay argues that gender and class mattered in the construction of Nation's message. Because she was a lower-middle-class, uneducated woman, Nation had to prove what her educated male counterparts could take for granted: the credibility to speak on a public issue. Rural midwesterners cheered her as a heroine and a prophet, affirming her as a preacher for prohibition. But urban northeasterners, fearful of blurring traditional gender roles, castigated her as an Amazonian or as a masculinized, menopausal woman. Nation and her agents turned castigation into commercial advantage, however, by making her rowdiness a selling point for inhibited urbanites.

While Nation rejected many aspects of the consumer ethos—exemplified by her affiliation with the anticonsumerism, antidecadence sect of Free Methodism—she nonetheless manipulated a growing consumer ethos and a commercialization of religion to advance her own crusade. Her use of Chautauqua and vaudeville stages, performative costume, street theater, crusade relics, and religious periodicals (she created and edited two papers) points to a strategy for modern self-promotion. Even her name reflected her commercial savvy and religious vision. In 1903, at age fifty-seven, she had her name legally changed to "Carry A. Nation" to reflect her belief that God had providentially chosen her to "carry a nation" to prohibition.[1] As a self-appointed "New Deborah," she would lead Kansas—and then the nation—into a liquor-free, tobacco-empty, sex-abstaining, decadence-rejecting American promised land (which some east-erners viewed as a promised land not worth going to). Perhaps she did not reach the promised land, but she certainly did entertain the people of God as they wandered through the wilderness of the late Victorian age.

Sacralization of Secular Entertainment Stages

Carry Nation did what few other entertainers (religious or secular) did in her time—moved back and forth between religious and secular venues. She went from Chautauqua, revival, and church pulpits to Broadway, vaudeville, bur-lesque, and music-hall stages. Her first lecture tour to Chicago, made while her Topeka, Kansas, crusade was in full swing during February 1901, exemplified her at-homeness in quite diverse venues: she made formal lectures at Willard Hall to middle-class Protestant reform patrons during the day and gave rowdy addresses from atop saloon tables to unchurched prostitutes and drinkers at night. The admission fees she charged for the middle-class audiences often wound up in the pockets of her saloon-going listeners. She was, in effect, a com-mercial Robin Hood who milked the pockets of white Protestant middle class consumers and passed along the proceeds to the economically and ecclesiasti-cally marginalized. A former press agent of hers complained bitterly that, despite her sensational knack for raking in cash, the "money vampire" (Nation) annoyingly refused to stay in "first class" hotels and preferred to give her money to the "blood suckers" who yanked at her heartstrings. Carry expressed a clear preference for the "down-and-out" dives of the working classes over the pious platforms of social higher-ups, but she always kept a foot on both stages.[2]

Nation was practical enough to know that the spreading of her message depended on meeting the people where they were. Back in the rural areas and small towns of Kansas where her crusade first took off, Nation garnered support for her crusade at community picnics, church revivals, and schoolhouse meet-ings. In northeastern urban areas, however, she had to adapt her religious mes-sage to secular entertainment platforms that drew widely varying audiences. She was surprisingly successful at marketing her Protestant evangelical prohibition gospel to urban consumers of entertainment. Despite the criticism of others that she should not taint God's word by commercializing morality, Nation believed that the salvation of society depended upon such commercialization.

She claimed she had God's authority to carry the gospel of prohibition to entertainment seekers, whether they claimed to be religious or not. Just as she believed God had commanded her to pick up the hatchet and smash saloons, Carry Nation saw her entertainment career as a God-given vocation: "I got hundreds of calls to go on the stage before I did. Gradually I got the light. This is the largest missionary field in the world. No one ever got a call or was ever allowed to go there with a Bible but Carry Nation. That door never was opened to anyone but me. The hatchet opened it. God has given it to me." God, she believed, called her to places that other entertainers disdained: "My managers have said: 'You do not wish to go to a variety house.' . . . If Jesus ate with publicans and sinners I can talk to them. Frances Willard said: 'The pulpit and stage must be taken for God.'" Nation intentionally marketed her gospel message to multiple audiences, including those at vaudeville and burlesque events: "I am fishing. I go where the fish are, for they do not come to me. . . . I found the theatres stocked with the boys of our country. They are not found in churches." She never stepped onto a stage without her Bible, which she identified as the real hatchet: "I take my Bible before every audience. I show them this hatchet that destroys or smashes everything bad and builds up everything that is good. I tell them of their loving Deliverer who came to break every yoke and set the Captive free." Nation delegated her speech preparation to the Holy Spirit, claiming that God inspired the very words that came from her mouth: "I never made a note or wrote a sentence for the platform in my life. Have spoken extemporaneously from the first and often went on the platform when I could not have told what I was to say to save my life, and for weeks God compelled me to open my Bible at random and speak from what my eyes fell on. I have literally proved that 'You shall not think of what you shall speak but it shall be given.'"[3]

A few fans believed her to be a divinely appointed prophet, a few rapscallions aimed to make her a martyr, and many simply found her amusing regardless of her status with the Almighty. They wanted entertainment. Nation's Holiness background caused her to reject many aspects of the consumer ethos of the Gilded Age and to counter with an ethic of self-denial, but these very same roots sacralized the performance stage as a venue that was appropriate for religious events. A Holiness revival was often the best show in town in the southern and western states, and Nation took from her experience of the revivals the assumption that the gospel was too important to be treated blandly or with dainty reserve.

Her use of Chautauqua and vaudeville stages exemplifies her determination to take advantage of commercial and leisure entertainment for God's glory. These were two very different kinds of stages. Although the Chautauqua Association was founded in 1873 as a Protestant Sunday school training camp in wooded western New York, it had become by 1900 a well-marketed retreat for middle-class urban consumers of leisure. As historian R. Laurence Moore has argued, Chautauqua popularized the expectation that "churches owed their members some good times" and was a principal agent in "selling God" to Americans who wanted a "moral vacation" that wedded inspirational messages to playful entertainment and recreation. Some who attended found the insularity to be stifling. When he attended in 1896, psychologist William James found the "middle-class paradise, without sin, without a victim, without a blot, without a tear" to be so unsettling that he yearned for the "relief" of the outside world where "something primordial and savage" might "set the balance straight."[4] Though a popular speaker at Chautauqua events until her death in 1911, Carry Nation also found its middle-class insularity to be lifeless and callow. Audiences cheered her raw wit and enticing informality, but managers sometimes endured complaints about her habitual sermonic use of "hell" and "damnation," a vocabulary seen as unfit for the children and women who attended Chautauqua. Even up to the year before her death, Nation wrote to a relative that she drew "the biggest crowds of any speaker on the Chautauqua platform."[5] Nation gave these Protestant consumers what they wanted: the fantasy that they could have both "old time religion" and an urban, middle-class life.

The staid and irenic middle-class Chautauqua audiences contrasted sharply with those of Nation's vaudeville and burlesque performances, but she was just as successful in exploiting them as commercial opportunities. In contrast to what some historians have suggested, Carry Nation's experience suggests the vaudeville milieu was a rowdy one, with much bantering from half-drunk, working-class audiences and the occasional food fight.[6] These audiences seemed drawn, just as the riotous mobs were in the Kansas towns of her smashing escapades, to Nation's ability to evoke God's presence in the midst of the carnivalesque. She successfully drew on the rhythm of revival language about conversion in secular environments.

In his magazine, Brooklyn editor Will Carleton described one of her shows in a New York City vaudeville "dive." "Smoke If You Want To" read a sign on the wall and, according to Carleton, most in the audience wanted to. The liquor flowed freely from a saloon in the basement, and so did the noise. He noted that occasionally the crash of glass and streams of profanity echoed up the stairs into the dingy, smoke-filled theater, seamlessly mingling with the ribald wit of the black-faced humorist and the much-abbreviated red taffeta dresses of the singers onstage. The half-drunken, unshaven patrons in this "free and easy" vaudeville "dive" hooted and hollered with gusto. After the acrobats, harlequins, singers, and humorist finished their acts, Carleton heard a stagehand announce "Carry A. Nation, loving home defender and famous Kansas saloon smasher." A grandmotherly woman plainly dressed in black alpaca, a Bible in her hand, stepped onto the stage. According to Carleton, the audience stopped yelling. She launched into a sermon about what utter sots they were making of themselves—drinking, smoking, and the like. She made her points so emphatic that they cheered her, and many converted to temperance (or at least agreed to sign a pledge).[7] In addition to the vaudeville circuit, she traveled with burlesque companies, such as the "Through the Centre of the Earth Burlesque Company," which took her to performances throughout the Northeast. "Hell Is No Joke" was the title of her routine performance, and it was introduced by "a chorus of twenty-five maidens in much abbreviated skirts." In the midst of dancing girls onstage and liquor-guzzling audiences, she preached about the judgment day to an attentive crowd.[8]

Hawking Holy Souvenirs

In addition to turning vaudeville dives into revival meetings, Nation sought to maintain consumer attachment to her gospel message by selling souvenirs and "relics." She sold hatchet pins, broken glass from saloon-smashing escapades, autographed copies of her autobiography, copies of her newspapers, signed photographs of her posed with Bible and hatchet, and custom-made flasks (for pure water, not "liquid damnation"). Far from undermining her Protestant message about prohibition, the selling of crusade objects broadened its impact, especially to women and children, who were less likely than men to attend her performances.

Ever since a stranger had given Nation the idea of selling her little hatchet pins, she was never without them and was able to pay all of her expenses, legal fees, and fines with the income she earned from sales. In a letter to a friend, she noted that "people are eager to get the little hatchet as a souvenir," and in her autobiography she marveled at how much revenue they produced.[9]

At a mythical level, the hatchet recaptured the integrity ("I cannot tell a lie") and revolutionary fervor of George Washington. For example, in Figure 9 a cartoonist depicts the connection to Washington by placing a hatchet-holding Carry Nation with folded arms and proud tilt of the chin in a completely demolished saloon with this caption: "I cannot tell a lie; I did it with my little hatchet." There was a level at which she really did exude Washington's legendary integrity because she was authentic and bluntly honest in an age when, as T. J. Jackson Lears and others point out, many people were not. Her "holy hatchet" brandished in the cause of western vigilantism against forces of eastern incorporation symbolized a revitalization of Washington's revolutionary plea for self-preservation and popular sovereignty. Perhaps consumers liked the pin because it bought them symbolic participation in the Puritan myths of antiauthoritarianism and divine chosenness.

Like some of the religious objects that Colleen McDannell describes, the pin "signals who is in the group and who is not" and helps people to articulate a self-identity—something especially appealing in urban environments where people often must reinvent themselves without the safety net of church community or family roots.[10] The hatchet's self-identity function was apparently very powerful

"I CANNOT TELL A LIE--I DID IT WITH MY LITTLE HATCHET!"
Mrs. Nation's Reform Crusade in Kansas, as the Globe Artist Understands It From the Press Dispatches.

_____ *Figure 9* _____

This New York cartoon pictures Carry Nation as many urban northeasterners saw her: a mannish Kansas firebrand, yet one with mythic appeal as a latter-day embodiment of George Washington's proverbial cherry-tree honesty and unstoppable commitment to sovereignty.

to women; most of the anecdotal stories about the pin are of its intergenerational transmission within families by mothers and grandmothers to daughters and granddaughters.[11] Nation commented that mothers pinned the hatchets on their little children to remind them of their mother's love and inspire them toward purity.[12] Buttons with hatchets on them inspired single women to "reject men with bad habits," according to a University of Kansas student who visited the crusader in jail and took four hundred of the buttons to campus to distribute to female students.[13] The hatchet paraphernalia, representative of both caring and violent motherhood, was the perfect commercial-religious-political symbol for the New Deborah who sought to recover what she said was a biblical model of warrior motherhood. However, women's wearing of the hatchet pin must have, at least at an unconscious level, connoted the threat to men of castration and androgyny—especially in urban society where men were preoccupied with effeminacy. A cartoon in *Life* magazine, for example, depicted a clench-jawed, football-shouldered Carry Nation heaving two battle-axes with the caption, "Look out, boys!"[14]

But Nation did not begin her smashing career with a hatchet. Rather, she viewed herself as a New Deborah carrying out the biblical mandate of idol smashing and saw rocks as the most biblical of weapons. However, once she used the hatchet in Wichita for the first time, the press latched on to it as a symbol for her crusade. Nation immediately adapted to this commercialization of her crusade. She sold the hatchet pins, always posed for commercial photographs with a Bible in one hand and a hatchet in the other, named her second newspaper the *Hatchet*, and named her last residence Hatchet Hall.[15] But even in adapting to the symbol that was imposed on her as her crusade developed, she continually tried to redefine—one might say with only limited success—its meaning away from an antimale message and to infuse it with religious overtones.

For example, in the masthead for the *Hatchet*, she made the pro-woman (but not anti-male) comment that "the ballot is to be your hatchet" and proposed that the hatchet was a "Home Defender" and "Home Builder" by "cutting out evil." She included Bible verses that sanctified the hatchet, such as this provocative one: "I will make thee a new sharp threshing instrument having teeth (Isaiah 4:10–15)." And in naming her last home Hatchet Hall, she was again trying to define the hatchet as a domestically friendly, not threatening, symbol. Yet there was a double edge, because her home was not the traditional one with male headship but a community of women over which she functioned as matron. Even if she was not entirely convincing in domesticating her hatchet, other entrepreneurs were. The Art Stove Company of Detroit, which manufactured Laurel Stoves and Ranges, gave away as an advertising scheme pins in the shape of Nation's hatchet with the message to consumers: "Buy Laurel Stoves and Ranges." Maybe the advertisement's idea was that if a husband stopped drinking, he could save that money and purchase a new stove for his family. In this way, the hatchet reinscribed the values of white, urban, Protestant, middle-class family life.[16]

In addition to her hatchet paraphernalia, Nation also marketed glassware that promoted her crusade's agenda of moral purity. She advertised "The Nation's Water Bottle" in her newspaper. They could be ordered in plain or imitation cut-glass, with the engraving: "Oh, let me drink as Adam drank," with a hatchet and "Carrie Nation" underneath. The idea was to have God-given, pure, healthy water as "the universal beverage" rather than the "liquid damnation" of whiskey. At least one Chicagoan expressed that his Carry Nation carafe was "one of his choicest treasures."[17] Nation's liquor enemies, however, had their own countercrusade marketing strategy using glassware. They sold the broken pieces of liquor bottles, windows, and mirrors from her actual saloon attacks as "relics." Antiprohibitionist companies also made and sold gin and decorative bottles that resembled Nation's fully clothed and bonneted form. Thus the space of commercial exchange became a place—just as important as the actual streets where booze and bonnet forces clashed—in which the battle for and against prohibition was waged.

Nation's commercial use of water continued at Hatchet Hall in Eureka Springs, Arkansas, where she—in a Protestant version of Bernadette's vision at Lourdes—dreamed of an underground spring across the street. A dynamiting of the place in her dream indeed resulted in a stream of "Protestant holy water" that served all of Steele Street. Such a vision of natural flowing, pure water would have been particularly compelling for urban dwellers who faced constant water and sanitation problems.

Nation took common utilitarian household items for the two most important commercial objects of her crusade—the hatchet and glassware. They represented the life experiences and roles of both sexes. She invested both of these objects with biblical and religious meaning and then used them as boundary-setters, fund-raisers, and self-promoters in her crusade. From Nation's perspective, the souvenirs helped to advertise, solidify, and immortalize her crusade.

The Commercial Appeal of Muscular Christianity

Nation's speedy co-optation of the hatchet mania palpable in newsrooms and on the streets illustrates a larger point: she commercially exploited the urban Northeast's growing consumer fascination with muscular Christianity and religious primitivism. In order to make her religious message about prohibition appealing, she packaged it and herself as representative of the robust health (moral and otherwise) that muscular Christianity and midwestern religious primitivism had to bring the urban, "effete" Northeast.

Northeastern urbanites were initially hostile to her arrival, mostly lambasting her muscular and rural ways. A woman from Waterbury, Connecticut, wrote that she hoped Carry would "see the error of [her] ways and go back to what God intended" for "a decent woman"—doing "right in [her] own home" and leaving out "all the rowdyism."[18] Even Woman's Christian Temperance Union (WCTU) members and women suffragists in the Northeast waxed rather condescendingly about the "barbarism" of Carry Nation's methods and their incompatibility with eastern refinement. Julia Colman, corresponding secretary of the New York WCTU, told reporters that her branch's nonendorsement was based on regional differences: "New York City is not Kansas. Methods that may be pursued with success in Kansas would not work here." Dr. Ellen Miles punctuated this comment by declaring that "Mrs. Nation's methods are peculiarly wild and westernly and would not do at all in the effete East where we have policemen seven feet high and believe in moral suasion and not muscle."[19]

Some easterners expressed support for Nation's visit to New York, making direct appeals to her embodiment of muscular Christianity. One woman wrote to Nation and begged her to "give us some of your valuable time . . . to start a crusade in New York City" where "we need a leader—someone with the backbone to lead the immense army awaiting the command of the Generaless." A male fan was most excited about her potential as a cure to boredom: "Come soon, for . . . New York is getting so good and quiet it is hardly worth living in it, so come soon. We want some excitement to wake the people up, and you are the one to do it."[20]

Thus her muscular Christianity style frightened some but compelled others—raking in commercial sales from both groups. Although she always packed in a full house, she sometimes left her urban performances with raw eggs plastered to her clothes. Even those who bombed her with raw eggs and vilified her as "unsexed" nevertheless bought her miniature hatchet souvenirs. For example, young men at Harvard played all sorts of pranks on Nation during her visit to their campus in 1902; however, they also donned her hatchet pins en masse: "All Harvard today is going around with little stick pins, in the shape of hatchets, which the enterprising Carrie sold to the crowds today." One first-year student from Ohio, probably to his parents' dismay as they read his letter, declared Nation's visit the highlight of his first year at Harvard. He said her no-frill wit, brash style, and western grit won over students who were not necessarily agreeable to an abstinence pledge or signing up to be all they could be in her Home Defender's Army.[21]

Why did she incite such a range of responses, sometimes from the same people? The divided response to her crusade illustrates larger cultural conflicts over gender, religion, and region. The "lived religion" of the consumers who eagerly purchased singular moments of intensity at her performances yet hit her with vegetable projectiles at the same time was practiced along the unformed borders of urban ambivalence, hope, and fear. Regional differences were significant. Northeasterners were drawn to her vigilante verve but were threatened by her blurring of gender roles. They liked to buy her hatchet pins, but they ridiculed her as unwomanly. The less urbanized and more evangelical midwesterners thought she was womanly enough, but they did not like her commercialism and accused her of money-grubbing.[22]

The backdrop to this schizophrenic response to her commercialized crusade was an emerging fascination in northeastern cities with western "primitivism" and muscular Christianity as a way to bolster an enervated Anglo-Saxon bourgeoisie. Nation's religious fervor, spicy vocabulary, and western rowdiness would have been a welcome relief for late-Victorian urban northeasterners, described as stifled, softened, neurasthenic, overcivilized, passionless, feminized, buttoned-up, self-restrained, and superficial. According to Lears, they had "won freedom from fear but lost possibilities for ecstasy. . . . The depth of emotional life seemed shallower, the contours of spiritual life softer." Little wonder they went in droves to see and hear an emotionally charged and spiritually robust Kansas woman. People who had lost touch with their own potential for passion could live it vicariously by hearing the neo-Puritan crusader tell her tale of rambunctious saloon-wrecking. As Robert Smith Bader puts it: "In her monomania, her fearlessness, and her God-driven determination, she became the fleshy embodiment of the geometric theorem that the shortest distance between two points is the straight line."[23] Perhaps the commercialization of her violence helped to contain the more threatening aspects of her crusade. It was better to have her onstage than in the streets, and it was safer for women followers to buy her hatchet pins than wield real ones.

Nation and her agents exploited her commercial draw to urbanites longing for old-time religion, purposeful determination, and muscular morality. They turned negative newspaper images to her advantage. Lengthy descriptions of her smashing attire filled the New York papers, often accompanied by surprisingly severe estimations of her physical appearance: "Mrs. Nation is not a pretty woman. Perhaps it is not too much to say that she never was pretty. Her features do not conform to any accepted style of beauty, and her nose is far too small for the rest of her face . . . she is inclined to stoutness. She confesses to 54 years and shows her age in her face."[24] Urban northeastern accounts were notoriously hyperbolic in reference to Nation's size; for example, they pictured her as a hyperthyroid Amazon of nearly six feet, who required "policemen seven feet high" to handle her, when in fact she was not much over five feet tall according to relatives. Perhaps the most bizarre of such accounts occurred not in the press but in a personal letter written to Nation from W. H. Collins, who speculated about her size and compared her to the notoriously mean general of the Kansas-Missouri border wars in the 1850s: "As I understand it you are a great strapping big, big dash skinned double-fisted savage looking woman who wears about a No. 9 shoe and that you are just as fearless as old Quantrill."[25] Nation and her agents, rather than fighting these negative portrayals, embraced them by marketing her "primitive" religiosity, masculinized rowdiness, and no-frills manner as an answer to urban aimlessness, religious mediocrity, and feminized overcivilization.

Carry Nation was threatening (but commercially appealing) because she seemed to blur the sexes. She was a woman who behaved like a man. But despite such speculations of sexual perversion—or maybe because of them—urban northeasterners responded with gusto to Nation when she, a regular cyclone of excitement, touched down in their city.

Her first visit to New York City exemplifies her intentional self-presentation as primitive, muscular, provocative, and rowdy. Upon signing in at the Hotel Victoria as "Carry Nation, Your Loving Home Defender, Kansas," she ordered the press to her hotel room, where she entertained the reporters with her rendition of a Mother Goose song:

> Sing a song of six joints,
> With bottles full of rye;
> Four and twenty beer kegs,
> Stacked up on the sly.
> When the kegs were opened,
> The beer began to sing,
> Hurrah for Carry Nation,
> Her work beats everything.

Her audience must have been both intrigued and shocked at this crass revision of a childhood rhyme. But they did not have time to ponder its deeper meanings because, dressed in her "Quakerish gown," she whizzed out to find the police commissioner, Michael Murphy. Their exchange was reported in one local paper as a heated blast of insults. Onlookers were reportedly thrilled when the two got into a tussle and he bounced her out of the office. From there, she participated in a mass at St. Patrick's Cathedral, tried to barge into the exclusively male Democratic Club (claiming that "God did not intend for men to be alone"), visited the seedy Tenderloin section of town, caused a ruckus on a streetcar at Fourth Street when she began snatching cigars out of the mouths of male passengers, and was arrested at Eighth Avenue. She ended up at Carnegie Hall, where she delivered a curious lecture, "The Lord's Saloon," to an overflowing crowd that, according to the newspaper accounts, constantly interrupted her address with "shouts of laughter" and "storms of applause."[26]

Carry later visited Coney Island, where she addressed herself to a more "common" Bowery audience. On the steamboat trip out from Battery Park, she spent her energy stripping cigars from men's mouths and throwing glasses from the bar; all of this caused the captain to threaten to lock her up until the boat touched solid ground. Once disembarked, she headed straightway for a cigar stand at the Steeplechase Auditorium, where she was to speak; the police responded immediately to the pandemonium and hit her more than once with batons. But the worst was to follow when, during her afternoon address in front of thousands, she saved her most blistering rhetoric about "rummies" for a dying President William McKinley, shot on September 6, 1901. Her audience responded with strangely midwestern cries for a lynching. While some purportedly went searching for rope, most stayed in the auditorium and satisfied themselves with pelting the rowdy grandmother with peanuts, hot dogs, and popcorn. Nation herself commented on the rabble-rousing she seemed to evoke from her audiences and indicated that her manager, James Furlong, knew it was a selling point. But this time her rabble-rousing nearly threatened her life. She barely escaped the hostile mob, protected by Furlong, who broke her contract with Steeplechase and rushed her to Rochester and then on to the Pan American lectures where she spoke eight times in a single day. At Rochester, Nation paid a visit to suffragist Susan B. Anthony who was not home but punctually wrote the smasher a letter of apology. The two finally met for a cordial visit, but their difference of opinion was clear. Anthony sent a note signed, "Yours for all peaceful methods to put down evil," and Nation remarked that Anthony "didn't seem to understand the need for the hatchet" because of her elite insularity: "if she went into the dens that I did . . . she would understand."[27]

Nation exploited consumer desires for intensity and rambunctiousness. Northeastern urban consumers were drawn to the white-haired, shabbily dressed grandmother from an obscure town in a rural state because she quenched their emerging fascination with western "primitivism" and muscular Christianity. Psychologists, ministers, and physicians were all touting the health and spiritual benefits of rough western life and old-time religion for an enervated Anglo-Saxon bourgeoisie struggling with nerve disease and "feminized" theology. Rejecting the old-style Calvinism, they had stuffed the "crabbed and joyous qualities of old-style evangelicalism" embarrassingly into the wastebasket along with the pioneer people's "religious enthusiasm." Critics of urban life concluded that the "buttoned-up bourgeoisie" had outcivilized its Puritan past.[28]

Much like Aimee Semple McPherson (1890–1944), the famous cofounder of Foursquare Gospel churches, Carry Nation radiated old-time religion, practicality, and simplicity.[29] In her autobiography and her public speeches she exuded a revivalistic charisma that brought her listeners back in touch with the vocabulary and narrative of conversion and sanctification. Her practicality meant a down-to-earth approach that favored homespun bits of wisdom over pretentious intellectualism. And her unguardedness, simplicity, and candidness seemed to communicate an authenticity that was disarming. She was freely herself. According to contemporary critic of Victorian malaise Agnes Repplier: "The old springs of simple sentiment are dying fast within us. It is heartless to laugh, it is foolish to cry, it is indiscreet to love, it is morbid to hate, and it is intolerant to espouse any cause with enthusiasm." What a breath of fresh air, then, to have a Kansas cyclone of revivalistic enthusiasm and boisterous personality sweep through as the evening's entertainment and the morning's reading, her "rough and tumble Populist manner" creating a chaotic excitement. Consumers begged for the excitement of her presence: "intensity of feeling—physical, emotional, even spiritual—became a product to be consumed like any other."[30]

Western religion and western folklore offered something salvific to overcivilized easterners and urbanites according to physicians, psychologists, and ministers; in fact, some experts saw western ways as a cure for "neurasthenia"—a catch-all diagnosis of mostly Anglo, middle- and upper-class men who seemed listless, drained of a certain masculine vitality. According to Gail Bederman, between 1870 and 1915 the medical and psychiatric establishments took "neurasthenia" as a very serious threat to "highly evolved" Anglo-Saxons. Ultimately, she concludes, it was framed as a "racial disease" because it only affected the overcivilized Anglo-Saxons. Tom Lutz further identifies it as a disease that late Victorians viewed as a mark of social distinction for upper-class Protestant "brain-workers."[31] In part, according to Lears, the disease was traceable to the "discordant noises of urban life."[32]

So if urban, effeminate, cultured overcivilization was the cause of the disease, experts suggested that part of the cure lay in recovering the rigor and peacefulness of an idealized rural life and a revitalized manly religiosity. "The curse of our age is its femininity, its lack of virility," mourned one observer.[33] As psychologist G. Stanley Hall conceived it, by reliving primitive masculine emotions—such as those seen in tales of western frontier heroes like Daniel Boone and Davy Crockett—adolescent boys could be "vaccinated" against nervous breakdown with doses of western virility.[34] President Theodore Roosevelt, the paragon of self-invented western manhood, agreed with Hall, writing him that "barbarian virtues" might indeed keep boys from becoming "milksops."[35] One way to inculcate such virtues was to participate in the "strenuous life" that had both martial and athletic dimensions expressed in the emergence of military imperialism and an obsession with sports at the turn of the century.[36] Ministers and theologians also believed in the potential of masculine feats for religious revitalization (that is, remuscularization). For example, a New York paper reported in 1902 that Congregationalist pastor John Scudder had opened a gymnasium at his church and was teaching "boys to box," thereby "inculcat[ing] virtues of highest moral value" since "manly sparring tends toward Christian growth."[37]

Urban northeasterners did not have to travel to the West to experience its robust manliness; it came to them. Eastern consumers expressed fascination with the West by purchasing large quantities of western art, magazines, and fiction and by attending the popular Buffalo Bill Cody shows, something of a commercial precursor to Carry Nation. She and her promoters were aware of the consumer currency of western "primitivism." They advertised her performances by emphasizing the "primitive" qualities of her personality and crusade: the savagery of her beer-stained hatchet, her steel-willed courage, her "utter informality," and her old-time religious fervor.[38] These personal and perform-ance qualities coincided with the rise of muscular Christianity, which Susan Juster describes as a "collective cry for a more virile form of religion" that sought to "rescue" the "sagging fortunes" of Protestantism "from the grip of women."[39] Nation's urban audiences not only lived out her western tale of mar-tial conquest, but they also gave themselves over to a certain rambunctiousness by indulging in revivalistic fervor, hearty laughter, loud cheering, and some-times more physical forms of acting out like egg throwing.

Nation's commercial appeal lay in her hearkening urban northeasterners back to what was perceived as a better time—a more religious, authentic, and manly time. With Bible in one hand and hatchet in the other, she intentionally evoked the sacred civil religious mythology of George Washington's righteous rebellion against godless British tyranny. Her hatchet symbolized national unity to those urbanites who feared social unraveling due to immigration; muscular Christianity to those who believed the churches had become feminized; and primitive religiosity to those who sought an antidote to nervous disease. Thus, as an entertainer in multiple venues, a seller of prohibition movement para-phernalia, and an icon of muscular Christianity, Nation successfully used vari-ous aspects of urban commercial culture to promote herself and her message of Protestant morality to a diverse turn-of-the century audience.

Notes

1. Jennie Small Owen, annalist, and Kirke Mechem, editor, *Annals of Kansas: 1886–1925*, vol. 1 (Topeka: Kansas State Historical Society, n.d.), 376–377.
2. John Gregory, "The Tragedy of Carrie Nation," *Topeka Daily Capital*, June 18, 1911.
3. Carry Nation, *Use and Need* (Topeka, Kans.: F. M. Stevens, 1909), 270–272, 177–178.
4. R. Laurence Moore, *Selling God: American Religion in the Marketplace of Culture* (New York: Oxford University Press, 1998), 150; William James, *Talks to Teachers on Psychology and to Students on Some of Life's Ideals* (1900; reprint, Cambridge: Harvard University Press, 1983), 152, quoted in Jeanne Halgren Kilde, "The 'Predominance of the Feminine' at Chautauqua: Rethinking the Gender-Space Relationship in Victorian America," *Signs* 24, no. 2 (winter 1999): 449–450.
5. Virginia Scharff, "Beyond the Narrow Circle: Women and Chautauqua, 1874–1898," 4, unpublished paper, University of Arizona, 1983; Carry Nation, Marshalltown, Iowa, to Alex McNabb, August 15, 1910, Fort Bend County Museum, Richmond, Tex.
6. See Robert Snyder, *The Voice of the City: Vaudeville and Popular Culture in New York* (New York: Oxford University Press, 1989). R. Laurence Moore argues that by the late nineteenth century, vaudeville offered family-style entertainment that was derided as "the Sunday School circuit"—probably true in general, but Nation's experience does not fit; Moore, *Selling God*, 195–198.
7. Will Carleton's eyewitness account in *Everywhere* (Brooklyn), is excerpted in Nation, *Use and Need*, 298–301.
8. *New York World*, November 18, 1902.
9. Carry Nation, Crookston, Minn., to the *Fulcrum* editor, June 29, 1902, Kansas State

Historical Society; Nation, *Use and Need*, 179. She advertised for "agents to handle my paper, buttons, pictures, water bottles and hatchets" in every state for a "handsome profit," *Smasher's Mail*, April 20, 1901. The buttons were "Home Defender" buttons that she called the "badge of our army."

10. Colleen McDannell, *Material Christianity: Religion and Popular Culture in America* (New Haven, Conn.: Yale University Press, 1995), 45.

11. *Relics: A Link to Our Pioneer Heritage* 3, no. 3 (October 1969), 19.

12. Nation, *Use and Need*, 179.

13. Carry Nation, Scrapbook, Kansas State History Center, Topeka, 47.

14. *Life*, March 14, 1901.

15. She advertised 11 by 14 inch photographs of "Mrs. Carrie Nation and her hatchet" for sale in *Smasher's Mail*, beginning with the March 23, 1901, issue.

16. *Relics*, 18; *Hatchet*, October 1, 1905.

17. Her advertisements of the water bottles are to be found in virtually every issue of *Smasher's Mail* (March–December 1901). See the March 30, 1901, issue for the Chicagoan's quote.

18. *Smasher's Mail*, March 30, 1901.

19. *New York World*, February 11, 1901.

20. Letter from Mrs. Frank Redman, printed in *Smasher's Mail*, April 20, 1901.

21. *New York World*, November 15, 1902. Albert Veenfliet, undated letter, Harvard University archives.

22. For more on Nation's midwestern milieu, see chapter 5 in Fran Grace, *Carry A. Nation: Retelling the Life* (Bloomington: Indiana University Press, 2001).

23. T. J. Jackson Lears, *No Place of Grace: Antimodernism and the Transformation of American Culture: 1880–1920* (New York: Pantheon Books, 1981), 44, 48; Robert Smith Bader, *Prohibition in Kansas* (Lawrence: University of Kansas Press), 154–155. Lears has been criticized for overstating the lack of religious vitality in cities; see especially Jonathon Butler, "Protestant Success in the New American City, 1870–1920: The Anxious Secrets of Reverend Walter Laidlaw," in *New Directions in American Religious History*, ed. Harry Stout and D. G. Hart (New York: Oxford University Press, 1997), 296–333.

24. A. M. Dickinson, *Saturday Globe* (Utica, N.Y.), April 2, 1901.

25. Letter from W. H. Collins, in *Smasher's Mail*, March 9, 1901.

26. *New York World*, August 27, 1901.

27. Nation, *Use and Need*, 81, 121, 122; *New York Times*, September 11, 1901; for Coney Island, see *Smasher's Mail*, October 1901, December 1901; Susan B. Anthony, Rochester, N.Y., to Nation, September 16, 1901, printed in *Smasher's Mail*, November 1901. The disagreement between Anthony and Nation illustrates the many layers of division among suffragists—regional, religious, strategic, and political.

28. Lears, *No Place of Grace*, 48. See Braude, "Women's History *Is* American Religious History," in *Retelling U.S. Religious History*, ed. Thomas Tweed (Berkeley and Los Angeles: University of California Press, 1997), for helpful interpretative comments on "feminization."

29. Edith Blumhofer, *Aimee Semple McPherson: Everybody's Sister* (Grand Rapids, Mich.: Eerdmans, 1993).

30. For Repplier quote and "intensity," see Lears, *No Place of Grace*, 48, 300; for "Populist," see Bader, *Prohibition in Kansas*, 154.

31. Tom Lutz, *American Nervousness, 1903: An Anecdotal History* (Ithaca, N.Y.: Cornell University Press, 1991), 6–7.

32. Gail Bederman, *Manliness and Civilization: A Cultural History of Gender and Race in the United States, 1880–1917* (Chicago: University of Chicago Press, 1995), 85; Lears, *No Place of Grace*, 51.

33. Orestes Brownson, "Literature, Love, and Marriage," in *Works*, vol. 14, 421, quoted in Barbara Welter, *Dimity Convictions: The American Woman in the Nineteenth Century* (Athens: Ohio University Press, 1976), 102.

34. For more on Hall, see Bederman, *Manliness and Civilization*, chapter 3; Carroll Smith-Rosenberg, "Davy Crockett as Trickster: Pornography, Liminality, and Symbolic Inversion in Victorian America," in *Disorderly Conduct: Visions of Gender in Victorian America* (New York: Knopf, 1985), 90–108; and White, *It's Your Misfortune but None of My Own: A New History of the American West* (Norman: University of Oklahoma Press, 1991), 620–621.

35. Quoted in Bederman, *Manliness and Civilization*, 100, see chapter 5 on Roosevelt; Richard Slotkin, "Nostalgia and Progress: Teddy Roosevelt's Myth of the Frontier," *American Quarterly* 33 (winter 1981): 608–637.

36. See John Higham, "The Reorientation of American Culture in the 1890s," in *Writing American History: Essays on Modern Scholarship* (Bloomington: Indiana University Press, 1978), 73–102.

37. *New York World*, November 16, 1902.

38. Madeline Southard, "Mrs. Nation," Nation, Scrapbook; William Railey, who remembers hearing her as a boy, says the same thing in *History of Woodford County* (Baltimore. Reginald Publishing, 1975), 215.

39. Susan Juster, "The Spirit and the Flesh: Gender, Language, and Sexuality in American Protestantism," in Stout and Hart, *New Directions*, 352–353.

Four

J. Terry Todd

New York, the New Babylon?

Fundamentalism and the Modern City in Reverend Straton's Jazz Age Crusade

Dayton, Tennessee, is often depicted as ground zero in the war between modernists and fundamentalists in American Protestantism. The Scopes trial, held in Dayton during the sweltering summer of 1925, sealed the association between fundamentalism and the rural South.[1] But if Dayton was a major site of contention between modernists and fundamentalists in the 1920s, so was New York City. In 1922 the Reverend Harry Emerson Fosdick took to the pulpit of New York's First Presbyterian Church to preach a plea for tolerance among Protestants in a sermon he entitled "Shall the Fundamentalists Win?"[2] Two years later Unitarian minister Charles Francis Potter squared off against Rev. John Roach Straton of New York's Calvary Baptist Church in a series of debates broadcast on radio and covered extensively in newspapers throughout the United States. Three of the debates were held in Carnegie Hall, where raucous crowds heard Potter and Straton spar over matters like the inerrancy of Scripture, the divinity of Christ, and the resurrection of the dead.

From 1918 to 1929 Straton presided over the venerable Calvary Baptist Church on fashionable Fifty-seventh Street, transforming a dying church of white Baptist elites into New York City's citadel of fundamentalism. Straton's use of the urban marketplace of ideas to spread his brand of the Gospel made him a celebrity in Jazz Age New York. He was the face of New York fundamentalism, and thanks to his aggressive radio ministry he was also its voice. No doubt because of his penchant for publicity, Straton became the target of urbane modernists like the journalist Stanley Walker, who called him "the Fundamentalist Pope," the "Scimitar of the Lord," "the ordained scourge of the whole hellish rabble of evolutionists, atheists, and free lovers." "He seemed a bizarre figure in the big city," Walker quipped in the *New Yorker*, "like Oliver Cromwell in a nightclub or Bishop Asbury at the Saratoga races."[3]

When Straton arrived in New York in 1918, he posed a question he had already answered for himself, "Is New York a Christian city or a pagan city?"[4] To this Jazz Age Jeremiah, New York was the New Babylon, the greatest contemporary battlefield in the ancient war between flesh and spirit, the devil and Jehovah, paganism and Christianity. Just about everywhere Straton looked in New York he saw signs of that war. A "jazz spirit" characterized modern urban life for Straton, a spirit he equated with the "impulses of animalism," "materialism," "sensualism," and above all "paganism." "Paganism is the exaltation of the flesh above spirit, the supremacy of matter over mind," Straton declared. "It is the apotheosis of the soulless and the sensuous, and its growth means the supplanting of Christian ideals by idolatry, the worshiping of Mammon, the glorification of brute power, and the passion for pleasure."[5] The jazz spirit was a sickness that corroded both the individual and the body politic, Straton believed, and he found signs of the disease in the city's streets, on the stages of its theaters, in speakeasies and dance halls, even in New York's Protestant churches. "We must either Americanize and Christianize New York," Straton declared, "or New York will speedily Europeanize and paganize us."[6]

Straton campaigned with particular vigor against the city's proliferating world of modern commercial amusements, but this did not mean that he opposed all things modern. In the following pages I explore how and why Straton selectively embraced modern commercial culture in his Jazz Age crusade. In particular, I focus on Straton's strategic use of attention-getting devices as a means of modern evangelism. Straton knew that bold measures were required to call attention to the Gospel in the endlessly varied urban parade of sound and image. The means he appropriated included some of the modern world's most impressive inventions, including the motorcar, the radio, and even the skyscraper. Straton outfitted his motorcar with a portable pulpit and went on preaching tours into the crowded streets of New York. Subsequently, Straton turned to radio, which he found to be an even more powerful instrument to spread the Gospel. New York's first church-owned radio was Calvary's WQAO. By penetrating the walls of urban apartments, the church's radio technology brought Straton's voice into domestic spaces he might never have visited in person. Finally, the centerpiece of Straton's plans to evangelize New York was the skyscraper church he built on West Fifty-seventh Street. As we will see, this structure was intended to house not only a new sanctuary but also an income-producing Christian hotel. Straton embraced these aspects of modern consumer culture in order to speedily Americanize and Christianize New York. The automobile, the radio, and the skyscraper were three of the modern means Straton mobilized to command attention in a city where nothing less than the future of Christian America was at stake.

John Roach Straton was born in 1875, just a year shy of the nation's centennial.[7] The son of a Baptist preacher, Straton's parents raised him within the fold of churches in rural Indiana, Alabama, and Georgia. It was in Atlanta where a young Straton first encountered the pleasures and dangers and possibilities of the city. In those years, Straton later confessed, he was living a life of sin. But that changed on the night he was born again at a revival meeting presided over by James Boardman Hawthorne at Atlanta's Baptist Tabernacle. Straton had gone to church in the company of some rowdy friends, expecting to be entertained by Hawthorne's flamboyant fire and brimstone preaching. Yet what awaited him was conviction of sin. "A miracle was worked in my life," Straton later said of that night, "and when we begin to tell the old, old story from the pulpits of America, we can fill our lands with miracles of that kind."[8] The experience convinced Straton that, although city life promoted sin, the work of dynamic preachers like Hawthorne could also promote salvation.

Straton's conversion so turned his life around that he gave up plans of becoming a lawyer to follow his father into the ministry. He studied at the Baptist Theological Seminary in Louisville, Kentucky, then went on to teach at Baylor, the citadel of Baptist higher education in Texas. Straton left the South to lead churches in Chicago, Baltimore, and Norfolk before arriving in New York to preside over Calvary, a church adrift in the wake of the retirement of its renowned preacher, Dr. Robert S. MacArthur, who had been at Calvary for over forty years. Sunday attendance had dwindled, and an internal schism threatened the unity and integrity of the church.[9] Straton came riding the winds of change. He immediately abolished pew rents, a move that roiled some of the older, wealthier members of his congregation. He also imported his brand of feisty, fiery, southern homiletics, peppering his sermons with language some considered unfit for the sanctuary. (Stanley Walker reported that one mother left the church in disgust after her daughter, having listened attentively to one of Straton's sensationalist sermons, turned to ask, "Mother, what is a prostitute?")[10]

In the spring of 1918, not long after Straton arrived in New York, President Woodrow Wilson declared a day of fasting and prayer on behalf of American troops fighting in the trenches of Europe. On that day Straton strolled through the city to note compliance with the president's orders. He found churches empty but restaurants and theaters packed with patrons. "The tables were piled high with luxurious food, though half the world was in the shadow of starvation," Straton reported, "and I saw men and women in the hotels, cabarets and clubs gorging themselves with luxurious viands and expensive drinks." Seemingly oblivious to President Wilson's call for prayer, New Yorkers kept on consuming and spending in a way Straton found "sinful and unpatriotic."[11] New York's vast economy did not bow to the president's call for national soul-searching. Pleasure was still the rule. Later in the same year, public celebrations of Armistice Day turned another national holy day into a wild debauch. "All up and down our streets we saw girls in short dresses—girls in their teens—trooping along with the arms of men around their waists. We saw men and women, including these very young girls, hugging and kissing each other upon the streets of our city, often in postures that were disgraceful." Straton declared the event "pagan to the core."[12]

In subsequent years Straton learned even more about the reach of New York's economy of pleasure. On a Saturday night in the spring of 1920, Straton doffed his usual black suit, donned a disguise, and set out on a night tour of New York.[13] He discovered that despite prohibition of alcohol sales, liquor flowed freely in New York. During a visit to a Manhattan dance hall, Straton found thousands of young people drinking and doing the bunny-hop—"more young men and women," he lamented, "than attended all the Protestant churches of Manhattan Island the following Sunday morning."[14] In the competition between religion and the world of commercial pleasures, Straton felt that religion was losing. The jazz spirit was alive not only in the city's dance halls but also in the precincts of high society as well. The annual charity event known as the *Bal Bleu* featured revealing evening dresses, couples dancing cheek-to-cheek, and the performance of scantily-clad "stage beauties" from the *Ziegfeld Follies*. What angered Straton most about the event was its sponsorship by Protestant churchwomen. He called the *Bal Bleu* "an appalling failure of Christian testimony," "treason against the Lord," and "an expression of pure paganism."[15]

Straton considered Protestant churches to be guardians of community moral standards, but he was convinced that New York's Christians had exchanged the stringent demands of the Gospel for a pale imitation that Straton derisively called "rag-time religion." Straton noted several examples of pagan advances into Protestant churches. One Manhattan church had hired a professional musician to entertain its congregation by whistling hymns. Another had engaged a Mr. Reef, "the banjo king," to perform his repertoire with organ accompaniment.[16] Some churches had moved up the hour of worship, freeing Sunday afternoons for leisure activities. Straton blamed the clergy for accommodating the modern spirit in such ways. Modernist-minded ministers were "animated question marks" whose tepid sermons failed to challenge or inspire. They were, Straton charged, "trying to heal the awful cancer of human sin with soothing syrup; they are sprinkling cologne water upon the putrid iniquities of a rebellious race."[17] Who would stand in the breach? Straton, of course, who called for an aggressive crusade to win the souls of New Yorkers through bold incursions into urban public space.

Straton's desire to Christianize New York ran squarely into the problem of how to capture the attention of the urban public. As it turned out, the very economy of getting and spending that that so distressed Straton produced the means by which he could reach the masses with his brand of the Christian Gospel. One of those modern means was the automobile. The motorcar has long been recognized for its contributions to cultural change in America, including its role in transforming courtship rituals and sexual mores.[18] Yet the automobile's role in Christian evangelism has been largely overlooked. These machines of personal freedom and mobility were no longer surprising sights in urban America in the 1920s, of course. But John Roach Straton hoped that a motorcar equipped as a church-on-wheels might still draw a crowd. Like generations of preachers before him, Straton knew that street evangelism required bold and dramatic gestures. From the nineteenth into the twentieth century, the Salvation Army paraded through the streets of urban America with loud brass bands and colorful banners to announce street revivals.[19] In Chicago, during the summer of 1893, evangelist Dwight L. Moody outfitted a horse-drawn wagon with lanterns and a portable organ, then journeyed into streets crowded with tourists visiting the city's Columbian Exposition.[20] By the late 1910s, the motorcar had displaced the wagon as a prop of urban evangelism. Aimee Semple McPherson drove a "Gospel Auto" in the early years of her ministry, draping it with signs announcing the location and hours of revival meetings.[21] Straton himself used a motorcar in his ministry at the First Baptist Church of Norfolk. He equipped a Ford with an organ and portable pulpit, outfitted it with a volunteer choir, and drove into Norfolk's Tenderloin district to hold impromptu street revivals.

In New York, Straton's motorcar served as both a portable pulpit and as a rolling billboard. Young Calvary members often took to the city's streets to sing, preach, and lure the curious back to Calvary for prayer meetings. On many occasions Straton accompanied them, standing at his portable pulpit on a platform attached to the car's hood. "If Jesus Christ converted an old fishing boat into a pulpit and preached from it," Straton was fond of saying, "I don't see why His followers today should not convert a modern automobile into a pulpit."[22] On Sunday afternoons when the weather was fair, Straton parked his motorcar at Columbus Circle and preached to Sunday strollers entering and leaving Central Park. Borrowing a strategy from the world of advertisers, Straton decorated his automobile with signs and banners. If cars bore advertisements singing the praises of consumer products to the urban public, why not use the automobile to announce the hours of Calvary's services and to herald the promise of salvation, "Jesus Saves"?

Radio broadcasting was yet another weapon in Straton's arsenal of modern evangelism. Radio was the new technology of the 1920s, and many evangelists

_____ *Figure 10*_____

In an attempt to evangelize New York, Straton took to the streets to preach from a pulpit mounted on the hood of his motorcar. At a time when advertisers decorated automobiles with signage praising consumer products to the urban public, Straton used his motorcar to announce the hours of church services and to herald the promise of salvation—"Jesus Saves."

American Baptist Archives, Rochester, New York.

quickly recognized its potential. Straton was one of them. Calvary became the first New York church to install and operate its own radio station, the 250-watt channel WQAO. The station took to the airwaves for the first time on March 4, 1923, with a broadcast of Calvary's Sunday-evening prayer meeting. In 1923 radio still had the capability to inspire awe, of course. Like the automobile, the radio carried the Gospel message outside the walls of the church. But here was a modern technology that could penetrate walls. Radio broadcast the voice of the preacher in a way that it had never before been heard—emerging from an electric box. The medium provided a virtual visit from the pastor and the real-time sounds of a church service. Straton often heard from members of what he called Calvary's "radio congregation." A Mrs. H., resident of East 230th Street in New York City, testified to the effects of the new technology. She wrote to Straton on behalf of her homebound husband who was unable to write for himself. An accident had deprived him "of his greatest pleasure on earth—going to church," Mrs. H. said, yet due to the miracle of radio the church came to him. The experience caused her husband to weep—"tears streaming down his face as he listened over our little radio to your sermon and service."[23] The members of Straton's radio congregation were not just passive listeners. They talked back through letters and telephone calls. During the broadcast of services, Calvary's switchboard buzzed with activity, Straton reported, as listeners phoned in their hymn requests.

In addition to prayer meetings, WQAO also broadcast classes of Calvary's *Bible College of the Air*. An advertisement published in the Calvary Church Sunday bulletin promoted a convenient education. "Now you can enjoy a thorough course in Bible Study without leaving your home," an advertisement promised. "No need to stir from your comfortable arm chair."[24] On Sunday afternoons at 3:30, WQAO broadcast Dr. Straton's class on the *Scofield Reference Bible*. In a cooperative venture with Oxford University Press, publisher of the Scofield edition of the Bible, Straton offered this popular Bible to his listeners for $1.95. Anyone with a radio and good reception could listen, of course, but students who actually enrolled received a certificate at the completion of their studies. Straton used the *Bible College of the Air*, the broadcast prayer meetings, and WQAO's other programming to publicize his Gospel message to New Yorkers. He also expected that more sophisticated radio equipment would one day widen his reach beyond New York. "I hope that our radio system will prove to be so efficient," Straton said, "that when I twist the Devil's tail in New York, his squawk will be heard across the country."[25]

The most ambitious of Straton's plans to capture public attention involved the erection of a skyscraper church on the site of Calvary's 1884 neo-Gothic sanctuary. Calvary's steeple had once commanded the skies over Fifty-seventh

Street, but by the mid-1920s Manhattan's explosive vertical growth had all but obscured it from view. Here as elsewhere in Manhattan, commerce now looked down on religion. Straton found that intolerable and began to make plans to transform the skyscraper into an instrument of evangelism. Straton had long recognized the skyscraper for what it was—an icon of the modern age, a tower intended to evoke a kind of holy awe in those who gazed upon it. He felt such power rightfully belonged to the church, not to commerce, so he wanted to reassert the cross over New York's corporate skyline by building a skyscraper church. "Should we not all desire to see here a new building that will once more tower up above all competitors," Straton declared in a question he had already answered, "to shine out in its beauty as a challenge and a call!"[26]

Straton's sense of competition between the church and the commercial skyscraper was already at play in an apocalyptic fantasy published in his 1920 volume, *The Menace of Immorality in Church and State*. Straton asked, "Have you ever thought what a good husky tidal wave could do to 'little old New York,' as we call her? Have you ever imagined the Woolworth 'sky-scraper' butting headlong into the Equitable Building, through such an earthquake as that which laid San Francisco's proud beauty in the dust? Have you ever imagined the Metropolitan Tower crashing over on Madison Square Garden some time, when there were tens of thousands of people in there at some worldly, godless celebration of the Lord's Day?"[27] In Straton's violent apocalypse, judgment is visited on the capital of modern commercial culture because of Sabbath-breaking. Madison Square Garden is packed with tens of thousands of spectators gathered on a Sunday afternoon to watch a sporting match, and these fans pay for pleasure with their lives. Yet what is so startling about Straton's fantasy is the prominence of skyscrapers. The appearance of the Metropolitan Tower here is no accident. The fifty-story Metropolitan Life skyscraper occupied the site of the old Madison Square Presbyterian Church, which was razed in 1906 to make way for its construction. By 1920 the new tower had become a spiritual symbol in its own right. Roland Marchand tells us that the beacon of light that stood at the tower's crown, visible for miles around, became known as "the light that never fails." In 1922 the Metropolitan Life Insurance Company turned to even more explicitly religious language with its adoption of a biblical verse for that year's advertising blitz: "Let your light so shine before men that they may see your good works."[28] Perhaps no other building in New York better symbolized the appropriation of religious rhetoric and imagery—and space—in the service of commercial culture. In Straton's theological universe, such an act of hubris was sure to stir God's wrath.

The skyscraper church was religion's revenge on the modern corporation. Dubbed "altitudinous Christianity" by one contemporary wag, the skyscraper church movement was surely one of the most novel and aggressive of all Protestant responses to the urban economy of the 1920s.[29] "The skyscraper was visible from afar, it was impressive in structure, it emanated solidity and progressiveness," Rolf Lunden has written, "and it was a very good business proposition."[30] In short, the skyscraper seemed to offer exactly what churches needed—a symbolic triumph and cash income from rental space. The first skyscraper church was the Chicago Temple of the First Methodist Episcopal Church. Completed in 1924 at a cost of four million dollars, it was the second tallest building in the world. By the late 1920s there were skyscraper churches in Miami, Pittsburgh, Philadelphia and, of course, New York City. In 1924 Rev. Harry Emerson Fosdick secured support from John D. Rockefeller Jr. to fund a massive skyscraper church on Morningside Heights adjacent to Union Theological Seminary. (The Riverside Church, as it became known, was formally dedicated in February 1931.) Straton was not to be outdone by Fosdick, his theological arch-rival. If Fosdick was to build a skyscraper church as a monument to religious modernism, Straton would erect a church that would "firmly entrench fundamentalism, old-time religion, and true Americanism at the heart of the world's greatest city."[31]

Planning for Calvary's sixteen-story skyscraper church was under way by 1925. Designed by the imminent architectural firm of McKim, Mead, and White, the building was to include a street-level auditorium seating fifteen hundred, three floors of administrative offices, and a fourth- and fifth-floor duplex to serve as a residence for Straton and his successors. The remaining space was to be occupied by an independently operated Christian hotel with 208 residential apartments. Straton's master plan required the destruction of Calvary's neo-Gothic sanctuary, the congregation's church home for over forty years. Predictably, this raised a howl of protests among some of Calvary's lay leaders, who charged Straton with gambling away the church's patrimony. Opponents complained that the plan was an affront to members past and present whose bequests had built and maintained the old edifice. Those with sentimental attachments to the old church interpreted Straton's skyscraper church as nothing less than an act of desecration. Straton countered by showing how the plan would give cash-starved Calvary an infusion of funds to bankroll its evangelism program. The church was sitting on a real estate gold mine, and Straton knew it. He estimated that rental income from the Christian hotel could yield the church somewhere between fifty and seventy thousand dollars each year.[32]

The Salisbury Hotel became the centerpiece of Straton's plan, not only because it would provide an infusion of income to the church but also because it would serve to promote conservative Christian values in an industry widely known for its indifference to matters of personal morality. Hotels promoted promiscuous public mingling and promenading in its bars and ballrooms—all within close proximity of private sleeping quarters. For Straton, this was a recipe for moral disaster. The Salisbury would be a place "where objectionable things would be rigidly excluded and the establishment would be conducted on the same clean, high and noble plane as right-minded people desire in their permanent homes." That included a ban on liquor sales in the hotel's restaurants. "Let us have at least one hotel in New York where there will be room for Him and those who love and serve Him."[33] He wanted the Salisbury to be a home for Christian transients living in the New Babylon. For years Straton had called for a return to "the old-fashioned home, where children were taught to obey their parents; where there was a family altar; and where members of the home found their chief satisfaction within the home, instead of in the dance hall, the theater, the card room, and other even more questionable places of amusement."[34] At last, Straton hoped, the Salisbury Hotel would institutionalize a commercialized form of the old-fashioned home at the heart of the New Babylon.

Straton's plan involved the risky step of taking a one-million-dollar mortgage on the church's property to leverage the funds required for constructing the tower. Straton tried to overcome any reluctance on the part of his congregation by urging them to "catch the spirit of Caleb and Joshua, who said: 'Let us go up at once and possess it, for we are well able.'"[35] In this revealing biblical allusion, Straton recalled the story of Caleb and eleven other Israelite spies whose reconnaissance mission served as a prelude to Joshua's successful assault upon Canaan. But Straton's call to action did not rally the troops for this particular mission. Some supporters saw Straton's plan as a courageous leap of faith, but others interpreted the skyscraper church as an irresponsible gamble. During Straton's pastorate Calvary had never known a time without conflict, but these plans provoked especially fierce challenges from the church's lay leadership. After failing to convince Straton to abandon the project, several trustees took the extreme measure of petitioning the civil courts to block it. Opposition delayed the start of construction for several years, yet by 1929 Calvary's neo-Gothic church was razed in the boldest and riskiest move yet in Straton's evangelism efforts.[36]

Straton's crusade to evangelize New York campaign was linked to a larger goal, the preservation of Christian America. He believed the presidential campaign of 1928 was a crucial moment in the struggle to maintain a Puritan America, a belief he shared with Protestant nativists who bitterly opposed New York Democratic governor Alfred E. Smith in his electoral battle with Republican Herbert Hoover. Like these nativists, Straton feared that Smith's election would hammer a nail in the coffin of the Protestant Republic. Yet Straton himself carefully insisted that Smith's Catholic identity was irrelevant. What really mattered, he claimed, was Smith's Tammany connections and the New York governor's opposition to the most fiercely contested political achievement of Protestant evangelical reformers—Prohibition. Straton spread the message on a whistle-stop speaking tour of the South, sponsored by local chapters of the Anti-Saloon League and the Woman's Christian Temperance Union (WCTU). Large crowds reportedly turned out to hear the fiery orator's public indictments of Smith and his band of wet Democrats from New Babylon.[37]

Hoover won the election against Smith, of course, but Straton did not live long to savor the victory. The rigors of the campaign trail had apparently exhausted him, and his health seemed to grow ever more fragile. Straton never lived to preach in Calvary's new pulpit. On a visit to Atlanta during April 1929, Straton was stricken with a heart attack. He returned to New York for a brief time in the autumn, then retired to a Protestant sanitarium at Clifton Springs, in the Finger Lakes region of upstate New York. There he suffered a fatal stroke on October 29, 1929, the very day the stock market crashed. Straton's funeral was held in New York's Pythian Hall, Calvary's temporary sanctuary until the fall of 1930, when the skyscraper church opened for business.

Straton's crusade made him a notorious figure in Jazz Age New York. In the character studies of Straton drawn by journalists like Stanley Walker, Straton became modernism's religious other, "lean, gray-haired, cadaverous and solemn," a caricature of the joyless Puritans and their spiritual descendants, the fundamentalists.[38] He was the emblem of a regressive American past, a real-life Elmer Gantry figure, a small town revivalist whose wrong turn off the sawdust trail had landed him uncomfortably in the capital of the modern world. Yet Straton was a far more complex figure than that. The point was made by an unnamed editorialist in the *New Republic* who wrote in the week following Straton's death, "In spirit he was a Baptist of the old school, attached to the letter of the Old Testament; in technique he was a New Yorker of the 20th century." "In general," the editors continued, "he used all the technical resources of modern life to oppose the modern spirit."[39]

Straton's relationship with the modern world was riven with ambivalence, a condition he shared with other American fundamentalists. Like generations of Protestant evangelists, Straton successfully integrated certain aspects of urban commercial culture in the service of Christian evangelism. In particular, he turned to the automobile, the radio, and the skyscraper as effective means of communicating the Gospel according to Straton. Yet if the modern commercial economy provided new techniques of evangelism, it also stood in the way of Straton's vision of Anglo-Saxon Christian civilization.

Straton's crusade was driven by his belief that the United States was God's New Israel, the last great hope of Christian civilization. Europe had degenerated into chaos through the destruction of war, but there was still hope for America. "Can anyone doubt," Straton asked, "that God has lodged with us in this free land the ark of the covenant of humanity's hopes? So surely as God led forth ancient Israel for a unique and glorious mission, so does He seem to have raised Christian America for such an hour as this. Where else can the children of men look for leadership and light?"[40] Until the 1920s such ideas were widely shared by American Protestants, yet in the Jazz Age decade, as Robert Handy reminded us years ago, this explicit brand of Christian nationalism was under attack by the realities of modern life. Handy writes, "The confident belief that America was basically Protestant and was progressing toward the kingdom of God had been an important foundation for evangelical Protestant crusading. But that foundation was crumbling under the pressures of population shifts, intellectual changes, and increased pluralism."[41]

When Straton talked about Christianizing New York, he also meant he wanted to Americanize New York. Straton was fond of saying that New York was home to more Italians than Rome, more Irish than Dublin, and more Jews than Jerusalem. He also added that New York was "the largest Negro city in the world."[42] What these people brought with them, Straton believed, was a love of pleasure that found a myriad of expressions in the city's commercial economy. They suffered from an "amusement madness" that shook the very foundations of Anglo-Saxon civilization. Straton hoped to bring a dose of Anglo-Saxon discipline to Catholic and Jewish and African American and other New Yorkers who had not yet been tutored in the values of "Americanism" and "old-time religion." That job belonged to Protestant churches, Straton believed, but ministers who had once been the guardians of public morality were no longer to be trusted since so many of them had succumbed to the allure of modern pleasure. The redemption of the city was a task to be entrusted only to those who, like Straton, held to the fundamentals of the faith.

Straton was right in his observation that the commercial spaces of modern urban life brought New Yorkers out of their homes and into public places, including retail stores, dance halls, cinemas, theaters, sports arenas, hotels, and crowded streets. In these urban public spaces, a new America had come into being. Of course, class and color and gender made some boundaries impenetrable, yet New York continued to be the promiscuous city Protestant reformers had always claimed it was, inhabited by what Straton called a "mixed multitude" of people whose social intercourse threatened the Puritan America of Straton's imagination.[43]

Straton was determined to reverse these trends toward a post-Protestant American civic order, yet New York's riotous economy of pleasure aimed a "pagan" arrow at the very heart of the Christian nation as Straton conceived of it. Modern techniques simply could not overcome his sense that the modern city was an alien place for Christians like himself. Thus Straton, like other fundamentalists, turned increasingly to apocalyptic thought to imagine a purge of the modern city. "Where is Babylon with its hanging gardens? Where is Nineveh with its vaunting pride? Where are Sodom and Gomorrah with their unspeakable infamies?" "These cities forgot God," Straton reminded his readers. "In the pride of their material glory, in their selfishness and their sins, they turned away from their Maker, and his righteous judgment and his holy wrath turned against them."[44] If Straton's crusade failed, God's old-fashioned anger waited in the wings to deliver the blow to the New Babylon. New York, that mongrel of a metropolis, might have to be destroyed so that a "pure" America could yet be preserved.[45]

Notes

1. For a riveting account of the Scopes trial and its place in American cultural history, see Edward Larson, *Summer for the Gods: The Scopes Trial and America's Continuing Debate Over Science and Religion* (New York: Basic Books, 1997).
2. Fosdick's sermon is reprinted in William R. Hutchison, ed., *American Protestant Thought: The Liberal Era* (Lanham, Md.: University Press of America, 1984), 170–182.
3. Stanley Walker, "The Meshuggah of Manhattan," *New Yorker*, April 16, 1927, 24.
4. John Roach Straton, *The Menace of Immorality in Church and State: Messages of Wrath and Judgment* (New York: George H. Doran, 1920), 191.
5. John Roach Straton, *Fighting the Devil in Modern Babylon* (Boston: Stratford Co., 1929), 138.
6. Straton, *Fighting the Devil*, 5.
7. For the most thorough and critical evaluation of Straton's career to date, see C. Allyn Russell, *Voices of American Fundamentalism* (Philadelphia: Westminster Press, 1976), 47–78. See also George M. Marsden, *Fundamentalism and American Culture* (New York: Oxford University Press, 1980), 161–163.
8. Quoted in William G. Shepherd, *Great Preachers as Seen by a Journalist* (New York: Fleming H. Revel, 1924), 71–82.
9. William R. de Plata, *Tell It from Calvary*, 2nd ed. (New York: Calvary Baptist Church, 1997), 44–45.
10. Walker, "The Fundamentalist Pope," *American Mercury* 8 (July 1926): 258.
11. Straton, *Menace of Immorality*, 176–177.
12. Ibid., 190–191.
13. Straton was accompanied that night by a journalist and a private investigator from a Progressive Era civic vigilance association, the Committee of Fourteen. The committee evolved out of the Anti-Saloon League and received funding from Andrew Carnegie, John D. Rockefeller Jr., and Felix Warburg, among others. See Timothy Gilfoyle, *City of Eros: New York City, Prostitution, and the Commercialization of Sex, 1790–1920* (New York: Norton, 1992), 303.
14. Straton, *Fighting the Devil*, 30.
15. John Roach Straton, *Fundamentalist* (July–August, 1923), 7.
16. Straton, *Menace of Immorality*, 154.

17. Quoted in Russell, *Voices of American Fundamentalism*, 51.
18. For example, see Beth Bailey *From Front Porch to Back Seat: Courtship in Twentieth-Century America* (Baltimore: Johns Hopkins University Press, 1988), 87.
19. Diane Winston, *Red-Hot and Righteous: The Urban Religion of the Salvation Army* (Cambridge: Harvard University Press, 1999), 40.
20. James Gilbert, *Perfect Cities: Chicago's Utopias of 1893* (Chicago: University of Chicago Press, 1991), 185–186.
21. See Aimee Semple McPherson's accounts of her "gospel auto" ministry in *In the Service of the King* (New York: Boni and Liveright, 1927), 177–206.
22. Quoted in Calvary Baptist Church, *Souvenir of Out Door Services*, n.d., John Roach Straton Papers, Box 1, American Baptist Historical Society (ABHS).
23. *Radio Program* 1 (April 27, 1923), 4.
24. John Roach Straton Papers, Box 11, ABHS.
25. *Radio World* 2 (March 17, 1923), 1.
26. *The Faith* 2 (April 19, 1925), n.p.
27. Straton, *Menace of Immorality*, 188–189.
28. Roland Marchand, *Creating the Corporate Soul* (Berkeley and Los Angeles: University of California Press, 1998), 184. See also Sarah Bradford Landau and Carl W. Condit, *Rise of the New York Skyscraper* (New Haven, Conn.: Yale University Press, 1996), 361–364.
29. Quoted in Rolf Lunden, *Business and Religion in the American 1920s* (New York: Greenwood Press, 1988), 82. On the skyscraper church movement, see also Thomas A. P. van Leeuwen, *The Skyward Trend of Thought: The Metaphysics of the American Skyscraper* (Cambridge: MIT Press, 1988), 71–78.
30. Lunden, *Business and Religion*, 80.
31. Quoted in the caption of the frontispiece, Straton, *Fighting the Devil*.
32. John Roach Straton, "The Center of Convenience" (pamphlet), John Roach Straton Papers, Box 17, ABHS.
33. *The Faith* 2 (April 19, 1925), n.p.
34. Straton, *Menace of Immorality*, 172.
35. *The Faith* 2 (April 19, 1925), n.p.
36. The conflict at Calvary regarding the skyscraper church building was covered extensively in the New York press. See *New York Times*, April 9, 1925, 3; May 20, 1925, 1.
37. Hillyer Straton and Ferenc Szasz, "The Reverend John Roach Straton and the Presidential Campaign of 1928," *New York History* 49 (April 1968): 200–217.
38. Walker, "Fundamentalist Pope," 257–258.
39. *New Republic* 60 (November 13, 1929), 335.
40. John Roach Straton, *The Old Gospel at the Heart of the Metropolis* (New York: George H. Doran, 1925), 251.
41. Robert Handy, *A Christian America*, 2nd ed. (New York: Oxford University Press, 1984), 170.
42. Straton, *Fighting the Devil*, 2.
43. Ibid., 65.
44. Straton, *Menace of Immorality*, 178–179.
45. The phrase "mongrel Manhattan" is from Ann Douglas, *Terrible Honesty: Mongrel Manhattan in the 1920s* (New York: Farrar, Straus, and Giroux, 1995), 5–6.

Part II

Protestant Transformation

_____ *Figure 11* _____

Leading citizens of Santa Barbara dressed as "Spanish Caballeros" parade on horseback in front of Mission Santa Barbara.
From Santa Barbara: Tierra Adorada *(Los Angeles: Security–First National Bank, 1930)*.

Five

Roberto Lint Sagarena

Building California's Past

*Mission Revival Architecture
and Regional Identity*

On June 29, 1925, a major earthquake in California destroyed most of Santa Barbara's downtown. Although the tremor claimed many victims—nine dead, hundreds of injuries, and many thousands of dollars in lost property— many Santa Barbara residents saw it as a blessing rather than as a tragedy. It allowed for a re-creation of the city's architectural landscape in a form that would promote a uniquely southern Californian sense of place, one founded on a peculiar and ecumenical religious imagination. Through its reconstruction, Santa Barbara could "now make itself the most beautiful city in America."[1]

Historians of American religious traditions have long studied the role of the urban environment on the development of religious traditions in the United States. They have examined the influence of ethnic pluralism, demographic density, and economic stratification on the American religious imagination in the urban context. But relations of influence between religious practice and their environs are reciprocal. Not only does religious practice adapt and change in the city, in many profound ways it also defines the city itself—most strikingly through the influence of religion on the built environment and in public processions and parades.[2]

The rebuilding of Santa Barbara presents a striking example of this reciprocal relationship. The regional identity of southern California was invented (largely) by and for Protestant settlers from the midwestern and eastern United States through a romantic articulation of the state's Catholic Spanish past. The opportunity to redefine the character of the city all at once after the earthquake allowed Santa Barbara to become home to perhaps the most successful citywide installation of stylized Mission and Spanish Revival architecture.[3]

The nation's first architectural board of review was assembled in Santa Barbara to maintain uniformity of design during the postearthquake building rush.[4] All new structures were required to conform to the city's Spanish colonial theme—even mailboxes and public trash receptacles were given Iberian stylings. By the end of 1926, the year after the earthquake, tourists encountered a uniformly "Spanish-flavored" city whose architecture was tightly integrated with its central attraction, Mission Santa Barbara.[5] One lighthearted commentator in the 1930s reported that "Santa Barbara is a little confusing—every building is a mission—At least that's the way the architecture affects you when you first see it. You feel like removing your hat when you drive into a service station."[6]

The development of southern California's regional character was directly influenced by the United States's encounter with established civic centers and architectural forms in the far West after the U.S.–Mexican War (1846–1848). Before the occupation and conquest of the West, annexed territories had, for the most part, been inhabited by nomadic and seminomadic Native American tribes. Historical narratives describing the nature of American expansion had not had to confront massive indigenous cities such as the Aztecs' Tenochtitlán or the Incas' Cuzco.[7] And as long as American historiography did not have to consider recognizable architectural monuments that marked a place as inhabited, it could still portray westward advance as a legitimate occupation of fallow territory. In the Southwest, however, the presence of Mexican towns and missionary outposts required the logic of Manifest Destiny to perform a radical reordering and restructuring of the narratives associated with the architectural landscape. By the late nineteenth century, as southwestern regionalism began to be codified, southern California's public history focused largely on its Spanish past and most explicitly on the Catholic missions.

Americans and the Missions

The first description of California to reach general audiences in the United States arrived in Richard Henry Dana Jr.'s autobiographical adventure story, *Two Years Before the Mast*, published in 1840. Dana's readers' first glimpse of California is of its architecture as visible from the deck of the aptly named Boston-based merchant ship, the *Pilgrim*, as it sailed into the Santa Barbara channel. Like most mid-nineteenth-century American visitors to Mexican California, Dana's assessments of adobe dwellings were generally critical, but he viewed the adobe churches with interest. Over time, American fascination with the missions would grow dramatically, in part because the buildings were quick to ruin; it often took much less than a hundred years for the unfired adobe bricks begin to be literally melted by the elements. The rapid disintegration of the missions provided ripe material for American imaginations, their ruins offering both historical solemnity and great interpretive possibilities.[8]

While the mission settlement of Santa Barbara was first dedicated in 1786, the church building that Dana saw was built in 1815, the same year he was born in Cambridge, Massachusetts. To the nineteen-year-old's eyes, "The Mission [was] a large and deserted looking place, the out-buildings going to ruin, and everything giving one the impression of decayed grandeur."[9] This trope of decay became common to American narratives about the missions because it added an ethical dimension to their history, deepening the buildings' appeal. The fact that these "stately monuments" were falling into disrepair was taken by many Americans as a clear sign of the moral failures of Mexican rule.

In 1850 (two years after the U.S.–Mexican War) Bishop Joseph Alemany was dispatched from Baltimore to administer the diocese of the Californias. His first tasks were to take control of Alta California's Catholic parishes and claim all church properties for the American Catholic Church. The transfer of church buildings was complicated by the fact that many of the missions lay in private hands after the war. But eventually the properties were acquired by Alemany— shortly before his assassination, President Abraham Lincoln "returned" the secularized California missions to the American Catholic Church by presidential decree. Initially, little came of this gesture; the Catholic brick-and-mortar priests of the nineteenth century were much more interested in building churches that looked respectably American than in restoring exotic-looking missions.[10]

Nonetheless, within fifty years the renovation and restoration of the Catholic missions did begin, but most significantly through the efforts of regional boosters (who were largely Protestants). In the early years after California was ceded (1848 to 1865), visitors' descriptions of adobe buildings often continued to condemn them as "squalid mud huts." But as social and political control of the state shifted into the hands of Anglo-Americans, these attitudes were inverted—by the 1870s romantic illustrations and travel narratives describing the missions began to circulate in the eastern United States. In time, all adobe buildings became valued historical treasures as they fell into ruin and disrepair.

The first decades of the American settlement of California centered largely in the north. These early years were defined by the gold rush and its attendant mass migration, the population boom in San Francisco, and the rise of a ruthlessly violent and xenophobic but also cosmopolitan culture.[11] Culturally and demographically, southern California changed much less in the first decade after the U.S.–Mexican War; the few Americans living in southern California during this period were mostly émigrés from the Southeast engaged in cattle ranching. But by the mid-1860s migrations (consisting largely of northeasterners) from the gold fields and into the region effected great changes and began the American appropriation of southern California in earnest.[12]

The Birth of Mission Romance

Despite the initial foreignness of its ranchos, presidios, and Franciscan missions, the distinctiveness of southern California's built environment was employed in the creation of a new regional history that redefined the formerly Mexican region into a "Spanish Arcadia." This was accomplished largely through the production of a constellation of historical narratives that encouraged enthusiasm for the history of Franciscan colonizers in order to valorize California's Spanish era over Native American prehistory and the recent Mexican past. In time, this retelling of California's history came to work powerfully and persuasively in the distinctions people made between one another, the stories Americans told themselves about the legitimacy of their presence in the region, and most enduringly in the way that they created and understood their lived environment.

While enthusiasm for the decaying missions became widespread quickly, two individuals are commonly acknowledged as the principal agents in the popularization of romantic portrayals of the missions, Helen Hunt Jackson and Charles Fletcher Lummis. In 1883 Jackson wrote a series of biographical essays about the life of Father Junípero Serra (1713–1784)—the Franciscan in charge of the establishment of Alta California's chain of missions. This first hagiographic treatment of "Father Junipero and His Work" appeared in *Century Magazine* in early 1883 and was read nationwide. In Jackson's prose, the Spanish priest was cast as a pioneer of California's barren spiritual landscape who Anglo-Americans should recognize and claim as an exemplar and hero.

Although Jackson appealed to a "Protestant biographer" of St. Francis of Assisi for proof that the Franciscan order was motivated by admirable values, she presented California's Spanish Franciscans as a legitimate alternative to New England's dour Puritans as American forbearers. She wrote: "On the Atlantic shore, the decedents of the Puritans, weighed down by serious purpose, half grudging the time for their one staid yearly Thanksgiving, and driving the Indians farther and farther into the wilderness every year, fighting and killing them; on the sunny Pacific shore, the merry people of Mexican and Spanish blood, troubling themselves about nothing, dancing away whole days and nights like children, while their priests were gathering the Indians by thousands into communities and feeding and teaching them."[13] Her enthusiasm for California's Catholic past is, perhaps, surprising given that she grew up in a strict Congregationalist family in Amherst, Massachusetts, that counted the staunchly anti-Catholic Beechers as family friends. But tours of Catholic Europe softened her antipathy, and, after the death of a son and husband in the 1860s, she (like so many other mourners in post–Civil War New England) experienced a deep and abiding spiritual crisis. In her later years the nostalgic and idealized image of California's pious Spanish Franciscans assuaged the feelings of religious longing that she often expressed in her poetry. And her empathetic biographical essays helped to make Fr. Serra, the Franciscans, and California's Catholic past broadly palatable to Americans regardless of religious affiliation.[14]

While Jackson's biography of Fr. Serra was influential, it was her novel *Ramona* (appearing in 1884) that reached the widest audience and formalized nostalgic tropes that influenced generations of American novelists, historians, travelers, and architects. She had hoped that *Ramona* would be "the *Uncle Tom's Cabin* of the West," bringing attention to the plight of California's Native American population and calling for social change, but the novel would instead effect a different sort of social change.

The simplicity of *Ramona*'s narrative is its greatest strength. The main protagonist is a "Cinderella" character, an adopted half–American Indian daughter raised by a cold Spanish stepmother, Señora Moreno. In typical form, Ramona's stepmother attempts to thwart her developing love affair. And even after Ramona escapes from her oppressive home and marries Alessandro, a Native American ranch hand, they face numerous trials and tragedies as a result of Yankee prejudice. In the end, Ramona leaves California to the Americans and heads to Mexico, where she makes her life anew as a grand dame in Mexico City. The novel bemoans the passing of the missions as a principal reason for the desperate condition of California's Native American population. But it casts the passing of Native Americans and Mexicans as tragically inevitable. This fatalism meant that while *Ramona* was one of the most popular novels of its time, it was read most commonly as a romance rather than as a call for social action and moral reform.

Nonetheless, *Ramona* did have a profound impact on California—most notably in the development of California's built environment. The novel clearly articulated the fact that architecture was to be a crucial component of the American reinvention and appropriation of California; the crumbling adobes were to serve as monuments to a fictionalized but commonly accepted portrayal of the past. Jackson described life during the colonial period (1767–1821) as "a picturesque life, with more of sentiment and gaiety in it, more also that was truly dramatic, than will ever seen again on those sunny shores. The aroma of it lingers there still: industries and inventions have not yet slain it; it will last out its century—in fact it will never be quite lost so long as there is standing one such house as the Senora [*sic*] Moreno's."[15] Señora Moreno's fictional rancho is the main stage for the drama that unfolds in the novel, and it was a place that fired the American imagination. The rich descriptions of the rancho helped to promote a distinctively Californian architecture connecting the past portrayed in the novel to the American present.

Railroad companies were quick to capitalize on Ramonamania. Rail tours of California that stopped at the missions to give easterners a taste of California's Catholic ruins soon began to stop at "the house of the true Ramona." Although Ramona was a purely fictional character, the Southern Pacific and Santa Fe rail lines each promoted California ranches that Jackson had visited during her stay in California as Ramona's home. Southern Pacific trains made a stop at Rancho Camulos near Santa Barbara, and the Santa Fe line stopped at Rancho Guajome near San Diego. Both ranches quickly became must-see attractions for travelers hoping to get a taste of the spirit of bygone California.[16]

Frank Miller, owner of the Mission Inn at Riverside, estimated in the 1920s that *Ramona* had "brought at least fifty million dollars into this region."[17] Journalists fanned the flames of enthusiasm for Ramona's story with endless articles speculating about the actual location of events in the novel. In 1919 D. W. Griffith brought a screening of *Ramona* to the nation in a cinematic adaptation starring Mary Pickford. By 1923 an annual Ramona theatrical pageant with a cast of over two hundred (that continues to this day) began at Hemet, California.[18]

Jackson provided the popular narrative and drama but passed away a year after the publication of *Ramona*—never seeing the effects of her writings. Soon after, Charles Fletcher Lummis became the principal mastermind of marketing Old Mission romance. Using his positions as editor of both the *Los Angeles Times* and *Land of Sunshine Magazine* as soapboxes for rallying popular support, Lummis established California's first historical preservation society, the Landmarks Club. Many prominent southern California boosters and supporters of the Landmarks Club such as Joseph Widney (a medical doctor and ordained Methodist minister who was an early president of University of Southern California) and Harrison Grey Otis (owner of the *Los Angeles Times* and famous union-buster) championed the restoration of the Catholic missions and the rights of Native Americans and also believed that southern California was destined to become the capital of New World Anglo-Aryan culture.

These seemingly incongruous causes and beliefs were linked by a common interest in southern California's developing regionalism, strong antimodernism, and eugenic theories about the influence of climate on race. Idealized depictions of the Spanish past worked to create a distinctive regional identity that stood in contrast with the American East. And writers such as Widney promoted the idea that after centuries of westward movement, Anglo-Aryan peoples had finally fulfilled their destiny by arriving at California's Southland. The journey across the continent as pioneers had changed these people and made them more like the "noble Redman" that they displaced, "tall, spare, muscular but not obese; taciturn men of few words, eyes always on the watch, rifle almost constantly in their hands."[19] Arrival in sunny (but not hot enough to cause tropical laziness) California marked the apotheosis of the Anglo-Aryan race. In this historical scheme, by moving west, Americans could become healthy, adopt the best features of the Native Americans and Latin Americans they displaced, and still retain their "superior civility, industry, and moral order."[20]

Although most of the leadership of the Landmarks Club was male, its foot soldiers and organizing muscle were primarily upper-class Anglo Protestant women. In 1905 one of the club's most prominent members, Eliza Otis, known affectionately as "California's Beloved Mission Poet," wrote in the pages of the *Los Angeles Times* that

> Catholicism and Puritanism are looked upon generally as opposing forces, but here each had its work of preparation to accomplish, and each did it well, and today they stand face to face without a thought of conflict. Puritanism commends the work accomplished by those early Mission Fathers, and comes here to sow and to reap in the soil which they made ready for the larger and grander life of this later century. The work proposed by the Landmark Club, "to conserve the missions and other historic landmarks of Southern California" is a most commendable one and should have the hearty support of every public-spirited citizen of the State.[21]

Enthusiasm for the missions and comparisons of the Spanish Franciscans to the Puritans became central to California booster literature. As the Spanish past became an anchor for southern California's regional identity, the Franciscans soon began to receive the more positive assessment in comparisons with their New England counterparts. Fr. Serra and other Franciscans were seen as having been as industrious, pious, and self-denying as the most devout Puritan but with the benefit of a "cheerful" Latin disposition instead of a "dour" northern European one.

Lummis, himself a Methodist, spearheaded a Protestant effort to have Fr. Serra canonized by the Catholic Church. He enquired to Fr. Zephyrin Englehardt, a Franciscan historian of the missions and caretaker of the mission archives at Santa Barbara, as to the why the Church hadn't already declared Serra a saint and what the probability of it happening soon might be. Lummis wrote that he believed that "this man—whom, as a historian, I count foremost among all missionary pioneers and administrators or the New World—should have the proper recognition. It isn't for me to meddle with the programme of the church; but I have a right to work as an American and a Protestant and a Californian in recognition of the hero whom not even the A.P.A. seems to hate."[22] When Fr. Englehardt expressed his doubts about the likelihood of Fr. Serra's beatification, much less canonization, Lummis seemed all the more determined and enthusiastic about his campaign. He responded to Fr. Englehardt that "I am a good deal disappointed at the improbability that we can secure the canonization of Junipero Serra. . . . However, I am a somewhat obstinate person; and am going to keep at this until whipped off the circuit. We have vague whispers of miraculous affairs; and I am going to trace them down."[23] Unfortunately for the cause of turn-of-the-century boosters, Lummis was unable to document any miracles directly attributable to Serra. But in time a controversial movement for Serra's canonization emerged within the Catholic Church itself.[24]

While these Protestants' efforts did signal some reconciliation between American Protestants and Catholics, the silk glove of the historical preservation committees hid the fist of racism. The decay of the mission buildings was used by preservationists as evidence of Mexican laziness and greed. In 1920 another Landmarks booster wrote in the *Los Angeles Times* that "Mexican politicians were filled with greed for the wealth that had been created by the Indians under the supervision of the padres, and desired possession of the resources already developed. The undeveloped wealth of California surrounded them. But do you think they would do a lick of work themselves? . . . It was downright greed, coupled with laziness and heresy which brought about the downfall of the missions."[25]

Revival of Religious Architecture as a Response to Immigration

As Americans, Protestant and Catholic alike, eagerly claimed the Spanish Franciscans' efforts as part of their own genealogy, they began to make clear ethnic distinctions between Mexicans and Spaniards. Up until the turn of the century the two forms of ethnic ascription were fairly interchangeable in the United States, but the romantic portrayal of the missions required clear boundaries to explain and legitimize the American presence. John Bodkin addressed the Catholic Newman Club of Los Angeles in 1905, claiming, "The Priests at the various Missions were usually men of very pure character. Those who established the Missions were directly from Spain. They were superior men in point of talent, education, moral and executive ability, as the successes of the Missions under their establishment and administrations showed."[26]

Bodkin's enthusiastic praise of the Spanish settlement of the state ignored the fact that many of the Spanish missionaries who came to California were of the same mixed ethnic and racial background as the deplored Mexicans. Often the only difference between them was a semantic one resulting from the Mexican War of Independence in 1821. Before the war, everyone in New Spain's northern frontier was a subject of the Spanish crown; after the war, everyone swore allegiance to Mexico.

Racial and ethnic distinctions often presuppose pure identities, but in actual fact the "lazy" Mexicans and the "industrious" Spaniards were often one in the same people. The instability of racial and cultural boundaries between Indians, Mexicans, and Spaniards had to be blocked, however, in order to maintain the order and symmetry of the American portrayal of California's past:

Spanish Franciscans = west coast Puritans

Mexicans = lazy foreigners who laid waste to the idyllic past

Americans = rightful and appreciative heirs to California

Native Americans = tragic characters who had passed away

In short order, regional histories came to rely on the brief period of Mexican rule (1821–1848) as a foil that explained the legitimacy of American rule. Secularization (that is, the transfer of Franciscan missions to control by diocesan clergy and the redistribution or sale of mission properties that occurred largely after Mexican independence) in particular was seen as powerful proof of Mexican responsibility for the collapse of the idealized Spanish era. In 1916 R. J. Cotter mournfully contemplated the fate of the missions, "Their children are scattered, their flocks and herds gone, their fertile fields and vineyards have passed to other hands. The mission bells are silent, the padres dead and gone, while all along the King's Highway, like bones of murdered men, are the ruins of God's churches, now fallen in the dust, mute but mournful monuments to Mexican misrule."[27] By adopting Spanish Catholic missionaries as "California's Pious Forefathers" who were "driven to ruin by Mexicans," claims for the legitimacy of the American presence and proof of Mexican inferiority could be accomplished in a single historiographical gesture.

The narrative of public history and invented tradition often follows a romantic pattern of golden age, period of decay, and final renewal. The historical record becomes "a drama of the triumph of good over evil, of virtue over vice, of light over darkness."[28] This tripartite division of history ascribes ethical value to a division of time—a particular period of history (in this case the Mexican) is obscured and cast as the nadir of human existence. The final stage is then seen as a triumphal return to an original state of grace or virtue. While this form of emplotment has structured southern California's history for most of the twentieth century, its impact on public historical understanding has been less through its presence in history books than through its influence on the urban environment.

But the romantic portrayal of the Spanish colonial past was not only cast in the static shapes of buildings, it was and is still performed in the Fiesta—citywide pageants and festivals with Spanish themes. The first Fiesta (modeled after the New Orleans Mardi Gras) was organized by Charles Lummis in Los Angeles in 1894 and was quickly adopted by cities throughout the Southwest, taking firm root in Santa Barbara as the "Old Spanish Days Fiesta." While Spanish Revival buildings served as the sets, the Fiesta parade allowed the American population to dress up in stylized Spanish colonial costumes and act out their appropriation of the imagined Spanish past. By dressing as Spaniards (but not Mexicans), Fiesta participants playfully and powerfully made connections between themselves and idealized wealthy and noble "Spanish Grandees."[29]

Santa Barbara's Fiesta parades became public history lessons as floats passed the crowd, each representing a particular era of California's past. These processions reproduced the narrative of the boosters' presentation of California's history by often omitting the Mexican period and mention of the Mexican War altogether. The presentation of the "benevolent conquest" of the Spanish Franciscans was often abruptly followed by the inheritance of the land by the American settlers.

Significantly, popularity for this reworking of California's public history coincided with the explosive growth of Mexican and Mexican American communities. Mexican immigration to the United States increased dramatically during the 1910s as the Mexican Revolution raged and thousands upon thousands of Mexicans fled for their lives. In the 1920s Mexican immigration intensified even further with the growth of agribusiness in the American West. U.S firms actively and illegally recruited Mexican laborers to come to work in the United States. Between 1900 and 1930, the Mexican-born population of the United States grew from 103,000 to 1,400,000, with the largest waves of immigration occurring in the 1920s.[30]

While many Catholic and Protestant churches were built during this period in the Mission Revival style, they were not necessarily hospitable to their Latino/a parishioners. For American Catholics, the early decades of the twentieth century were a time of growing confidence in their place in American society. The Church hierarchy placed a great deal of emphasis on the Americanization of immigrant Catholics in an attempt to create a unified American Catholic Church, but this unified front faced a serious threat in the west with the arrival of Mexican Catholics. However, with minor exceptions of Americanization campaigns and efforts to counter Protestant missionary efforts in Mexican American barrios, Mexican immigrant communities were largely neglected by the American Catholic clergy until well into the 1940s.[31]

Selling Old Mission Romance

Given the coincidence of the popularization of the Spanish past with the advent of Mexican immigration, this popularity can be seen as a response to social challenges brought about by drastic changes in demography. But enthusiasm for the Spanish-built missions also had clearly recognizable economic benefits. In "Stand Fast Santa Barbara," an essay published near the end of his life, Charles Lummis makes a point of emphasizing this to his Santa Barbara audience:

> In 1916, at the Landmarks' Club "Candle Day," at San Fernando Mission (where we had re-roofed and saved the enormous monastery and church,) after a Catholic Bishop and a Church of England Bishop, and a Methodist Bishop and a Jewish Rabbi and other men of many creeds had paid eloquent tribute to Junipero Serra and the Franciscan Missionaries, who founded Civilization on the Pacific Coast and left us these noble monuments of Faith and Architecture—then came the Apostle of Business, John S, Mitchell, President of the Los Angeles Chamber of Commerce. . . . He said, earnestly and emphatically, to the audience of 7,000 gathered there: 'I have a confession to make that should have been made long ago. We business men, who like to think that we are shrewd and far-seeing, have long been blind. It took us a great while to realize that the Old Missions had anything but a sentimental interest. . . . We realize today that the Missions have not only a commercial value, but the greatest! We realize today that the old missions are worth more money and are a greater asset to Southern California than our oil, our oranges, even our climate!' . . . Romance is the greatest asset of California. . . . To all this centuried Romance, Santa Barbara is legitimate and favorite heiress—about the only one left that has not traded away her birthright.[32]

Lummis believed that Santa Barbara should articulate this romantic past through "an architecture of its own," one that was authentic and true to the model of the missions.[33] He thought that "most of the so-called 'Mission Style' now going up all over California, isn't Mission at all, nor architecture, but obvious, awkward and detestable FAKE."[34] Lummis died shortly after the Santa Barbara earthquake and never saw that Santa Barbara did not exactly heed his call for authenticity in its architectural style.

While recognizably different from earlier Mission Revival architecture, Santa Barbara's Spanish Revival architecture drew its strength and inspiration from the popularization of the mission preservation movement.[35] This new architectural vocabulary worked in concert with the reconstructed missions to Americanize California's Latin American past. The architects of Spanish Revival were largely unconcerned with historical accuracy but rather attempted to create a feeling of affluence, exoticism, and regional distinctiveness.

Designers such as Bertram Goodhue, George Washington Smith, and Reginald Johnson quickly transformed the architectural vocabulary borrowed from colonial adobes by adding ornate Spanish and Italian architectural forms that provided a more attractive look than the rough frontier architecture of the missions.[36] Its popularity soon made the city's built environment resonate with a single voice. Just as there is erasure and loss of meaning in the repetition of a word, the ubiquitous presence of fanciful Spanish Revival architecture blurred any meaningful connections to a Latin American or indigenous past.

In *The Necessity of Ruins*, J. B. Jackson discusses the relation between social change and the built environment. He tells us that

> monuments are likely to be numerous in any landscape where the inhabitants share a strong sense of a religious or political past, and moreover are concerned with their beginnings. That is why every new revolutionary social order, anxious to establish its image and acquire public support, produces many commemorative monuments and symbols and public celebrations. That is what we see in the Soviet Union, or China or Cuba or for that matter Nazi Germany: a proliferation of public symbols of all sorts, not to please the public but to remind it of what it should believe and how it is to act.[37]

So, too, in southern California—Mission and Spanish Revival architecture acted in a monumental form for the American portrayal of the region's history. It evoked the golden age of the pious Spanish Franciscans, made references to the Mexican "period of decay," and showed that the region had been restored to a semblance of its former splendor as an idyllic Iberian paradise for Americans.

And paradise would command a stiff price from newcomers. Just two weeks after the Santa Barbara earthquake, a banker, Dr. L. R. Sevier, predicted, "Just as sure as I am alive, it will only be a matter of time until real estate value [*sic*] in the present wrecked city will stand at a figure of twice what they were before the disaster."[38] And he was soon proven right. The portrayal of pre-American California as a place and time of carefree Latin affluence and indolence served as a foundation for the presentation of Santa Barbara as an exclusive and wealthy community by boosters.

While railroad companies owning vast tracts of land were eager to promote the sale of real estate, they also saw that the region's greatest future assets lay in its drawing power with tourists. And local merchants concurred. One Santa Barbara businessman believed that if you "add our historical charm, as represented in the Queen of the Missions, to the charm of a typically Spanish city and its wonderful setting of mountain and sea and you have a lure that the tourist cannot resist. And there is no better 'business' than the tourist business."[39]

With the "historic charm" of California's Catholic Spanish past as a lure, the promotion of tourism and real estate worked hand in hand in the development of Santa Barbara. Desirability as a vacation spot helped to make the cost of living high, ensuring exclusivity, which in turn propelled property values to higher and higher levels. Santa Barbarans were not only aware of the role of tourism in the local economy as they rebuilt their city, they were aware of just exactly who the tourists were. A month after the earthquake one editorial in the *Santa Barbara Morning Press* highlighted the considerations of gender that had to be made to promote tourism in southern California at the time. The editor wrote, "In rebuilding our city, I wonder if we remember how many of our tourists are women? . . . It is largely the women who decide where the family shall spend its vacation and how long shall be the stay. . . . Through their clubs and various organizations women are becoming interested in civic betterment. We must win their approval of the way we rebuild our city."[40] The women who participated in restoration and historical societies such as the Landmarks Club were often the same ones who toured the missions with their families on holiday. Santa Barbara captured these tourists' hearts with an architecture that was convincingly and attractively coordinated with its mission.

Santa Barbara, California, a tourist tract written by John Steven McGroarty (author of the *Mission Play*) that was widely distributed by the Southern Pacific Railroad in 1926, described the city as a charmingly rustic but nonetheless up-to-date haven for the affluent. He advised tourists that

> progress and modern ideas have come to Santa Barbara, of course, as they have come to other places in the world. . . . But in Santa Barbara, *gracias a Dios* has not permitted unromantic and brazen Progress to destroy the vast beauty that is its heritage from the splendid past. It soothes the heart and rests the soul to think that there were once times when the world was not crazy. Times when men did not hurry and scurry and rush feverishly to their graves   as a result   it was inevitable that wealth should lay claim to a corner of the world so favored, even as the wealth of Rome had seized upon that sunny flank of the Bay of Naples to which the roadstead of Santa Barbara is so often compared.[41]

Thus the place was sold through the promotion of an antimodernist sensibility that still celebrated the latest cosmopolitan fads and convenient amenities. To be in Santa Barbara was to be wealthy, fashionable, and relaxed.

But not all residents were convinced of the desirability or equity of the economic benefits of the promotion of "Old Mission Romance." One concerned citizen, writing well before the earthquake, cajoled the editor of the local paper to forget the idea of modeling downtown as a "Street in Spain" and instead fight to make Santa Barbara

a city where any good square American citizen who has to work for a living can live and do as well as he can anywhere else and boost for some good stable industries so that Santa Barbara will be a truly American City, self-supporting, not living off the largess of the rich, but a producer that will be a credit to our great State of California and not an imitation of Greenwich Village. Why not in all fairness Mr. Editor, does not the Chamber of Commerce put a big sign at each of the entrances to the city,
"Millionaires Welcome"
"Plain Americans, Abandon Hope All Ye Who Enter Here."[42]

No doubt this Progressive writer was heartbroken by the postquake building boom and the subsequent sustained rise of Santa Barbara's real estate prices. However, the powerful cultural incentives and economic benefits that fostered the promotion of "Old Mission Romance" were simply too great for there to be much resistance to them at the time of their inception.

The popularization of Mission and Spanish Revival architecture by both Protestants and Catholics served to create an ecumenical regional history that integrated Catholic colonizers into the narrative of American history. It offered American Catholics a central place in Californian society and allowed Protestants to lay claim to Americanized historical monuments as exotic and stately as the Catholic churches of Europe. However, this spirit of ecumenism also worked to create lasting racial and ethnic boundaries within the region. The exclusive qualities of southern California's regionalism are perhaps most clearly seen in the border patrol checkpoints that dot coastal Highway 101 with their red tiled roofs and plastered walls recalling the romantic glory of California's colonial Latin American past while aggressively guarding the U.S. border with Mexico. At base, this romantic presentation of California's history gained its tremendous popularity from its ability to promote the economic growth and development of the region, largely to the benefit of wealthy elites. Fr. Englehardt noted in his diary that after being invited to a Landmarks Club meeting at the lavish Mission Inn, he thanked his entrepreneurial host, Frank Miller (a Congregationalist), by saying that "St. Francis will repay." "Ah, he has already" was the reply.[43]

Notes

1. *Santa Barbara Morning Press*, July 5, 1925, 1. Prodevelopment Santa Barbarans quickly portrayed the destruction of their city as a great opportunity to enact earlier proposals to unify Santa Barbara's architecture along a Colonial Spanish theme. The day after the earthquake, June 30, 1925, an article on the front page of the *Santa Barbara Morning Press* reported that "Santa Barbara will rise from its ruins more beau-

tiful and substantial than ever, businessmen of the city declared with unanimity following yesterday morning's earthquake."

2. See Robert Orsi, ed., *Gods of the City: Religion and the American Urban Landscape* (Bloomington: Indiana University Press, 1999), for an excellent sampling of contemporary scholarship on the effects of the urban setting on American religious life.

3. Santa Fe is another southwestern city that is notable for its unified architecture. See Chris Wilson, *The Myth of Santa Fe: Creating a Modern Regional Tradition* (Albuquerque: University of New Mexico Press, 1997).

4. This board was promoted and chaired by Bernard Hoffman, an influential businessman, and also by several architects known for their Mission and Spanish Revival works.

5. David Gebhard, *Santa Barbara: The Creation of a New Spain in America* (Santa Barbara: University of California at Santa Barbara Art Museum, 1982), 21.

6. Reg Manning, *Reg Manning's Cartoon Guide to California* (New York: J. J. Augustin, 1939), 28.

7. While Americans were fascinated by the North American mound-building cultures, these mounds were not generally seen as architectural forms in a conventional sense.

8. Richard Henry Dana Jr., *Two Years Before the Mast, a Personal Narrative of Life at Sea* (New York: Penguin Books, 1981), 101.

9. Ibid., 189. The original Santa Barbara Mission was destroyed in an earthquake in 1812, and the current church building was erected in 1815.

10. John Bernard McGloin, S.J., *California's First Archbishop: The Life of Joseph Sadoc Alemany, O.P. 1814–1888* (New York: Herder and Herder, 1966), 115–146.

11. See Grey Brechin, *Imperial San Francisco: Urban Power, Earthly Ruin* (Berkeley and Los Angeles: University of California Press, 1999).

12. For a discussion of the transition of political and economic control in Southern California at the time, see Albert Camarillo, *Chicanos in a Changing Society: From Mexican Pueblos to American Barrios in Santa Barbara and Southern California* (Cambridge: Harvard University Press, 1996), 33–52; Douglas Monroy, *Thrown Among Strangers: The Making of Mexican Culture in Frontier California* (Berkeley and Los Angeles: University of California Press, 1990), 233–277; and Leonard Pitt, *The Decline of the Californios: A Social History of the Spanish-Speaking Californians, 1846–1890* (Berkeley and Los Angeles: University of California Press, 1998), 229–248.

13. This unnamed Protestant biographer is cited in Helen Hunt Jacskon [signed H. H.], "Father Junipero and His Work (pt. 1)," *Century Magazine* 26, no. 1 (May 1883): 4. Quote is taken from "Father Junipero and His Work (pt. 2)," *Century Magazine* 26, no. 2 (June 1883): 201.

14. For the details of Helen Hunt Jackson's life during this period, see Ruth Odell, *Helen Hunt Jackson* (New York: D. Appleton-Century Co., 1939). Although dated, it offers a well-researched, accurate portrait of the author.

15. Helen Hunt Jackson, *Ramona* (New York: Signet Classic, 1988), 12.

16. See James A Sandos, "Historic Preservation and Historic Facts: Helen Hunt Jackson, Rancho Camulos, and Ramonana," *California History* 77, no. 3 (1983): 168–185, 197–199; and Richard Griswold del Castillo, "The del Valle Family and the Fantasy Heritage," *California History* 59, no. 1 (1880): 2–15. These essays provide a history of both of the ranches and the competing claims regarding their authenticity that were put forward by their respective owners and the rail companies.

17. Frank Miller is quoted by Charles Lummis in his essay "Stand Fast Santa Barbara," which was originally published in the *Santa Barbara Morning Press* and later reprinted as a small book by the Santa Barbara Plans and Planting Committee of the Community Arts Association (June 1927), 10.

18. For a critical assessment of Ramona's popularity and role in the creation of southern California regionalism, see Carey McWilliams, *Southern California Country: An Island on the Land* (New York: Duell, Sloan and Pearce, 1946), 70–83. It should be noted, however, that *Ramona* was popular with Mexican and Mexican American audiences as well as American ones. The popular Mexican actress Dolores del Rio starred in an adaptation of *Ramona* filmed in Spanish, and the novel itself was translated and distributed in Mexico City.

19. Joseph Widney, *Race Life and Race Religions: Modern Light on their Growth, their Shaping and their Future* (Los Angeles: Times Mirror Press, 1936), 79.

20. It is important to note that the promotion of American Anglo-Aryan culture had little to do with a positive assessment of England and northern European cultures. These thinkers were heavily invested in contrasting the Anglo-Aryans of the western United States with their more "effete" ancestors in the Old World. On the one hand, West Coast hispanophilia allowed for a critique of English culture, and, on the other hand, racism against contemporary Mexicans ensured that Latin American culture was safely contained and defined in exoticized and idealized archaic forms.

21. Eliza Otis, "The Romance of the Mission Period" (1905), in *Some Essays About the California Missions in Honor of the V Centenary of the Evangelization of the Americas*, ed. Msgr. Francis J. Weber (Santa Barbara: California Catholic Conference, 1992), 45.

22. Letter from Lummis to Englehardt, April 1, 1909, transcribed in "The Correspondence of Charles F. Lummis with Fr. Zephyrin Englehardt, O.F.M.," in *Franciscan Provincial Annals, Province of Santa Barbara* 3, no. 4 (July 1941): 52.

23. Ibid., 53.

24. In 1943, two decades after Lummis's death, a historical commission was convened by the Catholic Church in California to investigate the life and character of Junípero Serra. In 1988, amid contentious debate, Serra was beatified by Pope John Paul II.

25. George Law, "Purpose of the Missions" (1920), in Weber, *Some Essays*, 174.

26. John Bodkin, "The Romance of the Mission Period" (1905), in Weber, *Some Essays*, 39.

27. Fr. R. J. Cotter, "Missions of California" (1916), in Weber, *Some Essays*, 145.

28. Hayden White, *Metahistory: The Historical Imagination in Nineteenth-Century Europe* (Baltimore: Johns Hopkins University Press, 1973), 9

29. Presently, debate over the inclusiveness of the name of Santa Barbara's "Old Spanish Days" has escalated. Some have proposed changing the name to "Old California Days" in recognition of the Native American and Mexican past. However, others argue that Santa Barbara's "Fiesta is different from other fiestas, because the others, in cities like San Antonio are only Mexican. We're the only ones who try to keep alive the part of Spain we all have in us." See David Amerikaner, "Under the Influence," in *Rhythms and Music of Fiesta* insert, *Santa Barbara News-Press*, August 2, 1998, 4.

30. For persuasive consideration of mission boosterism as a response to immigration, see William Deverell, "Privileging Mission over Mexican," in *Many Wests: Place, Culture and Regional Identity* (Kansas City: University of Kansas Press, 1997). For a discussion of Mexican immigration during this period, see Matt Meir and Feliciano Ribera,

Mexican Americans/American Mexicans: From Conquistadors to Chicanos (New York: Hill and Wang, 1993), 120.

31. Sandoval, Moises, *On the Move: A History of the Hispanic Church in the United States* (Maryknoll, N.Y.: Orbis Books, 1990), 50. See also George Sanchez, *Becoming Mexican American: Ethnicity, Culture and Identity in Chicano Los Angeles, 1900–1945* (New York and Oxford: Oxford University Press, 1993), 157–159.

32. Charles Lummis, *Stand Fast Santa Barbara* (Santa Barbara: Santa Barbara Plans and Planting Committee of the Community Arts Association, 1927), 7–8.

33. Ibid., 13.

34. Ibid., 14.

35. See Karen J. Weitze, *California's Mission Revival* (Los Angeles: Hennessey and Ingalls, 1984), for a history of the development of the architecture that preceded and informed Santa Barbara's Spanish Revival.

36. Gebhard, *Santa Barbara*, 13–17; see also David Gebhard, "Creating the Santa Barbara Style," *Santa Barbara Magazine* (winter 1996): 35–41.

37. J. B. Jackson, *The Necessity of Ruins* (Amherst: University of Massachusetts Press, 1980), 92.

38. *Santa Barbara Morning Press*, July 2, 1925, 9.

39. *Santa Barbara Morning Press*, July 15, 1925, 4.

40. *Santa Barbara Morning Press*, July 22, 1925, 4.

41. John Steven McGroarty, *Santa Barbara, California* (n.p.: Southern Pacific Lines, 1926).

42. Editorial, *Santa Barbara Morning Press*, March 23, 1922.

43. "The Correspondence of Charles F. Lummis with Fr. Zephyrin Englehardt, O.F.M.," in *Franciscan Provincial Annals, Province of Santa Barbara* 4, no. 4 (July 1942): 67.

Six

Paul E. Ivey

Christian Science Architecture in the American City

The Triumph of the Classical Style

> *. . . to say that God has no relation to our business or work is like saying that for eight or ten hours (or more) each working day God has retired from His creation. . . . [The] peace of God is ceaseless activity."*
> —Bicknell Young, *Christian Science: Its Principle and Rule in Business*, 1917

In 1894 the Mother Church of Christian Science was built in Boston. The small Romanesque edifice with a spire mimicked H. H. Richardson's magnificent Trinity Church, which was located several blocks away. The inside of the church was noted in a *Craftsman* article for its excellent acoustics and ventilation, the modern simple use of mosaics and marble, and the sociability of the foyer.[1] With the completion of the Mother Church, the Christian Science building boom, which lasted into the early 1930s, was under way in earnest. During this time, Christian Science congregations began to solidify their religious teachings and practices in built form as branches of the Mother Church. What style of architecture was appropriate for the new indigenous, mainly urban religion, criticized by the growing medical field and other religious groups, which was still expanding rapidly? For most of their large, urban church buildings, rather than the traditional architecture of their Mother Church Christian Scientists chose a monumental classical architecture, with imposing Greek porches and Roman domes, inspired by the classical revival architecture of Chicago's World's Columbian Exposition of 1893. These grand edifices, all of them debt-free upon dedication, were not only important departures in church architecture in America, which utilized traditional spires and tended toward the

Gothic and Romanesque styles, but they forcefully declared the institutional-ization of Christian Science ideals of worship and publicity by congregations made up primarily of businessmen, young newcomers to the city working to succeed, and women who had been attracted to Christian Science through its promises of healing and moral regeneration. Also, the congregations provided a community setting in which morality and integrity in business were viewed as an individual demonstration of the practicality of Christianity, scientifically ver-ifiable in improved health and secure lifestyle at a time of great demographic, social, and economic change in American cities. These congregations, culled from dissenters from other mainstream Protestant denominations, believed that Christian Science stood "in every community for pure government, social purity, honest popular elections, business integrity, the purification of literature and journalism, and the elevation of the stage."[2] The church grew especially rap-idly in Chicago, New York, Boston, and later in Los Angeles, San Francisco, and Seattle.[3]

During the first three decades of the twentieth century, Christian Science congregations self-consciously employed classical revival architecture as a defining visual motif within the world of urban commercial culture and opened public reading rooms in the burgeoning business districts of American cities and towns to provide quiet places to communicate their spiritual ideals in the world of commerce. The classical architecture of these churches corresponded both with Christian Science theology and also broader urban reform move-ments such as City Beautiful, which emphasized the importance of aesthetic unity and monumentality as a way of constructing civic values and associated architectural style with conscientious civic behaviors. This emphasis on beau-tification and civic pride also promoted the free expansion of capital in improved cityscapes and therefore was supported overwhelmingly by businessmen. Architecture became a primary aspect of the movement's aspirations to meet the needs of urban populations. A unified classical architecture, then, was con-structed as an early device of advertisement and as a triumphal proclamation of what was, to the adherents of Christian Science, a new healing gospel that would unite humanity. These church edifices were often viewed as a means of demonstrating key spiritual principles and were effective worship spaces for attracting and capturing an audience of the faithful.

However, debates by architects at the time concerning the appropriate archi-tecture of Christian Science churches revealed an ambivalence toward insti-tutional self-representation. Should church architecture be aligned with progressive civic movements in architecture and society, or should it be based on Christian Science's continuity with historical and traditional Christendom? This ambivalence was tangibly expressed by 1904, when the Scientists started on an extension of the Mother Church that contrasted sharply with the earlier Mother Church building (Fig. 12). The choice of architectural style was not clear-cut for Christian Science. As a new religion, concentrated in cities, the church entered into the cultural debate concerning religion and architecture in American culture: How were churches to integrate into cityscapes increasingly defined by secular institutions yet retain their theological sensibilities?

Two decades prior to the erection of the Mother Church buildings, Christian Science had mostly a local appeal in the small factory towns of New England, where Mary Baker Eddy, the founder of the church, wrote in isolation and taught a few students. Born in 1821 in rural New Hampshire and raised a Congregationalist, Eddy's early life was marked with personal struggle and difficulty. By midlife her health deteriorated, attended by acute nervous and physical weakness. In her search for relief, she investigated a number of healing practices then available, including homeopathy and mesmeric healing. By 1866 she claimed to have discovered the decisive curative power of a spiritual understanding of the Scriptures.

In 1875 Eddy published the complete statement of this methodology in her book *Science and Health*. In 1879 she and several faithful members founded the Church of Christ, Scientist in order to "commemorate the word and works of our Master, which should reinstate primitive Christianity and its lost element of healing."[4]

In 1881 Eddy chartered the Massachusetts Metaphysical College in Boston and attracted attention among women and professional businesspeople. Pupils of the college began disseminating her teachings throughout the United States. The church—with its institutes, academies, and branches—spread across the country, grew rapidly, and began attracting popular and critical attention in the secular as well as religious and medical presses. By 1910 there were approximately eleven hundred organizations attached to the Mother Church in Boston. In a broader context, Christian Science as a new religion traversed its charismatic phase in the era of laissez-faire reconstruction and expansion following the Civil War. After a reorganization in 1892, the following period of triumphal self-assertion and representation through architecture coincided with the growth of a corporatist and monopolistic imperial American culture at the end of the nineteenth century and continuing into the Progressive Era.

Because of the concentration of its membership in urban areas, Christian Science has always been associated with the dynamically changing great cities at the turn of the century, the arenas of the church's maximum success, early on supported by Eddy, who admonished her students to, "locate in large cities, in order to do the greatest good to the greatest number."[5] Religion historians such as William Sweet also associate Christian Science with the rise of the American

_____ *Figure 12*_____
Franklin Welch, The Mother Church, The First Church of Christ Scientist (1894), with
Charles Brigham, Extension of the Mother Church (1906), behind it.
From E. S. Van Horne, Some Christian Science Churches *(Columbus, Ohio, 1912).*

economy: "Belonging in a peculiar sense to the era of big business and prosperity and the rapid rise of the city is the Church of Christ, Scientist," though
academic geographical studies of the religion indicate that it also did well in
cities with populations under one hundred thousand people.[6] E. L. Thorndike
suggests that the memberships for Unitarians, Universalists, and Christian

Scientists were particularly exceptional in the city because "these more secu-larized groups exhibited a greater degree of apparent affinity for urban moder-nity, and their numbers in the population correlated strongly in a positive direction with a city's quality of life."[7]

The Christian Science church represented itself through its daily, weekly, and monthly periodicals as the new religion for modern times based on an indi-vidualism and pragmatism that were both Christian and American. Its reform-ing methods would purify the masses, one individual at a time, through spiritual healing, through modern methods of church work, and through its compelling new church services, publications—including the daily *Christian Science Mon-itor* newspaper—and architecture. Early in the movement, the moral and busi-nesslike approach of its adherents and its support of individualism, the free market, and the Protestant work ethic, together with its emphasis on salvation as self-fulfillment, made Christian Science particularly popular with entrepre-neurial businessmen, who were challenged by the increasing growth of corpo-rate models of business. The Christian Science approach seemed like a page out of economist Simon Patten's book: it emphasized the growth, progress, and social cohesion of a primarily Anglo middle-class group of males by supporting an individualism within the free market. But it stated clearly that only the unselfish and honest businessman, governed by the Golden Rule, could demon-strate the abundance of God's "supply," and it supported these individualistic ideas through an organization that Mark Twain suggested was the best-run Trust in America; if Twain was right, it was an antitrust Trust.[8] As a prominent New York follower put it: "[Christian Science] ought to regulate the masses and heal their differences. . . . Go after the individual, and make him satisfied. Indi-vidual happiness and prosperity make national and international peace."[9] One prominent church spokesperson proposed that Christian Science revealed divine justice by enabling individuals to think along correct, scientific lines: "Think right and you will do right and be right! Be a man: take possession of yourself and do not let circumstances take possession of you! After that, turn around and help others do the same!"[10] This practical approach to individual spiritual dominion caused a Chicago Theological Institute student to suggest that Christian Science, unlike Protestantism and its new Social Gospel, put the sacred and secular in a special proximity to one another and Gerhardt Mars to say that Christian Science's "insistence upon the individual's rational freedom" made it "peculiarly compatible with democracy."[11]

With its promise of healing and moral regeneration as well as its general pos-itive individualism and reform spirit, Christian Science successfully found a niche within an increasingly challenged Protestant tradition. Through its emphasis on spiritual growth in personal and professional life and its teaching that Christianity was practical in everyday situations, the church succeeded in the changing city.

Seek Ye First the Kingdom of God . . . and All These Things Shall Be Added unto You: Christian Science, "a Business Man's Religion"

From its inception, the church began to attract women, young people, and businessmen to its ranks.[12] Many secular periodical articles reported on the striking importance of women in the pulpit as readers of the Bible and *Science and Health*, the preponderance of women at the services, and the overwhelming number of public practitioners who were women. Many called Christian Science a religion primarily for women.[13] But the number of men attending Christian Science church services also attracted comment and were sometimes reported to exceed women followers.[14]

As the church grew rapidly and began to build its large edifices, usually with small committed memberships but with overflowing services, friends and enemies alike were interested in defining the social status of the Christian Science congregations, particularly since the new church was noted for moving aggressively into the city while other churches were abandoning it. Newspaper articles by both the church's Committee on Publication insiders and usually critical outsiders reiterated that prominent people were attending services and were supporting the new church. A Presbyterian account suggested that many of the finest upstanding church members were leaving for Christian Science, particularly because of what it called healings of "business despondency."[15] As a Christian Science lecturer put it: "There can be no doubt that Christian Science is having a decided and beneficial effect on the commerce, the religion, the literature and the art of the world today. . . . It is a stay to the capitalist and a strength to the toiler."[16]

Businessmen were undoubtedly attracted to Christian Science for many reasons. Certainly one important reason was that they could meet others who approached business transactions similarly and create important spiritual and material support networks. These men viewed themselves as part of a moral revolution that would improve their personal lives and business profits. The emerging urban business elite was well represented, and Christian Science writers often cited these influential members in an attempt to defend themselves against the idea that Christian Scientists were simply sentimentalists or emotional faddists.[17] As an 1899 *Kansas City Times* article said, "Any man of wide acquaintance in Kansas City would probably have been surprised to look over the congregations which gathered. . . . Among those who came and went he would have found many men whose names are prominent in the business world and many women who are figures in society. . . . Christian Science, founded though it was by a woman, is not only a woman's religion, . . . its truth appeals to men of culture, of intelligence and trained thought." The article went on to list the number of businessmen interested in Christian Science.[18]

However, others perceived the need for more men in Christian Science, and in 1910 Eddy said that "men are very important factors in our field of labor for Christian Science. The male element is a strong supporting arm to religion as well as to politics, and we need in our ranks of divine energy, the strong, the faithful, the untiring spiritual armament."[19] Eddy requested that the frontline defensive wing of the church, the Committee on Publication, in charge of responding to press criticism and legal problems, be made up primarily of men, and her most important personal secretaries were men.[20] But Eddy tended to call for restraint when businessmen associated with her church proposed aggressive promotion of Christian Science, sometimes questioning their motives for action. It wasn't business acumen that was suspect—it was often lauded in the Christian Science periodicals—but it was a business sense that was exclusively worldly. Eddy wrote, "What is your model business man—the real Scientist who plants in Mind, God, who sows in Mind and reaps in Mind, or he who begins with political economy, human plans, legal speculations, and ends with them, dust to dust?"[21]

As Christian Science grew in influence, its organization at its headquarters in Boston included many successful businessmen from Chicago, Kansas City, and New York, and it tended to borrow its vocabulary and structures from business and education. Christian Scientists were awarded degrees within a hierarchical structure defined with terms from corporate America, with its board of directors, trustees, and committees. Mark Twain's comment that the church was one of the most successful business monopolies in America caused William McCracken to reply, "There is no doubt that executive and business skills are needed to manage the affairs of so great and active an organization; but because this management succeeds, is it necessary to call the denomination a 'trust,' a 'bargain counter' or a 'factory?'"[22]

The number of businessmen associating themselves with the church attracted much comment, and these men were often cited by name in secular periodical articles often penned by church officials.[23] Businessmen met together for regular lunches in Chicago to talk about Christian Science, and another group set up a Christian Science Department associated with their business in St. Louis in order to "spread the truths of Christian Science."[24] Christian Science lecturers, such as Bicknell Young, spoke to hundreds of businesspeople in the United States and Great Britain concerning the practicality of Christian Science in gaining peace, happiness, and business success.

During a Wednesday evening meeting at one of the largest branch churches, First Church, New York, investigative journalist William Johnston told the readers of the *Broadway Magazine* in 1907 that half of the twenty-five hundred people attending were men and that the service was overflowing. When asked who were the prominent New York Christian Scientists, a church spokesperson replied that they included the president of Otis Elevator company, the president of the Aetna National Bank, the president of Western Union Telegraph Company, a prominent attorney, a well-known author, and a Broadway playwright. "New York would marvel if it knew them all." Johnston spoke with playwright Charles Klein, who said that "there's the spirit of Broadway here . . . as it typifies this great city, which in turn typifies the New World—progress, discovery, mental and physical evolution, in short the spirit of the twentieth century, the determination to get at the real gist of things and then apply them to a practical end." Nearby, a prominent lawyer added, "One of the greatest reforms worked by Christian Science [is] it has unclasped the Bible. . . . Now it's my business guide. I apply its truths each day. I read it as eagerly as a young girl reads a novel. It is filled with vivid interest and practical value."[25] The sentiment echoed by many was summed up by Christian Science lecturer and prominent Chicago teacher Edward Kimball, who claimed that Christian Science had "purified and exalted the motives, desires, and aims of man; increased his wisdom, his executive and business capacity; arrested the havoc of vice; refined character and elevated manhood and citizenship."[26]

Early issues of the weekly *Christian Science Sentinel* often featured brief articles on Christian Science and business, and a steady stream of articles appeared in other Christian Science periodicals from 1894 onward, during an unprecedented economic depression, that addressed the relationship of Christian Science to business. Many included outpourings of gratitude from businesspeople, with several articles by commercial travelers, many of whom were impressed by the uniformity of Christian Science services across the country and were concerned with listing the various occupations of the men associating themselves with Christian Science.[27]

All of the church periodical articles emphasized the purifying Christian atmosphere that Christian Science provided businesspeople and pointed out that Christian qualities such as honesty and purity defeated dishonest business practices, one speaking of honesty as "the true religious element in man," another suggesting that "honesty, integrity, and strict fidelity of trust lie at the base of every act and motive of the true Christian Scientist."[28] These were considered, above all, spiritual values that impelled business success. A writer in the *New England Grocer* reported that an Indiana businessman testified in the Mother Church that his business grew rapidly when he told his clerks to "call cotton, cotton, and wool, wool" instead of following the "band wagon fashion" of then popular techniques of false advertising. To the *Grocer*, this line of reasoning would lead to absolute honesty in business and would therefore "make unnecessary pure food laws—it would hasten the coming of the trade millennium."[29]

Others criticized the moral idealism of Christian Science as merely a mask for greed in commerce, but the standards of business morality and efficiency supported by the church were also applauded in the press.[30] One commentator stated pointedly that Christian Science simply allowed businesspeople to ignore the problems of labor represented by the Industrial Workers of the World (IWW).[31]

But defenders, such as Unitarian and muckraking magazine editor B. O. Flower, supported the public importance of the moral idealism of the Christian Science position. Others warned traditional churchgoers that Protestantism might have to adopt Christian Science methods if it was to keep abreast of the changing times. As the Reverend J. Winthrop Hegeman, a priest in the Protestant Episcopal Church, told the readers of the *North American Review*,

> Hundreds of thousands bear witness to having risen through Christian Science into a spiritual consciousness in which sin, poverty, and sickness cannot exist. Here is the dynamic of Love, which can regenerate the world. . . . The fine type of Christian character, the striving to have the mind of Christ Jesus, the art of healing as an expression of its practical theology, the business prosperity, pure living following clean thinking, the spirituality, the loyal citizen ship to the Kingdom of God with its ardent missionary spirit—these are the undoubted fruits of the Spirit. Such fruitage is not common in the average church. To them, the primary quest is the Kingdom of God, and they realize that in their increasing material prosperity things are indeed thrown in as the promised by-product.[32]

Later Christian Science historians, such as Stephen Gottschalk, would lament this utilitarian "loaves and fishes" approach to Christian Science, noting that Eddy said virtually nothing concerning the relationship of Christian Science to business affairs but that she demanded a dedication to Christian Science practice that was "not coordinate with a secular quest for a fulfilled bourgeois existence."[33] However, sociologists and historians such as Stuart Knee consider that the spiritual encouragement and confidence-building of Christian Science was attractive to "an ambivalent, sometimes guilt-ridden industrial class requiring assurances that Heaven still loved them" and also responded to those in the middle class under the "unendurable pressure exerted by business rigidity and labor militancy upon the center stratum of society."[34]

Christian Science Architecture:
The Triumphal Face of the Movement

To those challenged by the rapid changes in urban economics and culture, Christian Science offered a stabilizing lifestyle and projected a confident rationality onto daily routine. Christian Science's optimistic approach to human problems, its easy relationship with business, and its promise of self-fulfillment motivated its followers to build edifices to gather congregations to usher in a Christianly scientific community. The architecture of the church, as the public face of the movement, was also peripherally caught up in civic reform conceptions being debated surrounding the beautification of the city and the function of civic architectures in the creation of moral citizens. The new edifices joined the urban arena as part of a broader social conception of moral reform. Christian Science never viewed itself as merely a harmonial healing movement but as an institution that challenged the very basis of much of public discourse about religion, morals, health, and reform, and therefore its architecture was particularly important in engaging a critical public with its message of healing and spiritual growth.

Gothicists had long claimed that the moral position of churches set them apart in the city and that a steepled architecture was the most honest expression of the highest goals of Christianity. Eddy seemed to concur. She preferred what one church official called a "churchy church" with "something pointing upward," similar to her Mother Church and one she donated to the citizens of Concord, New Hampshire.[35] Her buildings were recognizable as churches. Bernard Maybeck modernized the Gothic style in his well-known Christian Science church in Berkeley, completed in 1911. Its poured concrete foundations and pillars, fir and redwood beams, medieval-looking glass placed in factory sashes, and painted stenciled decorations expressed the unity, harmony, sincerity, and honesty requested by the congregation's building committee.

At the time of the erection of First Church, Berkeley, the architectural rhetoric about classicism was acknowledging the style's simplicity and honesty, and apologists and polemicists were beginning to identify the classical style with the Christian Science building boom. In the same year as Maybeck's innovative design, several other congregations in southern California completed large classical buildings, such as Second Church, Los Angeles, and First Church, Pasadena (Fig. 13). Clearly the needs of Christian Science congregations could be answered by several architectural styles.

Two Christian Science architects were central to the debates on how to successfully represent the new religion architecturally. They were Solon Spencer Beman, an important Chicago architect, and Elmer Grey, a Milwaukee architect who settled in California. Briefly, Beman's camp believed the church should

———— *Figure 13*————————————————————————————————
Alfred F. Rosenheim, Second Church of Christ, Scientist, Los Angeles, 1910.
From E. S. Van Horne, Some Christian Science Churches *(Columbus, Ohio, 1912).*

pronounce itself as the modern dispensation of the original primitive Gospel.
The notion that Christian Science was a complete revelation led them to promote the more classicized architecture of the Mother Church Extension as the
appropriate idiom. Classical revival architecture represented a restoration of a
perfected architecture associated with the time of primitive Christianity, and it
was also aligned with broader modern reform movements supported by business. To Beman, his churches were moral statements that would inspire citizens
with their public beauty.

   Others, including Grey, believed that Christian Science was the culminating
moment of the history of Christianity. They thought that Christian Science

emphasized the resurrection of the human condition from matter to Spirit: it was a progressive unfolding from suffering to Christian Science. The religion's self-representation, therefore, should underscore this continuous relationship with ecclesiastical Christendom.

Regardless of their opinions, what is striking about these debates was the idea that there should be a "Christian Science architecture." That is, the exterior style of the church should be indicative of a congregation's ideals of religious association, social appeal, and public reform. Gothic architecture seemed to orient the church around ecclesiastical Christianity—the very tradition that reacted so strongly against Christian Science. Within the architectural and design professions, classical architecture was increasingly presented as part of the progressive modern solution to urban space because it was monumental and idealistic, was not overly decorated, and was often less expensive than traditional architectures because it responded easily to new steel post and beam construction. The classical style separated the church from traditional Protestant denominations and also associated the new institution with public authority, respectability, and permanence. Moreover, it was undoubtedly attractive to businesspeople, who by this time were the primary supporters of urban renewal movements such as City Beautiful, which suggested that classical architecture with its rationality, purity, and calm order was the appropriate architectural idiom for public buildings.

Generally, Protestant church architecture in this "Gilded Age" was in its own identity crisis. The cities filled with immigrants while the older, wealthier, and more prominent members of the Protestant community moved to the suburbs. Many churches were faced with a loss of authority and social influence. The secularization of many Protestant churches demanded new architectures, with room for an increasingly large number of educational and social activities. Debates in professional periodicals on the appropriate architecture for churches often included important Christian Science commissions. In 1903, for example, leading architectural critic Montgomery Schuyler gave particular attention to the newly built First Church of Christ, Scientist, by well-known architects Carrère and Hastings, as a new model for the metropolitan church in an article on recent church buildings in New York (Fig. 14).[36] Pundits and apologists alike noted that the members of the growing New York Christian Science churches were important representatives of newly emerging businesses in the commercial metropolis.

In describing the churches in New York, Johnston told his readers about Carrère and Hastings's "magnificent" new edifice for First Church of Christ, Scientist on the fashionable Upper West Side, as well as architect Frederick Comstock's beautiful marble edifice of Second Church, a little over twenty-five

_____ *Figure 14* _____

Carrère and Hastings, First Church of Christ, Scientist, New York City, 1903.
From E. S. Van Horne, Some Christian Science Churches *(Columbus, Ohio, 1912).*

blocks south of First Church on Central Park West. Johnston put the memberships of the nine churches in New York City at four thousand but pointed out that attendance at Christian Science services revealed that nearly fifty thousand followers of this faith lived in New York City.

The organizer of First Church of Christ, Scientist, New York, was Eddy's student Augusta Stetson, who Eddy had sent to New York by 1886. Stetson's reputation as a teacher and healer were press-worthy and widespread throughout the city. In the building of the most expensive branch church in the movement, at nearly 1.2 million dollars, Stetson had secured important revenues through relationships with businessmen in her church who, in exchange for "absent treatment" on behalf of their enterprises, offered her shares of stock.[37] Stetson insisted on a tower being added to the architects' composite structure.

Besides this church, Fifth Church, New York, stood out for its emphasis on the importance of providing a spiritual basis for the business world (Fig. 15). The branch was originally founded at Eddy's request on the east side of Manhattan in 1901, grew rapidly when it began meeting in Aeolian Hall in 1915, and desired to build in midtown. Other churches in midtown had been selling their properties for large profits and moving uptown. But this congregation believed that "the spiritual demand for healing in the business and commercial world, as well as the healing of sickness and sin, through the teachings of Christian Science, was evidently a need for this church to fulfill."[38] Ironically, the site at Madison Avenue and Forty-fourth Street was an earlier locale for St. Bartholomew's. The church/office building's location next to Grand Central Station and near Pennsylvania Station ensured that the church would afford facilities for local members in business and those guests and members from out of town. Soon the idea of cooperating with the business needs of the area yet reserving "God's acres" intact caused the congregation in 1919 to help erect the twenty-one-story Canadian-Pacific Building, with a suitable edifice to be inserted as a completely separate structure into the building in which the congregation would have no ownership. In exchange, the congregation was responsible for selling two million dollars of bonds secured by the building and would receive a ninety-nine-year lease at a rental of one dollar a year. The *New York Evening Post* reported that the Scientists had basically rented fifteen million dollars in office space for only ninety-nine dollars and that it was "one of the cleverest and most ingenious real estate deals ever put over in New York City," with both parties "convinced that the transaction will prove profitable."[39]

Architects A. D. Pickering and Starrett Van Vleck designed the office building and church. The grand edifice, fronted by four Ionic columns, seated eighteen hundred in opera seats in its commodious, marble-faced auditorium with galleries. Eight great columns of kasota marble supported the office building above the forty-four-foot-high ceiling, which was decorated with ornamental plaster. Completed in 1921, the office building enjoyed "great prosperity" while Fifth Church "steadily grew in its spiritual mission of healing and serving mankind through the ministry of Christian Science in the heart of this world center of business activity."[40] Foreclosure was necessary in 1938, and the church's lease was canceled, but the membership made the bonds secure and in 1938 received the deed to its land and edifice.

_____ *Figure 15*_____

The Canadian-Pacific Building with Fifth Church of Christ, Scientist in the lower left-hand corner, New York City, 1921. *New York Evening Post*, January 24, 1920.

Though the denomination never had an official position on the style of church architecture, in 1902 the clerk of the Mother Church wrote to a congregation that they should construct an edifice recognizable as a church rather than a "city building, library, school or hall."[41] But by 1907 the classical style was being defended as the style of the movement, at least in the secular press. The most significant reason for the use of classical revival architecture was the popularity and importance of Christian Science in Chicago and the influence of the World's Columbian Exposition on concepts of progressive architecture and religion, as well as the choice of Solon Beman to undertake the design of several prominent church buildings. Also, if church architecture represented religious ideals and associations, then the classical style harmonized well with law and the authority of government and dovetailed with architectural concepts conveyed by progressive businessmen who believed that commerce would thrive through municipal reform. This was important because the Christian Science movement was criticized as being too individualistic to contribute to civic morality. Another reason was the preponderance of important financial backers of the building movement who were undoubtedly attracted to a style that represented rational principles upheld in Christian Science and emphasized in business circles. The classical style was also sometimes discussed using the metaphysical language of Christian Science and could be justified through its theological ramifications.

In 1880 Christian Science was still a "Boston Craze"; by the 1890s it emerged as a national and even international religious movement. By 1893 Chicago stood at the geographical and demographic center of the Christian Science movement, and Christian Science in Chicago grew rapidly. A newspaper account from 1900 reported that in thirteen years it had attracted fifty thousand new adherents, primarily businesspeople and professionals, to its ranks. Between 1893 and 1910 eight classical revival edifices of stone were built, each seating between one thousand and fifteen hundred people. In this short time, Chicago built more Christian Science churches than any other city.

Christian Scientists undoubtedly presumed that the growth of their religion in the rapidly expanding commercial city of Chicago indicated that their message of healing and success, eloquently stated in a session at the World's Parliament of Religion Auxiliary Congress at the 1893 Columbian Exposition, was having a profound influence on the urban population. The Exposition launched Christian Science into the public limelight and inspired the style of its church buildings.

The impact of the Exposition on Christian Science architecture was immediate: the chief apologist architect was Solon Beman, who designed the large Mines and Mining Building and the small Merchant Tailor's building for the Exposition. Beman had a decisive impact on the architecture of the new church. Christian Scientists were inspired to build their own version of an architecture that seemed to embody reformative ideals—a progressive architecture read through metaphysical values as well as social ones. Christian Scientists seemed swept along by the new aesthetic growth that was ushered in by the Exposition.

By 1896 the large congregation of First Church, Chicago, had moved into Louis Sullivan's Auditorium Building. In the same year, Eddy requested that the Chicago Scientists should own their own edifice. Twelve leading architects were invited to submit plans by a conference committee of area congregations. Beman's design was selected and included a semicircular arrangement of tiered theater seating, derived from Sullivan's Auditorium, and a large foyer as requested by the congregation. In his proposal, Beman wrote that he had chosen the Erechtheion of the Athenian Acropolis as the prototype. He claimed that his studies of the basic principles of Christian Science led him to a model that would express "elements of dignity, strength, refinement, and beauty by crystallizing these high sentiments that your teaching inculcate [*sic*] into the architectural harmony."[42] The building was the first truly monumental Christian Science building and the largest Protestant church edifice in Chicago at the time, and its solid and attractive architecture received a lot of attention in the Chicago papers (Fig. 16). Nearly ten thousand Christian Scientists attended the dedication services. One visitor remarked that it was "almost like the World's Fair."[43] Beman's church was noted for its excellent acoustics. Also innovative were the new seating arrangements and the open spaces created by the absence of supporting columns, which allowed all participants to be seen. The unornamented auditorium was illuminated by "electric stars" that lit up the Tiffany glass dome. A *Chicago Evening Post* report observed that the building was "a unique and bold departure from the conventional lines of ecclesiastical architecture."[44] The church was often overcrowded, with many businessmen attending the services.[45]

After the building of Second Church in 1901, Beman was established as the leading Christian Science architect, and his designs for these two churches were soon imitated by the architects of other Christian Science commissions. Beman himself continued to influence the church by his connection with administrators in the Boston organization, especially Archibald McLellan, who had been a successful Chicago attorney before going to Boston to serve his church. Beman was asked to help with the completion of the Mother Church Extension.

By 1896 the original edifice of the Mother Church was overflowing. By 1904 construction on the huge Extension, one of the largest churches in America, had begun. The commission was awarded to Boston architect Charles Brigham, but Beman was called in to complete the plans and correct what he considered engineering and architectural problems with the edifice. He eventually took charge of the project. Beman classicized the building, which had been inspired by the Byzantine mosque of Ahmed I as well as Italian Renaissance architecture. The classical style had arrived in Boston, and Beman's ideas were recognized as authoritative.

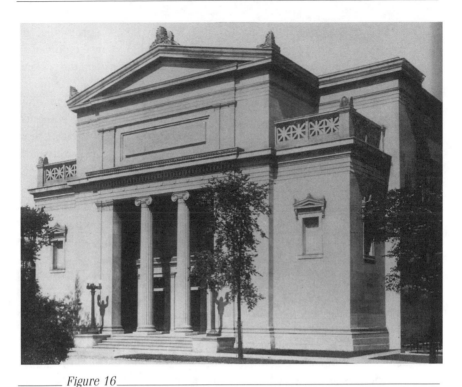

_____ *Figure 16*_____

Solon S. Beman, First Church of Christ, Scientist, Chicago, 1897.
From E. S. Van Horne, Some Christian Science Churches *(Columbus, Ohio, 1912).*

In 1907 Beman published a sweeping defense of the classical style for which he was gaining popularity. Christian Scientist congregations throughout the country now were beginning to turn to him for plans. The article, published in the popular Chicago *World To-day Magazine,* introduced Beman and his churches with: "No modern architectural development, not even that of the great office building, is more striking than that seen in the churches of the Church of Christ, Scientist." Beman's article was said to have "a real importance for all those who, whether or not Christian Scientists, are interested in public buildings." Beman stated that the classical style of church was not a "pagan temple" but a "vital force" of the "first principles of truth." The classical style had been the guidance and inspiration for great architecture throughout history. This style was, therefore, appropriate and logical for a religion that concerned itself with the well-being of the individual and society. The predominance of the classical style in Christian Science commissions, moreover, indicated to Beman that the church was progressive. Gothic architecture represented the past and the "ritualisms and [emotional ceremonies of the Orthodox Church]."[46]

If the Columbian Exposition's architecture was the stylistic prototype, the ideas developed in the City Beautiful movement provided a social model. City Beautiful was Daniel Burnham's urban renewal movement based on the success of the Exposition as a model for a dignified, efficient, civilized city. It promoted urban spaces defined by wide boulevards lined with grand classical buildings and flanked by gardens and open spaces. Many Christian Scientists aligned themselves with the projected unity of public architecture, believing that their churches would raise the moral and aesthetic standards of urban dwellers and contribute visually to the city as a whole—other City Beautiful ideals. In these cities, the Christian Scientists built monumental classical buildings in middle-class residential suburbs on fashionable boulevards and along parkways.

Classical Christian Science churches also related directly to new government and civic architectures then being built in Chicago and other cities, which denoted both official order and fiscal responsibility. This architecture, supported federally and locally, claimed to represent a moral civic order. Classical architecture also operated as an important visual language of commercial culture and was comforting and attractive to members of the urban business classes.

Many Christian Science congregations wanted to make these civic associations tangible. An important example is the style of First Church, Providence, Rhode Island, erected in a fashionable residential district between 1906 and 1913 as "a city set on an hill," which directly echoed the larger dome of McKim, Mead, and White's state capitol in the valley below. Earlier in Denver, the *Denver Sunday Post* wrote in late 1900 that the Christian Scientists had tried to get the lot "right opposite the Capitol" and that the plan of their church exterior was "wholly on the old Greek temple of justice style." The *Architectural Review* reported that the "Christian Science Tabernacle in Denver is quite properly civic, rather than ecclesiastical in its style" (Fig. 17).[47]

Indeed, Christian Science architecture associated the religion and its adherents with a range of monumental buildings devoted to governmental, legal, and administrative functions. This solidity caused some critics and members alike to compare Christian Science churches to banks and post offices. Nonetheless, classical architecture allowed Christian Scientists to relate to already existing social structures, which emphasized substantive civic and social values.

In theological terms, some Christian Science apologists asserted a rapport between Eddy's teaching and the forms of classicism. To many, the readings from the Bible and *Science and Health*, the central focus of the worship services, were simple, rational articulations that could be recognized in the stately classical architecture. Even prominent Gothicist Ralph Adams Cram, who in 1905

_____ *Figure 17*_____

Varian and Sterner, First Church of Christ, Scientist, Denver, 1903.
From E. S. Van Horne, Some Christian Science Churches *(Columbus, Ohio, 1912).*

condemned all classical forms in church buildings for denying the rich thousand-year history of Christianity, later asserted that the Christian Scientists had chosen classicism properly, because it was an honest architecture according to their theological position.[48]

Christian Scientists also reiterated the importance of Christian Science precepts in the commercial world through their commitment to maintaining public Christian Science reading rooms. These quiet rooms, with spaces for study and purchasing church-approved publications, were first started in Boston in 1888 and were similar to other reading rooms that had become outlets for publishers to sell their books and allow would-be purchasers the chance to peruse their publications.[49] By 1900 Eddy instructed all churches to provide these public spaces so that authorized Christian Science literature would be readily available, and 212 reading rooms were already operating. The clerk of the Mother Church reported at the 1900 annual meeting: "In these pleasant places,—these harbingers of rest,—in the midst of the rush of the business district,—the merchant and the shop-hand can escape from the whirl of daily life and find a resting-place where on a work-day they can think about God, and return to their tasks with sweeter thoughts, strengthened courage, and regenerated hopes."[50] These homelike spaces were quiet and attractive, and Christian Science periodicals mentioned several times that they were frequented primarily by businessmen.[51] One Saturday morning Johnston found the reading room of First

Church, New York, crowded with men: "brokers and financiers from Wall Street, manufacturers and merchants from middle Broadway, men of the professions, excluding none, men from the editorial sanctums of our great newspapers, men at the heads of our leading industrial and commercial enterprises. They seem to prefer the restful, spiritual atmosphere of these rooms to the amusement of the Saturday afternoon matinée."[52]

Increasingly, by the middle teens the classical trajectory of the architecture of branch churches was contested. Beman's conceptions of the timelessness of classical values were challenged chiefly by Milwaukee architect Elmer Grey. Grey asserted that Christian Science should not "exclude from its architecture anything worthy in the Christian architecture of the past."[53] He supported a regional and site-specific approach to church design and believed in what he called a liberated "new-world" architecture based in architect Louis Sullivan's ideals of a homegrown American architecture and not in historical forms.[54] Though he designed only three prominent Christian Science edifices—in Los Angeles (1911), Long Beach (1914), and Palo Alto (1916)–his writings offered strong antidotes to the idea that classical architecture represented Christian Science theology. By the teens, California was eclipsing the Midwest as the most popular domain for Christian Science. As Grey put it, the "Chicago architectural idea" could not possibly be successful in the last great American frontier, marked by a freedom from European examples.

Other Californians argued that a church needed a steeple in order to inspire. As George Wharton James told the readers of *Out West* magazine, church steeples "typify aspiration" that would remind the businessman that he is also a spiritual being, "seeking spiritual expression." James thought that more traditional structures, such as the Gothic, Romanesque, and Mission examples designed by Grey and San Diego architect Irving Gill, were more "striking in the community of other structures," because their "strength, power and simplicity," invite us to "thoughts over and above the material and commercial."[55]

By the mid-1920s the Colonial and Georgian styles began to compete with a purer revival classicism for dominance in Christian Science commissions, many of which were located in the growing suburbs. However, the classical style was unquestionably triumphant in urban areas and is still associated with Christian Science today. Clearly, church architectures negotiated the church's complex relationships with the social, cultural, civic, and business trends of the times and helped define the church's public image.

While the triumphal expression was isolated in the early century at the time of the religion's maximum success, the large Church Center in Boston, designed by Araldo Cossutta of I. M. Pei's firm and completed in 1977, continues to pronounce the religious values of architectural expression important to the early movement and echoes the spectacle of the 1893 Columbian Exposition's White City setting.[56]

Notes

1. *Craftsman* 7 (March 1905): 690–691.
2. Carol Norton, *The Christian Science Movement*, reprinted from the *New York Sun* (Boston: Christian Science Publishing Society, 1899), 19–20.
3. A specific example of this architectural movement is found in Paul E. Ivey, "Building a New Religion," *Chicago History* 23, no. 1 (spring 1994): 16–31. For a full-length study, see Paul E. Ivey, *Prayers in Stone: Christian Science Architecture in the United States, 1894–1930* (Champaign: University of Illinois Press, 1999).
4. Mary Baker Eddy, *Manual of the Mother Church, The First Church of Christ, Scientist, in Boston, Massachusetts*, 89th ed. (Boston: Christian Science Publishing Society, 1908), 17.
5. Mary Baker Eddy, *Retrospection and Introspection* (Boston: Christian Science Publishing Society, 1892), 82.
6. William Warren Sweet, *Story of Religion in America* (New York: Harper, 1939), 527; see A. J. Lamme III, "From Boston in One Hundred Years: Christian Science in 1970," *Professional Geographer* 23 (1971): 329–332.
7. Quoted in Kevin J. Christiano, *Religious Diversity and Social Change, American Cities, 1890–1906* (New York: Cambridge University Press, 1987), 192, from E. L. Thorndike, *Your City* (New York: Harcourt, Brace, 1939), 97. See Harold W. Pfautz, "A Case Study of an Urban Religious Movement: Christian Science," in *Contributions to Urban Sociology*, ed. Ernest W. Burgess and Donald J. Bogue (Chicago: University of Chicago Press, 1964), 284–303; Raymond J. Cunningham, "The Impact of Christian Science on the American Churches, 1880–1910," *American Historical Review* 72 (1967): 885–905.
8. Mark Twain, *Christian Science* (New York: Harper, 1907). For an excellent discussion on the economics of harmonial religion, see William Leach, *Land of Desire, Merchants, Power, and the Rise of a New American Culture* (New York, Pantheon, 1993).
9. William A. Johnston, "Christian Science in New York: History of the New York Organizations," *Broadway Magazine* 18, no. 2, 166.
10. William McCracken, "The Meaning of Christian Science," *Arena* 37 (May 1907): 466.
11. John Schwenke, "An Analysis of the Contributions of Christian Science to the Basic Human Needs of People Living in Modern Urban Society, with Special Emphasis on Evidence Collected in the Chicago Metropolitan Area" (B.D. thesis, Chicago Theological Seminary, 1948), 256–266; Gerhardt C. Mars, "Democracy and Religion," *Arena* 40 (August 1908): 287–292.
12. J. U. Higinbotham, "In the Business World," *Christian Science Journal* 20, no. 8 (November 1902): 471–472.
13. See Rodney Stark and William Bainbridge, *The Future of Religion: Secularization, Revival, and Cult Formation* (Berkeley and Los Angeles: University of California Press, 1985), 237.
14. See Alfred D. Kohn, *Christian Science from a Physician's Viewpoint* (Chicago: privately printed, 1906). See also "How New York Goes to Church, Completed Census of Attendance on Four Sundays," *New York Herald*, December 15, 1903.

15. Quoted in the *Christian Science Weekly*, 1, no. 2 (January 12, 1889), 4.

16. George Shaw Cook, "Growth of Christian Science in America: What Christian Science Is Accomplishing," *Fine Arts Journal* (May 1907): 201.

17. See, for example, B. O. Flower, "The Recent Reckless and Irresponsible Attacks on Christian Science and Its Founder, with a Survey of the Christian Science Movement," *Arena* 37 (January 1907): 59–60.

18. *Kansas City Times*, January 22, 1899; "Business Men Healed," *Christian Science Sentinel* 1, no. 26 (1899): 7.

19. Mary Baker Eddy, *The First Church of Christ, Scientist and Miscellany* (Boston: Christian Science Publishing Society, 1913): 355.

20. Mary Baker Eddy, *Manual of the Mother Church, the First Church of Christ, Scientist, in Boston, Massachusetts*, 89th ed. (Boston: Christian Science Publishing Society, 1908): 99.

21. Robert Peel, *Mary Baker Eddy: The Years of Authority* (New York: Holt, Rinehart, and Winston, 1977), 15–16.

22. See Twain, *Christian Science*, 86; W. D. McCracken, *Mrs. Eddy's Relation to Christian Science: A Reply to Mark Twain* (New York: North American Review, 1903), 3.

23. See, for example, Alfred Farlow, "A Glance at the Personnel of the Christian Science Movement: A Statement of Mrs. Eddy's Faith, and the Names of Some Prominent People Who Believe in It," *Human Life* 4 (January 1907): 5.

24. See Edward Kimball, *Lectures and Articles on Christian Science* (Chesterton, Ind.: Edna K. Wait, 1921), 475–476. See also *Christian Science Journal* 21 (1903–1904): 292; 26, no. 3 (June 1898): 193–195; 17, no. 2 (May 1899): 173.

25. Johnston, "Christian Science in New York," 166.

26. Kimball, *Lectures and Articles*, 69.

27. See, for example, *Christian Science Weekly* 1, no. 20 (January 12, 1899). See *Christian Science Sentinel* 3, no. 16 (December 20, 1900): 252; 3, no. 32 (April 11, 1901), 511; 6, no. 5 (October 3, 1903): 58; 8, no. 39 (May 26, 1906): 613. See *Christian Science Journal* 12, no. 11 (February 1895): 477–482, which features testimonials from businessmen; 12, no. 12 (March 1895), 497–502; 13, no. 7 (October 1895): 291; 15, no. 4 (July 1897): 203; 25, no. 5 (August 1907): 270–275; 25, no. 12 (March 1908): 743. See also Alfred Farlow, "Christian Science in Business Life," *American Business Man* 11 (May 1908): 155–157, in which he notes that a "Christian Scientist can judge better as to his real advancement by noting how many of his pet sins he is escaping, rather than by counting the amount of money he is gaining." Doubtless there are those who see in Christian Science a panacea for business troubles, for example, Remington Edwards Twitchell, "An Analysis of the Published Writings of Mary Baker Eddy to Determine Metaphysical Concepts That Christian Scientists Might Apply to Selected Business and Personal Financial Problems" (Ph.D. diss., New York University, 1977).

28. H. B. H. "The Christian Scientist in Business," *Christian Science Sentinel* 7, no. 31 (April 1, 1905): 485; "Editor's Table" *Christian Science Journal* 15, no. 4 (July 1897): 255.

29. Quoted in "Voices of the Press, Christian Science in Business," *Christian Science Sentinel* 3, no. 48 (August 1, 1901): 763.

30. See Francis Edward Marsten, *The Mask of Christian Science* (New York: American Tract Society, 1909); Herbert N. Casson, *The Crime of Credulity* (New York: Peter Eck-

ler, 1901); and James Campbell, *What Christian Science Means and What We Can Learn from It* (New York: Abingdon Press, 1920), 77.

31. Hugo Hume, *The Superior American Religions* (Los Angeles: Libertarian Publishing Co., 1928), 91.

32. J. Winthrop Hegeman, "Must Protestantism Adopt Christian Science?" *North American Review* 198, no. 6 (December 1913): 826–827.

33. Stephen Gottschalk, *The Emergence of Christian Science in American Religious Life* (Berkeley: University of California Press, 1973), 255. See the section entitled "Secularism and the Problem of Class," 249–259.

34. Stuart E. Knee, *Christian Science in the Age of Mary Baker Eddy* (Westport, Conn.: Greenwood Press, 1994), 143.

35. Alfred Farlow, "Christian Science Church Architecture," *New England Magazine* 32 (March 1905): 33–47.

36. Montgomery Schuyler, "Recent Church Building in New York," *Architectural Record* 13 (June 1903): 508–534.

37. Altman K. Swihart, *Since Mrs. Eddy* (New York: Henry Holt, 1931), 27. On Stetson, see also Sarah Gardner Cunningham, "A New Order: Augusta Emma Simmons Stetson and the Origins of Christian Science in New York City, 1886–1910" (Ph.D. diss., Union Theological Seminary, New York, 1994).

38. "Dedication, Fifth Church of Christ, Scientist," Field Collection of the Mother Church, The First Church of Christ, Scientist, Boston, privately published, 1949, 4.

39. *New York Evening Post*, Saturday January 24, 1920, 1, 10.

40. "Dedication, Fifth Church of Christ, Scientist," 6.

41. Lettor, William B. Johnson to clerk of Laurel, Mississippi, church, November 4, 1902, Archives of the Mother Church, The First Church of Christ, Scientist, Boston.

42. Quoted in "History of First Church of Christ, Scientist," ms. 1939, Field Collection of the Mother Church, The First Church of Christ, Scientist, Boston.

43. *Chicago Times-Herald*, November 15, 1897.

44. Quoted in the *Christian Science Journal* 15 (1897): 633.

45. See George Shaw Cook, "Christian Science in Chicago," *American Queen* (April 1907): 8–9.

46. Solon S. Beman, "The Architecture of the Christian Science Church," *The World Today* 12, no. 6 (June 1907): 582, 588.

47. *Denver Sunday Post* quoted in the *Christian Science Sentinel* 2 (December 13, 1900): 233; *Architectural Review* 10, no. 5 (May 1903): 59.

48. Ralph Adams Cram, "A Note on Architectural Style," *Architectural Review* 12 (1905): 181–195; Ralph Adams Cram, *American Church Building Today* (New York: Architectural Book Publishing Co., 1929), vii.

49. See John Tebbel, *A History of Book Publishing in the United States* (New York: R. R. Bowker, 1972).

50. William B. Johnson, "Annual Meeting Report," *Christian Science Journal* 18, no. 4 (July 1900): 206–207. See also Annie M. Knott, "The Christian Science Reading Room," *Christian Science Sentinel* 12 (May 7, 1910): 710.

51. See *Christian Science Sentinel* 2, no. 41 (June 14, 1900): 66; 10, no. 45 (July 11, 1908): 891. The *Sentinel* 4, no. 9 (October 31, 1901): 131, reported that "in the larger cities it is a common thing to hear of the successful business man, turning away from the

cares of the world, seeking the reading room where he may talk of that which relates to God, and thus be about his Father's business in Christian work. The help received in this retreat, gives him strength and courage to conduct his business on a Christian basis."

52. Johnston, "Christian Science in New York," 161.

53. Elmer Grey, "Christian Science Church Edifices and What They Stand For," *Fine Arts Journal* (October 1907): 43.

54. See B. O. Flower, "Elmer Grey and His Dream of a New-World Architecture," *Arena* 40 (September 1908): 198–204. See also Elmer Grey, "The Style of Christian Science Church Edifices," *Architect and Engineer of California* 49 (December 1916): 61–72.

55. Grey quoted in George Wharton James, "Christian Science Architecture of California," *Out West* 4, no. 2 (August 1912): 72, 73, 77.

56. See William Marlin, "Formed Up in Faith," *Architectural Forum* (September 1973): 25–39.

Seven

P. C. Kemeny

Banned in Boston

Commercial Culture and the Politics of
Moral Reform in Boston during the 1920s

At the famed Brimstone Corner on the Boston Common on the afternoon of April 5, 1926, the Reverend J. Frank Chase waited with the captain of the Boston police vice squad and several other officers for H. L. Mencken to arrive. A crowd of nearly five thousand, including a large contingent of Harvard students, had gathered at this corner of Park and Tremont Streets to witness the confrontation between Chase, the secretary of the New England Watch and Ward Society, an antivice organization, and Mencken, the famous critic of southern fundamentalism and the editor of the modernist *American Mercury*. As every member of the crowd knew, a battle was to be waged over what type of morality would dominate urban public life. Brimstone Corner had gained its colorful name when seventeenth-century Puritans allegedly spread hot ashes over the area to illustrate the texture of hell to unbelievers. Now Chase, a descendant of the original Puritans and a defender of twentieth-century Protestant values, was posed to preserve Boston from the onslaught of secular values and ugly aspects of commercial culture. Mencken, the notorious debunker of all things Protestant, had published a story about a small town prostitute in that month's issue of the *American Mercury*. Chase found the story obscene and, working with the Boston Magazine Sellers Association and the approval of the police, had it banned for sale in New England.[1]

Mencken, as he explained in a previously unpublished manuscript, intentionally set out in the fall of 1925 to subvert the "organized terrorism" that the Watch and Ward Society exerted over literature consumption in Boston. The plan, Mencken recounted, was "to proceed against them satirically" in the *American Mercury* until "they writhed under the attack." He was especially eager to unmask the Protestant elites, such as the retired president of Harvard University, Charles W. Eliot, and the other honorary vice presidents of the Watch and Ward Society, who lent their "great" names to the Society's "nefarious operations." Mencken was certain that if these "false faces" "could be brought to book," "the wowsers would lose their support." Mencken despised Watch and Ward Society secretary and Methodist minister Chase, whom he called "the most potent and impudent" of all American censors.[2] In a series of sarcastic articles in the *Mercury*, several authors mocked the Watch and Ward Society and especially Chase for being, as one put it, "an unctuous meddler." But it was Herbert Asbury's April 1926 article on the small town prostitute that pushed Chase over the edge.[3]

Chase's decision to ban the *Mercury* delighted Mencken. With the financial support of his publisher, Alfred A. Knopf, and the legal counsel of Arthur Garfield Hays, who had gained notoriety as the American Civil Liberties Union's (ACLU) lead attorney at the 1925 Scopes trial, the militant Mencken went to Boston to contest the ban and the cultural hegemony of the Puritan "blue noses." "Chase swallowed the bait," as Hays described it. Chase agreed to meet Mencken at Brimstone Corner, purchase the banned issue, and order Mencken's arrest. Arriving at the designated time, Chase, who typically worked clandestinely, had just stepped onto a vaudeville stage to play the straight man to Mencken's slapstick humor. The crowd cheered as Chase stepped forward and bought the banned issue. When Mencken bit the silver half-dollar to ensure it was real, the crowd roared again. While Mencken was hauled off to jail with a "joyous crowd" of supporters trailing, it was the Protestant establishment that was soon to be swept away by a coalition of cultural modernists, civil libertarians, and progressive publishers.[4]

By 1930 the Watch and Ward Society's censorship activity had collapsed. Writing in the *Harvard Graduates Magazine* in 1930, the novelist Bernard DeVoto mused that the Watch and Ward Society "is irresistibly funny." The only course of action for the "educated public of Boston" to take was "to laugh" at this "preposterous" organization. What had made the city "the laughing stock of the civilized world," as Horace Kallen opined a year earlier, was the fact that the "precious Watch and Ward Society" maintained "an *Index Expurgatorius*," or an index of morally objectionable texts, that prevented the legal sale of works by such modern authors as Theodore Dreiser and D. H. Lawrence.[5] By 1930 a coalition of critics had emerged to subvert the Watch and Ward Society's cultural authority in the city to determine what type of literature was morally acceptable for public consumption. The object of public ridicule, deserted by Boston elites, plagued by financial difficulties, the organization lost its cultural authority when the secularizing coalition successfully revised the state's censorship law in 1930.

Some of Boston's most prominent theologically liberal Protestant leaders, including Phillips Brooks, the Unitarian minister Edward Everett Hale, and

Boston University president William F. Warren, founded the Watch and Ward Society in 1878. Its original impetus was to investigate the growing number of inexpensive, mass-produced books, periodicals, tracts, pamphlets, and picture postcards and ferret out the threatening ones. Over the years, the organization's interests expanded to include gambling, illicit drugs, and "white slavery." The Watch and Ward Society was certainly not a unique organization. Similar antivice societies existed in New York, Philadelphia, Baltimore, Cincinnati, Chicago, and San Francisco. These organizations were part of a larger late-nineteenth-century movement of extralegal law enforcement agencies, such as the Society for the Prevention of Cruelty to Children, founded in 1872, that attempted to reform municipal governments and to curb police malfeasance. Other voluntary and professional organizations, such as the Woman's Christian Temperance Union, which established its own Department for the Suppression of Impure Literature in 1883, supported censorship. Protestant denominations, likewise, advocated censorship. For example, the Methodist Board of Temperance, Prohibition, and Moral Reform launched a national censorship campaign in 1925. In Washington, D.C., the International Reform Federation served as a lobbying organization for censorship and other moral reform causes.[6]

As part of the Protestant establishment, the Watch and Ward Society enjoyed a cultural authority disproportionate to its small numbers. The fourteen-member board of directors, which supervised the daily operation of the organization, included such prominent Bostonians as the physician William Norton Bullard, grandson of Harvard Divinity School dean Andrews Norton and nephew of Harvard English professor Charles Eliot Norton, and Edward Cummings, Unitarian pastor of the prestigious South Congregationalist Church (and father of the poet e. e. cummings). The board of vice presidents was also packed with Brahmins, such as Charles W. Eliot and George A. Gordon, the prominent liberal Protestant theologian and pastor of the Old South Church. In 1919, for example, financial support came from more than eight hundred individual and local churches as well as from a $130,000 endowment fund.[7] In short, the Watch and Ward Society was the Protestant establishment in action.

An examination of the secularizing activists' efforts in early-twentieth-century Boston to curtail the religiously inspired moral reformers' cultural authority over this one particular form of commercial culture, the publication of modernist magazines and other inexpensive forms of mass-produced print culture, reveals that conflict—persistent, violent, and very public—lay at the heart of the dynamic between religion and urban commercial culture in the early twentieth century. The history of the Watch and Ward Society demonstrates how the Protestant establishment enjoyed a preponderant influence over what kind of literature was produced and promulgated well into the 1920s and also reveals how and why it was forced to give up control over this one particular area of commercial culture. William R. Hutchison has argued that between the years 1900 and 1960 mainline Protestant churches were compelled "to relinquish the comforts of an earlier-taken-for-granted hegemony within American society."[8] The Watch and Ward Society certainly demonstrated this sense of custodianship over American culture. According to Hutchison, "Jews, Catholics, and others who considered themselves thoroughly accredited as custodians of American ideals found that stance at best disingenuous, at worst self-serving and outrageous." Among the unspecified "others" were secular activists who despised the Protestant establishment's dominance over literary products, detested its moral idealism, and saw their own social standing threatened by the Protestant control of this particular area of commercial culture.

Although Massachusetts had laws banning obscene literature that dated back to the early eighteenth century, the law that Mencken violated had its origins in an 1881 statute that the Watch and Ward Society had helped to write. The law prohibited the importation, publishing, or distribution of any kind of printed material "containing obscene, indecent or impure language or manifestly tending to corrupt the morals of youths." Massachusetts was just one of a number of states that passed anti-obscenity laws following the 1873 federal Comstock Act that barred the sale or distribution of "obscene" images in literature and art as well as birth control information.[9] The Massachusetts law was a critical institutional structure that helped empower the Watch and Ward Society as it exercised jurisdiction over literature in Boston. According to this law, a book could be found obscene based upon a single passage. Moreover, the law's definitions of the key terms "obscene" and "impure" were vague. These two factors gave the Society wide latitude in its efforts to suppress books it deemed obscene.

The Watch and Ward Society served as the region's unofficial censor because the organization had the cultural power to determine what was morally acceptable reading material for bookstores to sell. In 1915 the Boston Booksellers Association and the Watch and Ward Society formed a committee to review any allegedly objectionable material. When someone found a book offensive and issued a complaint to either the booksellers or the Society, the committee reviewed the work. If the committee unanimously decided that the work violated the state's obscenity laws, an "informal notice" was sent out to all Massachusetts booksellers. They would "quietly" withdraw the book or risk prosecution. The Society had a similar arrangement with the New England Magazine Sellers Association. To be sure, the Watch and Ward Society was not the only religious organization interested in suppressing "impure" literature. The fundamentalist Lord's Day Alliance, though most concerned with enforcing Blue Laws, supported censorship. Likewise, the Boston Catholic archdiocese established vigilance committees in 1913 to safeguard Catholic youths from salacious material.[10] However, unlike either Boston fundamentalists or Catholics, it was the theologically liberal Protestant Watch and Ward Society that held the cultural authority to dictate what type of literature was available for public consumption.

Several sources fueled the Watch and Ward Society's rationale for censorship. Most obviously, the Watch and Ward Society embraced the Victorian view of literature. In fact, many of the "apostles" of Victorian culture, such as Harvard English professor Bliss Perry, actively supported the work of the Watch and Ward Society. Speaking at the Society's 1923 annual meeting, Perry complained that "pernicious" literature not only dwells upon sexual obsessions and perversions but also "harps with cynical insistence upon the meaningless, the emptiness, [and] the futility of life." While every book might not be legally "actionable," every artist, Perry believed, has to answer to a higher law—"the eternal trinity of Truth, Goodness, and Beauty." This Neoplatonic trinity served as the standard by which literature was to be judged. For example, the Victorian William Dean Howells's best-known book, *The Rise of Silas Lapham* (1885), is a work of sober realism. In it, the protagonist Lapham is a modest Boston manufacturer whose prosperity parallels the postbellum industrial boom. Through circumstance and his own poor choices, he slips into corruption. However, his personal scruples intervene. Although Lapham's business and social standing collapse, his personal morality triumphs, and he makes a valuable contribution to society's ethical economy.[11] Judged by traditional literary culture, Howells's work embraces and expresses truth, goodness, and beauty. By contrast, pernicious books were simply not good literature because they violated such traditional literary values.

Pernicious books posed more than just a threat to the aesthetic sensitivities of Victorians. They thought that certain books were noxious because they imperiled the character of the reader. Victorians viewed character as a set of eternal and fixed virtues, such as perseverance, honesty, and self-control, that could be mastered and incorporated into the self. "Character" served as a code word that indicated the moral rectitude of a person or of a cultural product, such as a novel or magazine. Unlike upper-class Victorians who could pass on economic capital to their children, the middle class concerned themselves with the personal capital that character possessed. In America's nineteenth-century economy of scarcity, virtues like hard work, self-restraint, and faithfulness were considered valuable assets that could help individuals prosper. By the 1920s, however, the modern mass consumer economy had supplanted the economy of scarcity, and the Victorian cult of character had been eclipsed by the ideal of "personality." The personality ideal was neither bound to an external authority nor limited to a list of external virtues to be acquired. Instead, it became its own higher law and was considered to be an ongoing, dynamic process.[12] One of the cardinal features of the new consumer culture, William Leach observes, was that individuals achieved self-fulfillment through the acquisition and consumption of consumer goods and self-pleasure.[13]

Beneath these fears about the risk that pernicious literature posed to a reader's character lay certain convictions about the nature of culture and the consumption of cultural forms through reading. In a 1916 address before the Watch and Ward Society, William T. Sedgwick, a professor at Massachusetts Institute of Technology, insisted that "obscenity is clearly an infectious disease. It can spread like wildfire under the right conditions and in combustible material, as in a boys' or girls' school, where it has spread more than once."[14] If the "character" of literature was either pure or pernicious, then the consumption of this cultural form, the Society believed, would have either a morally constructive or detrimental effect upon the reader.

The Watch and Ward Society's rationale for censorship also resonated with the ideas of influential criminologists, psychologists, and sociologists of the day. "If the New Psychology is true," the Society reported in 1924, "that which affects the imagination deeply impresses the subconscious self and brings a 'trauma' to the spirit that it is not easy to heal. It gives rise to wishes that must be suppressed unless the home life is to be endangered. These suppressed wishes return and haunt life with an impure atmosphere." In the development of modern social thought, Ruth Leys argues that the "imitation-suggestion theory" of William James and of Gabriel Tarde "introduced a new approach to crime and delinquency by proposing that these were the product not of biological degeneration but of the appropriation or incorporation of deviant forms of behavior."[15] The social sciences gave warrant to the Society's fears about the impact of pernicious literature upon the behavior of readers. Put simply, pernicious literature was dangerous because a reader might imitate it.

Although the Watch and Ward Society worried over destructive literature's impact on individual character, its primary focus was on the institutional, not individual, expression of evil. The fact that the Watch and Ward Society conceived of pernicious literature as a "social problem" helps to identify the organization as one of many voluntary societies that emerged in the late nineteenth century that attempted to reform different troubling aspects of American society. To be sure, this concern with "pernicious literature" certainly makes the Watch and Ward Society appear to be like late-nineteenth-century religious conservatives. However, unlike conservatives, the Watch and Ward Society was not concerned with evangelizing and reforming individuals but rather with combating the commercialization of vice on an institutional level. The Society repeatedly insisted that "we concern ourselves with fighting vice as a business, not vice as a diversion; public immorality, not private immorality."[16]

"To me the interesting part of our preventive work," Society president Raymond Calkins, pastor of the prestigious First (Congregational) Church in Cambridge, explained in 1925, "has been the way in which the big business interests have come forward and accepted our leadership in this matter of suppressing obscenity." In spite of their vested economic interest, some evidence suggests that the older established publishers and booksellers shared the Society's opposition to certain types of modern literature. According to Perry, the "Boston booksellers, as high-minded a group of business men as any in this city, have shown their willingness to cooperate with any movement for decency." Some of the more staid publishing firms refused to publish works that they considered pernicious. For example, when Frank Doubleday and his wife, Neltje, read Theodore Dreiser's *Sister Carrie* in manuscript form in 1900, they were horrified and tried to back out of the contract. Dreiser refused, and the book was published. However, Doubleday did not advertise the book but rather let more than a thousand copies of it wilt in the basement of his warehouse. Although exact information concerning the growth of so-called pernicious literature is not available, the publication of fictional works in general grew exponentially in the 1920s. *Publishers Weekly*, the leading trade journal of the industry, reported that more than thirty million fictional works were published in 1925. Five years later, that figure had leaped to more than forty-five million. According to Oswald Garrison Villard, allegedly salacious magazines enjoyed a growing market in America's consumer economy in the early twentieth century. Villard reported in the *Atlantic Monthly* in 1926 that one "sex magazine" publisher had made more than 8.8 million dollars in 1924.[17]

In 1916 H. L. Mencken wrote to Theodore Drieser, "My whole life, once I get free from my present engagements will be devoted to combating Puritanism." The Puritan, Mencken's classic definition explained, suffered from "the haunting fear that someone, somewhere, may be happy." Beneath his witticism, however, lay a set of intellectual and professional grievances that aroused his opposition to the Watch and Ward Society. The term "Puritan" had a simple rhetorical function in Mencken's social philosophy: it embodied all of his antipathies. Nietzsche, Darwin, Shaw, and Huxley were the central influences who shaped Mencken's social philosophy. Not surprisingly, he favored the works of Joseph Conrad, James Branch Cabell, and especially Dreiser because of their skepticism and unyielding naturalism. By contrast, he alleged that the

Puritan reduces everything to a morality play. Not only had Puritanism's "moral obsession" discolored American literature, but it also endangered the social status of avant-garde writers. Puritanism, moreover, posed a danger to Mencken's concept of civil liberties. Puritans, he said, "have put an almost unbearable burden upon the exchange of ideas in the United States." Mencken served, according to Joseph Wood Krutch, as a "liaison officer between American intelligentsia and European ideas." In fact, he was a leader of the literary revolt against Victorianism.[18] Mencken opposed censorship most obviously because it threatened the economic well-being of his periodical. In April 1926 the *Mercury* had an impressive circulation of 80,500. However, if Chase persuaded the postal authorities that the periodical was obscene, it could lose its second-class mailing privileges, and this could spell economic ruin. Mencken himself had been censored in the past. During World War I, the *Baltimore Sun* suspended Mencken's regular column because of his militantly pro-German position. He had also fought moral reformers in the past and lost. After the New York Society for the Suppression of Vice banned Theodore Dreiser's novel *The "Genius,"* Mencken first attempted to rally support from avant-garde writes to publicly pressure the censorship organization to reverse its decision. After that effort failed, Mencken sat down with the organization's secretary, John S. Sumner, to excise the pernicious sections of *The "Genius"* in order to make it acceptable for publication. But Dreiser refused to compromise with the censors and reneged on the agreement.[19]

While Mencken had a well-earned reputation for deriding Puritanism well before the 1920s, the grand sociopolitical changes in America in the 1920s offered him a particularly propitious opportunity to subvert the cultural dominance of the Protestant establishment. The demise of the Progressive movement, the growing dissatisfaction with Prohibition (another Protestant effort to "reform" society), the spreading revolt against Victorianism among many of America's youth and intellectual leaders, the internal fracturing of mainline Protestantism because of the fundamentalist-modernist controversies in various denominations, the growing opposition to political or any other kind of censorship after World War I, and the increased number of upstart avant-garde publishers willing to risk censorship for the sake of profit made the Protestant establishment more vulnerable to attack in the 1920s than in previous decades. Although these forces created a larger cultural setting in which religiously inspired moral reform looked rather repressive in the eyes of many cultural modernists, it was the Scopes trial in Dayton, Tennessee, in the summer of 1925 that made the beliefs and activities of the Watch and Ward Society especially susceptible to challenge.[20]

Within this historical context, the April 1926 ban of the *American Mercury* provided Mencken with the perfect political opportunity to challenge the Protestant establishment, defend his own economic interests, express his ideological beliefs, and advance his cultural power. In this first major attack on the Watch and Ward Society's cultural authority, Mencken employed a two-pronged strategy: ridicule the censors in public and challenge them in court. After learning of the ban, Mencken, Knopf, and Hays determined that Mencken himself should travel to Boston and personally violate the ban. This act, Mencken explained, would not only "force an open court fight" but would also "arouse those Bostonians who were ashamed" of the Society and "eager to find a stick to flog it with." In court, Hays, as he wrote in 1928, "made the familiar argument that the Bible or Shakespeare would not stand the test of Chase's temperature. Reference was made to the illiberal spirit throughout the country pursuant to which small groups of people gathered together to compel others to accept their ideas." Taking the stand, Mencken argued that Chase's methods were "grossly unfair and disingenuous." While the judge was deciding his fate, Mencken dined that evening at the St. Botoph Club—one of the most holy places of the Boston Brahmins—as the guest of Ferris Greenslet, head of Houghton Mifflin. The judge dismissed the charge the next day with a simple, extemporaneous decision "that no offense has been committed."[21]

Mencken's strategies produced several results. First, Chase and other leaders of the Society were hard-pressed to defend themselves against public ridicule. Any response only further discredited the Society and undermined their social standing. Second, Chase and the Society were threatened with economic ruin because Mencken began legal proceedings in damage suits against Chase and his associates. Finally, the signs of an emerging anticensorship opposition surfaced. With his trial completed, Mencken lunched as the guest of honor at the Harvard Union. After complimentary speeches by noted civil libertarian lawyers Felix Frankfurter and Zechariah Chafee, students hailed Mencken, as he later recalled, as a conquering hero with the Harvard cheer, "three times *fortissimo*."[22]

The April 1927 trial over the sale of Dreiser's *An American Tragedy* and the subsequent 1929 appeal presented a second political opportunity to challenge the Watch and Ward Society's cultural authority. Although the Society was not directly involved in the trial, it had helped to write the obscenity law and stood to lose its ability to censor books if Dreiser's work was not found obscene. The trial and appeal also brought the specific legal factors preserving the Watch and Ward Society's cultural authority into bold relief. If the Society was to be overthrown, then the state's obscenity statutes would have to be rewritten. The trial, furthermore, revealed why the cultural modernists and their avant-garde publishers found censorship so offensive. Since literature constituted a form of cultural capital, book banning imperiled more than the economic well-being of the modernist writer and publisher. Censorship threatened their social status and, moreover, one of their most deeply held virtues, intellectual freedom. The trial was part of a larger "Book War" in Boston in the spring of 1927 that helped to mobilize an anticensorship coalition of cultural modernists, avant-garde publishers, and civil libertarians.

Dreiser's standing as the leader of the literary revolt against the genteel tradition in letters made his challenge to the cultural authority of the Watch and Ward Society especially significant. In his 1930 Nobel Prize speech, Sinclair Lewis observed that Dreiser, "more than any other man, marching alone, usually unappreciated, often hated, has cleared the trail from Victorian and Howellsian timidity and gentility in American fiction to honesty and boldness and passion of life." Like many other cultural modernists, Dreiser was an outspoken atheist. In 1930 he told a reporter for the *El Paso Evening Post* that "religion in America is just a total loss. . . . Boot out your El Paso ministers along with all other religionists and your city and America will be much better off. At least you will have cleared this country of just so much pure dogmatic bunk. That is all this religion is—just fool dogmatic bunk."[23]

The trial over the sale of *An American Tragedy* is also significant because Dreiser advocated a moral vision that represented the repudiation of all traditional Protestant values. Dreiser's stark naturalism inverted conventional morality, and his work boldly defied the Victorian literary notions about truth, goodness, and beauty. Because Howells's *Silas Lapham* lost everything but kept his virtue, the novel serves as a moral lesson about good character. By contrast, in his groundbreaking work *Sister Carrie*, Dreiser's protagonist, Caroline Meeber, is a wanton sexual libertine who uses several men in her climb to fame and fortune. In *An American Tragedy*, Dreiser traces the social rise of Clyde Griffiths from poverty to the cusp of prosperity. The protagonist, however, ends up in the electric chair for murdering a young woman whom he had gotten pregnant. As he had done in *Sister Carrie*, Dreiser only intimated that the couple had sexual relations. The central theme of the novel is that Griffiths did not have a free will but was driven to murder by circumstances and forces beyond his control. Dreiser's works are a social protest against the American Dream. To critics, Dreiser's naturalism reduced the human will to that of an animal. The New Humanist Stuart Sherman found neither "moral value" nor "memorable beauty" in Dreiser's fiction because his characters simply act upon their "jungle motive." Sherman called Dreiser's works a "sermon illustrating a crude and naively simple naturalistic philosophy, such as we find in the mouths of exponents of the new *Real-Politik.*[24] Spurning Victorian notions about character formation and human freedom, modernists deemed unbridled liberty the gateway to the full development of one's own personality. They found the restraint of individual freedom offensive and immoral.

While the modernist impulse in American fiction may have symbolically been put on trial, at the 1927 trial and 1929 appeal Arthur Garfield Hays unmasked the specific legal issues that had empowered the Watch and Ward Society. The vague definition of obscenity, critics complained, "is capable of broad interpretation, and therein lies its danger." At both trials, the district attorney read selected passages to illustrate the work's pernicious character. At the 1929 appeal, Hays put Dreiser on the stand and asked him what sections would demonstrate to the jury that those passages read by the prosecution "were not salacious." "The whole book," answered Dreiser. The district attorney objected, and only long passages were permitted to be read aloud. Lifting a passage out of its larger literary context clearly contradicted the most basic rules of scholarship; this had the potential of arousing widespread outrage among thoughtful people of every political and religious persuasion, not just enlightened intelligentsia. Not only was the defense unable to place allegedly obscene passages in their broader literary context, legal precedent precluded Hays from introducing expert testimony from leading professors, writers, and other intellectuals. Given these restrictions, perhaps the most damaging testimony came to the Society from the police officer who had arrested Donald Friede, the chief literary agent of Horace Liveright, Dreiser's publisher, for selling *An American Tragedy.* Hays asked him at the 1927 trial if his morals had been corrupted by reading the objectionable passages. He answered that they were not but added that he was not assigned to "the book-censor department." When the audience chuckled, Hays had successfully invalidated the "imitation-suggestion theory," or philosophy of reading, that informed the Watch and Ward Society's rationale for censorship. However, the jury at the 1927 trial still convicted Friede.[25]

The current obscenity statute left Hays little legal ground upon which to defend Dreiser's work other than freedom of the press and freedom of speech. Throughout the trial and appeal, Hays and his allies turned to these civil liberties for inspiration and, more important, as a basis for vindicating Dreiser's book. While waiting for the appeal of Friede's conviction to reach the higher court, Hays wrote a classic defense of civil liberties in *Let Freedom Ring.* He insisted in the preface that "I should not deny to any of these people the right to express their views; or to persuade others. I don't want to control them. But I don't want them to control me." Given the peril that censorship posed to modernist writers' income, identity, and social status, cultural modernist writers viewed censorship as a violation of their most basic civil liberties. In a remarkably ironic reversal of moral judgment, civil libertarians viewed censorship as "pernicious" and "indecent." Despite the appeal to basic civil liberties, the moral reformers' view prevailed. Friede's conviction was upheld on appeal, and he was fined three hundred dollars.[26]

After the Friede conviction in the spring of 1929, the Massachusetts Civil Liberties Union (MCLU) joined the effort to overthrow the Watch and Ward Society's jurisdiction over literature in Boston. "A well-organized program to fight censorship in all its phases was launched last night," announced a front-page *Boston Globe* story in October 1929. Sponsored by the MCLU, the meeting drew more than a thousand people. This was no publicity stunt intended to boost lagging sales for another banned novel. The roster of speakers included some of Boston's most respected citizens, including Harvard Law School professor Zachariah Chafee and Edward Weeks, the editor of the *Atlantic Monthly*. The secularizing activists now had the institutional support of an independent organization to contest the cultural authority of the Watch and Ward Society. Moreover, the social standing of many in this organization, such as Weeks, equaled that of the Brahmin supporters of the Society. The activists also had greater financial resources than in the past to try to match the Watch and Ward Society's endowment and donor list. Chafee announced the establishment of a "War Chest" to finance their effort to curb censorship.

Between the spring of 1927 and the fall of 1929, calls to end the practice of censorship in Boston had increased dramatically. *Publishers Weekly* called the Society's work "illegal" and suggested that a change in the law would be the only "way out of the ridiculous situation in which Boston has got itself." Whereas the Watch and Ward Society once depended upon Boston's newspapers for support, the local media had largely turned against censorship. A *Boston Herald* editorial succinctly summarized most newspapers' position with a question: "[Is] it a square deal to pounce upon a reputable bookseller as though he were peddling narcotic drugs in a dim alley, or caught in the act of burglary?" In an open letter to the city's business leaders published in the *Boston Evening Transcript* two days after Christmas 1927, A. Lincoln Filene, the department store magnate, was certain that censorship was hurting the region's efforts to sell goods across the nation. "Have the censors weighed against their moral triumphs the economic losses which they entail?" People in other parts of the country, he wrote, "think we take censorship seriously and diagnose our general mental outlook accordingly."[27] Censorship, the argument went, threatened the cultural status of Bostonians and therefore jeopardized their economic well-being.

In January 1928 and again in January of 1929 a loosely organized anticensorship opposition, comprised of publishers, the Massachusetts Library Club, and other civic leaders, such as Filene, attempted to revise the existing obscenity law. Both times, the Society successfully thwarted the revisionist movement by using a strategy similar to that which the Anti-Saloon League had employed to obtain and then maintain the Eighteenth Amendment. They applied direct political pressure to key legislators, issued press releases, and contacted ministers in critical districts and encouraged them to speak directly with representatives or have influential congregants attempt to persuade senators to vote against the proposed revision.[28]

Unable to limit Watch and Ward Society's cultural authority by revising the state's obscenity law, the anticensorship coalition turned to ridiculing the censors. On the night before the jury was to render its decision in the April 1929 appeal of Friede's conviction for his illegal sale of Dreiser's *An American Tragedy*, the intelligentsia gathered at the twenty-first anniversary celebration of the Ford Hall Forum to burlesque censorship. Placards were hung around the balcony with titles of banned books and signs reading "Verboten" and "taboo." Arthur M. Schlesinger Sr., professor of history at Harvard University and civil rights activist, served as toastmaster to the gala, which included various gags and speeches mocking censorship.[29]

In the aftermath of Friede's 1929 conviction, several developments in the nation at large and in Boston in particular helped to spur the civil libertarians to action. By the mid-1920s, the ACLU's interest in free speech rights extended beyond the defense of unpopular political views. More important, prohibition had convinced many civil libertarians and other citizens that religiously inspired social reform had trampled upon the Bill of Rights. The trial and execution of Nicola Sacco and Bartolomeo Vanzetti heightened many Bostonians' commitment to free speech rights. Boston was also the site of several other bruising fights over free speech in the 1920s. For example, three-time Catholic Democratic mayor James Curley refused to allow birth control advocate Margaret Sanger to hold public meetings.[30]

The alleged entrapment of a Harvard Square bookstore owner James DeLacey in 1929 for selling a banned copy of D. H. Lawrence's *Lady Chatterley's Lover* to an undercover agent of the Watch and Ward Society provided a decisive political opportunity for the emerging coalition of secularists, publishers, and civil libertarians to subvert the Society's cultural hegemony. In November 1929 a Middlesex County judge had convicted the owner of the Dunster House Book Shop and his salesperson on obscenity charges. At the December 1929 appeal before the State Superior Court, the booksellers' new lawyer, Herbert Parker, the retired attorney general for the state of Massachusetts, turned the tables on the Society and accused them of entrapping his clients by using an agent provocateur. The media reported the allegation as a statement of fact. Not only were the secularizing activists outraged by the Watch and Ward Society's alleged misconduct, but the organization also drew harsh criticisms from totally unexpected quarters. The controversy energized the renewed effort to revise the state's obscenity law. In fact, the secularizing activists, led by the MCLU, had just organized the Massachusetts Citizens Committee for Revision of the Book Law and held public meetings to cultivate wider support to overturn the key institutional structure that empowered the Society's jurisdiction over literary commercial culture in Boston.[31]

The Society had always found willing allies in the judicial system. Now, however, both the judge and district attorney turned against the organization. The judge, Frederick Fosdick, agreed with Parker: the Watch and Ward Society had "induced" DeLacey to sell the book. This entrapment "robs the offense of a great deal of its wickedness." Fosdick's criticisms proved to be gentle in comparison to the vociferous attack of the district attorney, Robert Bushnell. While Bushnell called *Lady Chatterley's Lover* the work of a "filthy degenerate" and said that since it was the obligation of his office to uphold the state's obscenity law he would prosecute the offenders, he described the actions of the Watch and Ward Society as "the best illustration of the futility of the existence of private, snooping societies." In his closing argument, Bushnell warned that if the Society even went "into a bookstore in this district, and procure[d] the commission of a crime which would not othrewise [*sic*] be committed, I'll proceed against them for criminal conspiracy." The courtroom, the *Boston Globe* reported, sat in stunned silence.[32]

The proposed revision of the state's obscenity law came up for consideration in the state legislature at the very same time that criticisms were cascading upon the Society. For example, William Allen Neilson, president of Smith College, wrote in the *Atlantic Monthly* that "the saving of a man's soul, which one must presume is the object of the censorship is after all a man's own affair, and is not to be achieved by external compulsion or guardianship." As critics berated the organization, the Society was internally weakened by the public defections of three prominent members. The first to defect was the director, Julian L. Coolidge, a mathematics professor at Harvard. While he claimed that he was overwhelmed by academic duties, the *Boston Globe* reported in a front-page story that Coolidge's association with the Society had cost him dearly at Harvard. He had recently been appointed master of the new Lowell House, but students were reluctant to sign up for rooms in it for the next academic year because they feared his *in loco parentis* oversight. On New Year's Eve, the Boston press reported that the retired Episcopal bishop of Massachusetts and Society vice president, William Lawrence, had abandoned the organization. Then word leaked out that David D. Scannell, a prominent surgeon and another director, had left the organization in protest. Whereas the Society's secretary, president, and directors ran the organization's daily operations, the honorary position of vice president proved to be a major organizational weakness in the structure of the Society because these individuals had little significant involvement in the management of the Society. When the press approached William Anderson, the bishop of the Methodist Episcopal Church of Massachusetts, for his position on the controversy, he said that he had read recent newspaper articles listing him as a vice president with "a good deal of surprise." He had never been notified of his "election." Anderson speculated that the honorary title was a "legacy" that he inherited from his predecessor.[33] Whereas the names of some of Boston's most prominent citizens provided the Society with a certain degree of social credibility, some members found their association to be a major liability due to the controversy swirling around the organization.

Despite efforts to rebuff the tirade of criticisms, many longtime Watch and Ward Society members abandoned the organization. Some wrote and demanded that their names be removed from the Society's rolls, as one person put it, because he wanted nothing to do with an organization that played an "unprincipled trick" upon the Cambridge bookseller. Not everyone disapproved of the Society's actions. One person increased his annual contribution, albeit by only three dollars, to demonstrate his "hearty approval of the recent action." If, however, support for the Society's role in the Dunster House Book Shop affair is judged by the annual financial contributions of members, then they overwhelmingly disapproved of the action. According to the treasurer's monthly report in July 1930, year-to-date contributions had dropped by almost 54 percent when compared to the previous year. The fact that this controversy coincided with the onset of the Great Depression could not have come at a worse time for the Society.[34]

While the Watch and Ward Society tried to save its reputation, the Massachusetts Citizens Committee gained support in its effort to rewrite the obscenity statute. In mid-December 1929 the committee announced that it was going to push for specific wording that only considered a book "as a whole" to be obscene. The committee had gathered the signatures of a broad coalition of religious leaders, including George Spencer, secretary of the Massachusetts Bible Society; Charles Slattery, Episcopal bishop of Massachusetts; educators, including Neilson and Vida Scudder, English professor at Wellesley College; publishers, such as Greenslet; politicians, including former mayor Andrew Peters; and civil libertarians like Chafee. In March 1930 the state legislature revised the obscenity law, thus curtailing the Watch and Ward Society's jurisdiction over literature in Massachusetts. The clearest evidence that the Watch and Ward Society's cultural authority over this one particular aspect of commercial culture had

South Church, Copley Square, Boston, Mass., April 22, 1923 (Boston: Printed for Watch and Ward Society, 1923), 11. On Victorian literary culture, see Henry F. May, *The End of American Innocence: A Study of the First Years of our Own Time, 1912–1917* (1959; reprint, New York: Quadrangle Books, 1964), 30–51; and Malcolm Bradbury, *The Modern American Novel* (New York: Oxford University Press, 1983), 1–19.

12. Stanley Coben, *Rebellion Against Victorianism: The Impetus for Cultural Change in 1920s America* (New York: Oxford University Press, 1991), 3–35; Alan Hunt, *Governing Morals: A Social History of Moral Regulation* (Cambridge: Cambridge University Press, 1999), 4, 121; Nicola Beisel, *Imperiled Innocents: Anthony Comstock and Family Reproduction in Victorian America* (Princeton, N.J.: Princeton University Press, 1997), 4–7, 162–163; Norman Clark, *Deliver Us from Evil: An Interpretation of American Prohibition* (New York: Norton, 1976), 12, 43, 174, 210–211; Daniel Rodgers, *Work Ethic in Industrial America 1850–1920* (Chicago: University of Chicago Press, 1980), 7, 95, 100–107, 121, 125–126; Richard Wightman Fox, "The Culture of Liberal Protestant Progressivism, 1875–1925," *Journal of Interdisciplinary History* 23 (1993): 639–660.

13. William Leach, *Land of Desire: Merchants, Power, and the Rise of a New American Culture* (New York: Vintage Books, 1993), 3–4.

14. *Annual Report, 1915–1916*, 37.

15. *Annual Report, 1923–1924*, 9; Ruth Leys, "Mead's Voice: Imitation as Foundation, or, The Struggle Against Mimesis," *Critical Inquiry* 19 (1993): 280; Parker, *Purifying America*, 21–22.

16. *Annual Report, 1914–1915*, 5, 21.

17. *Annual Report, 1924–1925*, 12; Perry, *Pernicious Books*, 15; W. A. Swanberg, *Dreiser* (New York: Scriber, 1965), 87–93; *Publishers Weekly*, March 28, 1931, 1686; Oswald Garrison Villard, "Sex, Art, Truth, and Magazines," *Atlantic Monthly*, March 1926, 395; *Annual Report, 1914–1915*, 5, 21. For a conservative Protestant approach to social reform through individual conversion, see Diane Winston, *Red-Hot and Righteous: The Urban Religion of the Salvation Army* (Cambridge: Harvard University Press, 1999), 17.

18. Mencken to Dreiser, quoted in Fred Hobson, *Mencken: A Life* (Baltimore: Johns Hopkins University Press, 1994), 190; H. L. Mencken, *A Mencken Chrestomathy* (New York: Knopf, 1949), 624; H. L. Mencken, "Puritanism as a Literary Force," in *A Book of Prefaces* (New York: Knopf, 1917), 198–199, 202, 210; Joseph Wood Krutch, "Antichrist and the Five Apostles," *Nation*, December 21, 1921, 733.

19. H. L. Mencken, *My Life as Author and Editor*, ed. Jonathan Yardley (New York: Knopf, 1993), 165, 355, 390–391.

20. Coben, *Rebellion*, 48–68; Steven Biel, *Independent Intellectuals in the United States, 1910–1945* (New York: New York University Press, 1992), 54–84.

21. Mencken, "Hatrack," 51–60; Hay, *Let Freedom Ring*, 168–169; Ferris Greenslet, *Under the Bridge: An Autobiography* (Boston: Houghton Mifflin, 1943), 178; "Mencken Decision to be Announced Tomorrow Morning," *Boston Evening Transcript*, April 6, 1926, 1, 9; "Mencken Wins His Case Over Watch and Ward," *Boston Evening Transcript*, April 7, 1926, 1–2.

22. Mencken, "Hatrack," 63–72; "Big Ovation to Mencken at Harvard," *Boston Post*, April 8, 1926, 2.

23. Sinclair Lewis, "The American Fear of Literature," in *The Man From Main Street: Selected Essays and Other Writings, 1904–1950*, ed. Harry Maule and Melville Cane (New York: Random House, 1953), 7; Swanberg, *Dreiser*, 361.

24. Bradbury, *Modern American Novel*, 25–26; Malcolm Cowley, "Sister Carrie: Her Fall and Rise," in *The Stature of Theodore Dreiser*, ed. Alfred Kazin and Charles Shapiro (Bloomington: Indiana University Press, 1955), 171–181; James Farell, "Dreiser's *Sister Carrie*" in Kazin and Shapiro, *Stature of Theodore Dreiser*, 182–187; Stuart Sherman, "The Naturalism of Mr. Dreiser," *Nation*, December 2, 1915, 648–650.

25. Editorial Note, *Nation*, April 27, 1927, 465; "Sustains Ban on Dreiser Novel," *Boston Globe*, April 11, 1927, 24; "Adult Books for Immature Readers," *Publishers Weekly*, April 30, 1927, 1709; "Jury Finds Friede Guilty," *Boston Globe*, April 18, 1929, 1, 17; "Friede Fined in Boston," *Publishers Weekly*, December 7, 1929, 2676.

26. Hays, *Let Freedom Ring*, xvi; Joseph Wood Krutch, "The Indecency of Censorship," *Nation*, February 16, 1927, 163.

27. "Still in the Limelight," *Publishers Weekly*, July 16, 1927, 206; "Put an End to This Absurd Book Situation," *Boston Herald*, June 2, 1927, 20; A. Lincoln Filene, "Letter to the Editor," *Boston Evening Transcript*, December 27, 1927, I:18.

28. Meeting at Boston City Club, Minutes of the Directors' Meetings, January 16, 1928, New England Watch and Ward Society Records, Harvard Law School Library, Box 14; "Revising the Censorship Law," *Publishers Weekly*, January 28, 1928, 349–350; "Would Amend Present State Censorship Law," *Boston Evening Transcript*, January 12, 1929, 7; "Censorship Discussion Before Massachusetts Legislature," *Publishers Weekly*, February 16, 1929, 761; "Boston Censorship," *Publishers Weekly*, March 23, 1929, 1504; "Senate Again Votes to Kill Book Censorship Bill," *Boston Evening Transcript*, April 2, 1929, 1, 7. On the Anti-Saloon League, see K. Austin Kerr, *Organized for Prohibition: A New History of the Anti-Saloon League* (New Haven, Conn.: Yale University Press, 1985).

29. "700 Cheer Mockery of Censorship Here," *Boston Globe*, April 17, 1929, 17; "Flout Censorship at Ford Hall Frolic," *Boston Evening Transcript*, April 17, 1929, 3.

30. Felix Frankfurter, *The Case of Sacco and Vanzetti: A Critical Analysis for Lawyers and Laymen* (Boston: Little, Brown, 1927); David Felix, *Protest: Sacco-Vanzetti and the Intellectuals* (Bloomington: Indiana University Press, 1965); James M. Curley, *I'd Do It Again: A Record of All My Uproarious Years* (Englewood Cliffs, N.J.: Prentice-Hall, 1957), 182–184, 188.

31. "Jail Sentences in Obscene Book Case," *Boston Evening Transcript*, November 25, 1929, 5; Secretary's Report, November 1929, New England Watch and Ward Society Records, Harvard Law School Library, Box 16; New England Watch and Ward Society, *The Dunster House Book Shop Case: A Statement* (Boston: New England Watch and Ward Society, 1930), 6; "Stage Set for Watch & Ward Statement," *Boston Evening Transcript*, January 11, 1930, 1.

32. "Hit Watch and Ward," *Boston Globe*, December 21, 1929, 1, 2; "Gave False Name, Agent Confesses," *Boston Globe*, December 20, 1929, 1, 28.

33. William Allen Neilson, "The Theory of Censorship," *Atlantic Monthly*, January 1930, 16; "Resigns Watch and Ward Post," *Boston Globe*, December 14, 1929, 1, 19; "Watch and Ward Silent on Report," *Boston Globe*, December 31, 1929, 27; "Watch and Ward Legacy to Bishop," *Boston Globe*, January 7, 1930, 32.

34. Marty Pierce to Watch and Ward Society, July 3, 1930, New England Watch and Ward Society Records, Harvard Law School Library, Box 10, Folder 6; William Brigham to Charles Bodwell, January 3, 1930, New England Watch and Ward Society Records, Harvard Law School Library, Box 12, Folder 1; Treasurer's Report for the Month of July, 1930, New England Watch and Ward Society Records, Harvard Law School Library, Box 15.

35. "Propose New Law on Book Censorship," *Boston Evening Transcript*, December 13, 1929, 1, 12; *Annual Report, 1930–1931*, 15–17.

36. For examples of Whiggish interpretations, see William E. Leuchtenburg, *The Perils of Prosperity, 1914–1932* (Chicago: University of Chicago Press, 1958); Paul Boyer, *Purity in Print: The Vice-Society Movement and Book Censorship in America* (New York: Scribners, 1968); Jay Gertzman, *Bookleggers and Smuthounds: The Trade in Erotica, 1920–1940* (Philadelphia: University of Pennsylvania Press, 1999); and James Elias, Veronica Diehl Elias, Vern L. Bullough, Gwen Brewer, Jeffrey J. Douglas, and Will Jarvis, *Porn 101: Eroticism, Pornography, and the First Amendment* (Amherst, N.Y.: Prometheus Books, 1999). For examples of the "status anxiety" interpretation, see Louis Zurcher and R. George Kirkpatrick, *Citizens for Decency: Anti-Pornography Crusaders as Status Defense* (Austin: University of Texas Press, 1976); and Beisel, *Imperiled Innocents*. Two recent studies successfully challenge these conventional interpretations but do not examine the Watch and Ward Society in any detail, Parker, *Purifying America*; Hunt, *Governing Morals*.

37. Whereas most sociological discussions of secularization have been framed by abstract and agent-less concepts, such as "rationalization," this study has drawn upon social movement theory in order to move concrete historical issues, such as human agency, to the center stage of analysis. Secularization, as Mark Chaves argues, is best understood not as the decline of religion per se but as the declining scope of religious authority. The coalition of anticensorship activists took away from the Watch and Ward Society the cultural authority to determine what was a morally acceptable cultural product for people to read. While the intention to secularize varied within this coalition, the result was the decline of a religious institution's cultural authority—secularization, in short. Mark Chaves, "Secularization as Declining Religious Authority," *Social Forces* 72 (1994): 750, 752. See also, Karel Dobbelaere, "Secularization: A Multi-Dimensional Concept," *Current Sociology* 29 (1981): 49–87.

Part III
Minority
Adaptation

Eight

Judith Weisenfeld

"Saturday Sinners and Sunday Saints"

The Nightclub as Moral Menace in 1940s Race Movies

Throughout the heyday of the Hollywood studio system, black American moviegoers consumed largely the same fare as did white Americans and sampled from genres that included comedies, musicals, melodramas, and mysteries.[1] While segregated viewing practices within theaters were firmly in place—most commonly, African Americans were required to sit in the balcony—in many cities black audiences also attended theaters that catered to them exclusively. In 1929, for example, the *Film Daily Yearbook* counted 461 "colored theaters" in the United States. The majority of these were located in the rural and urban South, but urban areas in the Northeast, West, and Midwest all had black theaters, some even owned by African Americans.[2] In addition to exhibiting the latest Hollywood releases, these theaters also provided African American access to a vibrant separate cinema of films produced exclusively for their consumption.[3] In producing these "race movies," as they were known, black and white filmmakers endeavored to tap into the same market that had proved so lucrative for record companies that marketed "race records."[4] In the context of pursuing profit, however, these race movie makers also sought to provide a counter to the powerful uses of film to promote and shape white supremacy, a goal most convincingly achieved in D. W. Griffith's 1915 *The Birth of a Nation* and pursued through a range of mainstream films throughout the twentieth century.

Race movies often featured representations of religious experience, expression, and institutional structures as the filmmakers addressed the distinctive uses of black religiosity in mainstream American culture. Mainstream American film has typically presented black religion as simplistic, sincere, instinctive, and emotional, as well as the primary diversion in black life—to the complete exclusion of interest in the political, economic, and social needs of the here and now.[5] In fact, mainstream Hollywood found images of black religiosity so compelling that the majority of the industry's "all-black cast" films use religious settings. These films include Paul Sloane's *Hearts in Dixie* (Fox, 1929), King Vidor's *Hallelujah* (MGM, 1929), Marc Connelly and William Keighley's *The Green Pastures* (Warner Brothers, 1936), the final segment of Julien Duvivier's *Tales of Manhattan* (20th Century Fox, 1942) and Vincente Minnelli's *Cabin in the Sky* (MGM, 1943). Each of these films predictably traps its black characters in a happy rural world in which no white people exist and in which their troubles are of their own making. The films' religious characters typically pine for heaven and rail against participation in the pleasures of this earthly existence (including or especially urban commercial entertainments) and yet engage in what the movies present as extraordinarily exuberant, embodied, and sexualized worship.

It is not surprising, then, given the uses of black religiosity in mainstream films as well as the importance of religious life and community throughout African American history, that religious themes appear regularly in many of the surviving race films produced by both black and white film companies. Responding to relentlessly negative and stereotyped images of the simple, emotional, irrational exuberance of African American religiosity in American film, makers of race movies often countered with representations of restrained, erudite Christians but also with images striking similar to those found in Hollywood films. But countering problematic images in mainstream culture with "positive" images was not, by any means, the only interest of these race film makers. The frequent appearance of religious themes in a variety of race movies across genres signals the interest of filmmakers in using the public medium of film as an arena to debate and to provide a range of examples of how black Christians should or should not comport themselves. Hovering in the background of these discussions was the broader issue of the contested Americanness of blacks, even of black Christians who could lay claim to a shared religious commitment with many white Americans. What kind of public presentation can and should African Americans make of themselves in order to make a strong bid for access to full citizenship rights, these films ask. And what place should religious institutions and their leaders occupy in an increasingly urbanized and "modern" community whose social life now included a range of nonreligious options?

This essay explores race movies' constructions of the urban nightclub as a profound, even primary threat to the integrity of black Christian life in the 1940s, with particular emphasis on the films of Spencer Williams, who directed eight movies in that decade.[6] Because race film companies made these movies for black audiences with no expectation that white Americans would see them, it is reasonable to expect such films to engage issues of particular concern to African Americans at the time, in addition to seeking to entertain. As in the Hollywood "all-black cast" films, these race movies generally oppose urban and rural life (valorizing the rural); a corrupt and backward church with an educated, modern one; and the ways of the worldly with those of the church. Rather than simply harkening back to an imagined idyllic rural past, as is so often the case in the Hollywood films, race movies present a much more complex and probing analysis of the impact of urbanization and urban commercial culture on black religious life. A survey of race movies that feature religious themes, characters, and institutions reveals a strong connection between anxieties about the urban environment and commercial culture and the films' interrogations of the possibilities and problems of black religious leadership. A heightened concern with the ministry—which by the 1930s had begun to be displaced by electoral politics and the arts, for example, as the primary avenue for developing social and political leadership—becomes clear in a range of race films from the 1930s and 1940s. As race movies moved through their final decade in the 1940s, the possibility of greater access to citizenship opened up by America's participation in World War II made an interrogation of black leadership even more pressing. There is a strong sense in the world of these films that a modern community cannot rely exclusively on ministers for direction, particularly when some have not served the community well in a variety of ways, and the films offer many representations of uneducated, corrupt, scheming, or ineffectual ministers in order to make the case for needed change.

In addition to a concern with the future of religious leadership, the films provide evidence of anxiety about the potential of the church's influence to be eclipsed by the world of entertainments. Beginning in the early twentieth century, the commercial landscape for urban African Americans expanded dramatically as they encountered more of the growing variety of popular entertainments such as film, theater, nightclubs, professional sports, and radio as well as consumer items like beauty products, records, literature, newspapers, magazines, and toys marketed specifically to their communities. While urban African Americans' engagement with commercial culture took place in ways that shared much with the experiences of other Americans, there were, of course, aspects of it that remained particular to black communities. In his study of black churches in Brooklyn, New York, Clarence Taylor observes:

> For the most part, African Americans embraced mass cultural forms with little resistance. Yet they were not just passive recipients who swallowed

mass culture whole. They molded it to suit their needs as African Americans in an urban environment. They made choices in music, clothing, products, movies and other forms of recreation. . . . Although blacks adopted mass cultural forms that were popular in the larger white society, the trend toward mass culture was part of the larger struggle led by African Americans that challenged the racist view of blacks as lazy and incapable of succeeding. African Americans used mass culture to become economically independent and make black communities viable.[7]

A range of race movies explore the issue of how these arenas of church and commercial entertainments would relate to each other in the urban environment.

In the context of an interrogation of the meaning for the church of both urbanization and the rise of secular entertainments, many race films also addressed the strong presence of women in black churches as a potential problem. The concern with the future of the ministry is directly related to the perception of the church arena as destructively feminized and with the nightclub as allowing for the unchecked expression of female sexuality. The perception of a feminized church as a problem is not confined to the history of African American Christians, but the importance of the church as a significant "public sphere" for African American communities makes taking account of representations of apprehension about feminization critical to an understanding of urban African American life in the early twentieth century.[8] The films seem to connect the potential to read the church as a feminized arena to the problems that result from African Americans having an exclusively ordained leadership. A number of films work around these issues and, not surprisingly, use female characters as vehicles for arguing either for a particular kind of ministerial leadership not tied to women's spiritual agency or to argue for looking outside the church for leaders. The question of what that new nonchurch leadership might look like and what relationship it would have both to the church and the increasingly influential arena of the nightclub looms large in many of these films.

By the time he embarked on his career as a race film director, Spencer Williams had already established himself as a distinguished entertainer and Hollywood insider (insofar as this was possible for an African American man in the period). Born in 1893 in Vidalia, Louisiana, Williams migrated to New York City sometime around 1910, where he studied acting and comedy with Bert Williams of the Williams and Walker comedy team, then a regular act in the *Ziegfeld Follies*. After military service in World War I, Williams made his way into the movies, eventually becoming a writer at the Christie Studios in Hollywood. His work at Christie in the late 1920s involved writing short, all-black talkies, and he was also involved in a number of projects at other studios.[9] In the 1930s Williams became a familiar screen presence for black audiences through his appearances in several feature-length race films, including a group of popular black westerns, *The Bronze Buckaroo*, *Harlem Rides the Range*, and *Two Gun Man From Harlem*, and a black horror film, *Son of Ingagi*.[10] In the 1940s Williams joined with Alfred Sack, a white film producer, and directed at least eight films with Sack Amusement Enterprises, work that placed him among the most successful race film makers of the decade. Of these eight films, two were religious melodramas and two were dramas featuring strong religious themes.[11] He, more than any other race film maker, popularized the religious race film, which film historian Thomas Cripps has asserted "constitute[s] the most self-contained subgenre of black film."[12]

The Blood of Jesus (1941), the first film Williams wrote and directed with the Sack company, established patterns for the religious melodrama that he attempted to reproduce in other films, both in terms of story and directorial technique.[13] The story in *The Blood of Jesus* revolves around the near-death experience of Martha (Catherine Caviness), a newly baptized woman whose husband, Ras (Spencer Williams), refuses to have anything to do with the church in the small, rural town in which they live. Ras accidentally shoots Martha, and for the rest of the film her spirit attempts to find its way back to her body but must withstand various temptations that the devil places in her path. In a very literal presentation of the journey back to life, we see Martha's travails in the city where, in a nightclub, the devil's agents attempt to lure her into prostitution. When she escapes this trap, the devil tries again to distract her with a dance party and jazz band. Eventually, Jesus and a guiding angel intervene and come to Martha's aid, permitting her safe return to her body, family, and church community. With his first film, then, Williams makes clear his concern with the lures of commercial entertainments and their impact on church culture.

Williams's approach to filmmaking, which distinguished his religious films from most other race movies that dealt with religious themes, involved creative use of special effects to represent divine interventions in the lives of believers as well as the activities of angels and the devil on earth.[14] Lacking access to the technology available to the Hollywood studios, Williams and his crew found simpler means of accomplishing the effects. Jack Whitman, the white cameraman on this film, recalled, "There was a lot of trick photography that I was able to do in the camera. I had learned that, it was a lost art really. Even in that time, all those things were done with an optical printer, but he [Williams] did not have the money to pay for it, so I used a matte box and double exposures and so forth . . . there were parts where the soul left the body and went through the walls, and where angels appeared, and the devil appeared, and you know they had to come from nowhere and suddenly be there."[15] In addition to the emphasis on effects, *The Blood of Jesus* and Williams's other religious films all contain the range of entertainment elements common to American popular films of the age—musical numbers, melodrama, comedy—set in the context of a deeply devotional presentation.

Where the action in *The Blood of Jesus* took place largely in a realm in between life and death, which Williams represented by superimposing figures representing the spiritual world onto the action of characters in this world, *Go Down, Death* concerns itself primarily with an earthly struggle between "Saturday Sinners and Sunday Saints" who "clash in the battle of good against evil!" as the advertising tells us.[16] Based on the poem "Go Down, Death" by James Weldon Johnson, the story involves the attempt of Jim Bottoms (Spencer Williams), a cabaret owner, to discredit Rev. Moons, the new pastor of Mount Zion Baptist Church.[17] Jim inaugurates his campaign to counter the minister's public opposition to the "ungodly" activities that go on in the nightclub. Indeed, on the very Sunday that Rev. Moons preaches a sermon against the ungodly, one that promotes purity as "the very essence of Christ's message," Jim sends three "fly chicks" to entrap the minister.[18] The women wait for him in his office after the service and pose as potential converts. One of them tells him, "We really do want to be Christians. I just think that one can be a so much better person with religion." The three then walk him home, and he gives each of them a New Testament with instructions to read various passages. Meanwhile, one of Jim's men waits outside the window, and when the women suddenly grab Rev. Moons, kiss him, and place a glass of whiskey in his hand, the man snaps a photograph.

As the story proceeds, Williams's characters find themselves interacting with spiritual beings who attempt to influence the outcome of events and ensure the victory of religion over the forces of the urban nightclub. Sister Caroline, Jim's adoptive mother and a faithful member of the congregation, is the character who proves most important in creating access to the spiritual world. Caroline rescues Rev. Moons from the women in his office and from Jim's man, and, after the others leave, she tells Rev. Moons that she will do everything she can to prevent Jim's scheme from working. She is committed to Rev. Moons, not only because he is her minister and she respects him but also because he is engaged to her niece, Betty Jean.

In the end, Caroline's faith, which actually makes things happen in the film, proves the most powerful force in protecting the minister from Jim's plot and the church from the saloon. Williams's commitment to the use of film techniques to represent divine intervention in the lives of believers becomes especially clear in his depiction of the results of Caroline's faith. In the crucial scene, Caroline sits on her bed in the apartment she shares with Betty Jean and Jim and gazes at a photograph on the wall of her dead husband, Joe, and asks him to tell God that "one of his faithful servants is in trouble and needs his help." Caroline lies down and looks at a reproduction of Warner Sallman's *Head of Christ*, which hangs on the wall, and then back to Joe.[19] She then sees Joe's spirit emerge from the photograph "as a ghostly superimposition on the frame" and pass through the closed door and out of the room. She follows him into Jim's room and watches as Joe's spirit opens the safe where Jim had hidden the incriminating photographs of Rev. Moons. Just as Caroline removes them from the safe, Jim returns and the two struggle. Jim wrests the pictures from her hand and pushes her, causing Caroline to fall and hit her head on the corner of the safe. When Betty Jean rushes in to find out what has happened, Jim tells her that a thief stole his money and injured Caroline. Caroline dies shortly thereafter, surrounded by family and friends, with the final words, "I'm going home." Rev. Moons comforts Betty Jean, telling her that "God will bring the guilty to justice in his own good time."

Although *Go Down, Death*'s story revolves around the threat that Jim poses to Rev. Moons and his ability to function as a leader in the church, the minister is strangely passive and appears at a loss as to how to maintain his standing in the community and how to insulate his community from the incursions of the world of the nightclub. Williams does not position Rev. Moons as the character who draws the line against the secularization that the film argues attends the expansion of commercial culture. Instead, Sister Caroline's religious commitments seem to anchor the congregation, while the minister appears merely as a moral, if ineffective, figurehead. He does not confront Jim, nor does he take any action to work against the image of himself and his ministry that Jim created through the staged photographs. In fact, Rev. Moons decides to resign from the church rather than declare his innocence and is satisfied to "turn it over to the Lord." Caroline is the agent of the minister's rescue, praying to her husband to intercede with Jesus. She is certain that her faith will be able to effect what she needs, and through the use of superimposed images, Williams permits us to see the product of Caroline's prayer as her husband's spirit appears to help. It is not the simple retrieval of the incriminating photographs that brings Jim's campaign to an end, however, but Caroline's death.

In the film's final sequences, Williams integrates events in this world and the next into a single frame and uses voice-overs to represent different modes of intervention of the supernatural in this world. Rev. Moons preaches Caroline's funeral service, telling the congregation, "Weep not, weep not, she is not dead. She is resting in the arms of Jesus."[20] In the pews sit the three women who

worked for Jim, dressed simply in white, an indication that they have been converted and have dedicated themselves to church and community. Jim sits next
to Betty Jean, both obviously distraught. Throughout the funeral sermon we see
rays of light streaming through clouds, stained glass windows, Death riding on
a white horse, and finally people marching up a staircase to the gates of heaven,
all images recycled from Williams's *The Blood of Jesus*. He edits these sequences
into the sermon so that they illustrate moments in the poem and in Sister Caroline's life, death, and life in heaven. Here it is not an intrusion of the miraculous into this world that Williams emphasizes, but he demonstrates instead
how powerful preaching conjures up such images.

After the funeral Jim retreats to his club—the source of his conflict with the
minister and Sister Caroline and, for Williams, an arena of commercial culture
that threatens to destroy the church community. Jim obviously regrets what he
has done but rather than repenting, simply sits drinking and smoking. Williams
brings the film to a close by showing the audience the consequences of Jim's
life in the saloon and his disregard for the church. In the film's final sequences,
we hear a devilish voice torment him that he's going home, just as Caroline did,
but that he will not be going to heaven but rather to the home that he deserves.
Williams then shifts the action to show us the vision that the devil has provided
to illustrate his anticipated torment of Jim, who collapses and dies.[21] As in all of
Williams's films that address conflict between the church and the world, the
wrongdoers receive their just punishment, and the church community (through
Caroline's sacrifice) protects itself from the incursions of sinful forces.

In this short devotional melodrama obviously made with very little money
(the film runs only fifty-four minutes and contains considerable amounts of
recycled footage), Williams employs a shorthand in referencing the set of problems he sees facing the church: urbanization, nightclubs, intemperance, smoking, and gambling. In his earlier film, *The Blood of Jesus*, Williams includes long
sequences set inside nightclubs—marked as urban through the use of an establishing long shot of a city at night—which provide a sharp contrast with the
world of the rural church. *Go Down, Death* contains only two short scenes in
Jim's nightclub, which serve to frame the story of Caroline's death. Nevertheless, the film's brief references to the secular, commercial sphere of the nightclub would have resonated with audiences, as would Caroline's references to
Jim's involvements with "streetwalkers" on "colored street." Equally brief are
scenes set in the church, with the exception of Caroline's funeral. Williams
simply makes reference to the conflict between the church and the world and
proceeds to focus on the issues of ministerial leadership and gender within the
church that are, for him, inextricably linked with questions of urbanization and
the impact of commercial culture on the church and its members.

Although Williams made abundant use of special effects to represent the supernatural—most commonly through the superimposition of one image on another—the general quality of the films is quite poor when compared to many other race films of the day and certainly when viewed alongside almost any Hollywood film.[22] Nevertheless, his focus on making the divine present on film through special effects distinguishes his work from that of other directors of race films. In the sequence in which Caroline prays before the photograph of her husband, Williams implies a connection between visual intimacy and religious experience, an assertion that ultimately may make the film industry immune to the criticism he directs at other arenas of commercial culture. It is not merely Caroline's prayers that give rise to the appearance of Joe's spirit but the interaction between her prayers and her gaze upon the images of Joe and of Jesus. Williams makes a similar equation between looking and religious experience in a number of important scenes in *The Blood of Jesus* in which Martha prays before an image of the sacred heart of Jesus. Williams's heavy emphasis on the visual aspects of film serves to overcome the severe technical limitations under which he labored, requiring him to include inadequately synchronized postproduction sound rather than dialogue recorded at the time of filming. In taking this approach, which layers the visual within the frame of the largely visual medium of film, he rejects the notion that to simulate miracles on film demeans the power of the divine and instead affirms the possibility of using the viewing of films to direct and enrich religious experience. Thus, while he cautions viewers about the dangers of some aspects of commercial culture, film remains outside the scope of his critique.

In *The Blood of Jesus* and *Go Down, Death*, Williams presents women as the most important moral agents in black church life and praises them while at the same time requiring these women to step aside, sacrificing themselves for the greater good. Williams relies heavily on melodrama in his religious films, no doubt because of the identification of the genre as a women's genre and its emphasis on revealing the virtuous nature of a victimized character.[23] The generic choice of melodrama permits him to explore the conflict between church and world and the fluid relationship between this world and the spiritual world with particular intensity. In considering the question of why early black melodramas almost necessarily have no appeal to audiences of today, Jane Gaines concludes that "melodrama reenacts a moral pattern that coincides with the value system in operation within a community at a particular point in history. In the parallel world constructed by melodrama, it is safe to raise emotionally volatile issues and test traumatic outcomes. Because the moral pattern, the distribution of reward and punishment in melodrama, is always tailor-made to fit local assumptions and prevailing theses, it stirs an audience in its time but may never strike a chord for another generation." In addition, she notes that "the family context serves to intensify" the nature and the implications of conflicts that melodramas explore.[24] In *Go Down, Death*, Jim's betrayal of his surrogate mother sits at the center of the moral conflict, but the family melodrama also points to a variety of larger issues, most notably the impact of urban entertainments on family and community and to class conflicts.

In addition, in keeping with conventions of melodrama, Williams's film reflects community values by depicting both the current state of affairs and imagining a more morally satisfying one from his perspective. As Christine Gledhill argues "[melodrama's] enactment of the continuing struggle of good and evil forces running through social, political and psychic life draws into a public arena desires, fears, values and identities which lie beneath the surface of the publicly acknowledged world."[25] In this context, Williams takes the extraordinary approach of using the presence of demonic and heavenly forces in this world to speak the unspeakable concerning his own vision of morality. Thus Williams demanded more from his audiences than a simple identification with the heroes of the story or unexamined acceptance of his religious beliefs. Instead, *Go Down, Death* and *The Blood of Jesus* provide opportunities for viewers to contemplate the nebulous relationship between the religious and the secular, between the world of the church and that of commercial entertainments.

Williams took up similar questions of the relationship between the church and the nightclub, as well as of the efficacy of black religious leadership, in the 1946 comedy *Dirty Gertie from Harlem, U.S.A.* In his earlier and explicitly religious melodramas, Williams creates a great deal of dramatic tension concerning the fate of his characters, but the outcome is never in doubt. God punishes the wicked, and the church community emerges renewed. The generic choice of comedy permits him to take narrative chances and to probe more deeply questions about the impact of the nightclub on black life and about the future of the ministry. The direction of the narrative in *Dirty Gertie* is much less formulaic than in either of the melodramas, and the film, which includes music and comedy, contains no special effects and no scenes depicting divine or satanic intervention in the lives of humans.[26] Despite the obvious differences between *Dirty Gertie* and Williams's religious melodramas, the themes the films takes up are quite similar, especially in their explorations of tensions between the church and the nightclub and of issues of gender and black religious leadership.

Set on the fictional island of Rinidad, the story follows Gertie La Rue (Francine Everett), a cabaret dancer who is billed as the greatest performer "this side of Harlem." Because of Gertie's infidelity to and subsequent breakup with Al (John King), a club owner in Harlem, she fled New York, and her troupe has followed her to Rinidad, where they have an engagement at the Diamond

Palace. While on Rinidad, Gertie entertains herself with two servicemen, and her sexuality run amok wreaks havoc on the community. The film concludes as Al arrives determined to punish Gertie, eventually killing her. Gertie's death at Al's hands comes as something of a surprise because Williams establishes the film's primary conflict as one between Gertie and two missionaries who arrive on Rinidad on the same day she does. Throughout much of the film, Gertie, the embodiment of the frightening aspects of urbanization and commercial entertainments, engages in an all-out war with the representatives of the church.

In contrast to his presentation of the dedicated and well-meaning (if ineffectual) ministers in *The Blood of Jesus* and *Go Down, Death*, Williams draws the characters of Jonathan Christian (Alfred Hawkins) and Ezra Crumm (David Boykin) as problematic moral exemplars. Jonathan, the senior of the two missionaries, shows himself to be excessively concerned with his comfort as he complains bitterly about his hotel room. Finding that Gertie's troupe has been assigned the best rooms, Jonathan whines, "Why, I just don't see how I'm going to stand it. And we expect to stay here quite some time. Why, if we're going to teach these people what sin is, we've got to be in more comfortable surroundings." In the course of observing Gertie's behavior with the servicemen and expressing concern to the nightclub owner about the troupe's show, he becomes obsessed with Gertie. For her part, Gertie sees Jonathan as nothing more than a "dirty psalm-singing pole cat" who desires her as much as any other man does. Although Jonathan does not give in to his desires, his resistance is not sufficient to make him an admirable example of the fortitude of the ministry. In addition, neither Jonathan nor Ezra can contain their prurient interest in the show that Gertie's troupe is doing at the club. Ezra sneaks around, peeking in on rehearsals, and begs Jonathan to let him see the show so that he can attest to what a sinful exhibition it really is. Jonathan forbids him to go but is able to justify his own attendance as God's will in response to his prayer:

> Oh God, I beseech thee to show me the way. This woman, this sinner, this temptress of men whose flesh is weak. Please Lord, tell me, must I stop this dreadful performance, this horrible exhibition of flesh? You know Lord, I'm loath to witness such a spectacle of filth, but if it is thy will, I will slip into the Diamond Palace tonight, unseen, and watch unnoticed, this show of lewdness that I may be better able to judge in thy sight. Tell me oh Lord, must I go? Yes, Lord, I'm listening. You want me to go! Then if it is thy will, I shall not disobey. Thank you, oh Lord, thank you. Amen.

Jonathan and Ezra both attend the performance, with Ezra sneaking in. Ezra clearly enjoys it, but Jonathan mounts the stage and interrupts the proceedings, slapping Gertie in the face while comparing himself to Jesus chasing the moneychangers out of the temple. In the end, the missionaries do not play a significant role in the progress of the narrative and function in many ways as comic relief. Gertie's past comes back to kill her in the person of Al, and the ministers simply observe the course of events, presenting no answers to the question of how the church can productively engage the entertainment world.

In addition to exploring the conflict between the church and the nightclub, the film also comments on another type of commercial enterprise that Williams posed as a threat to the moral integrity of black communities. In a scene toward the end of the film, Gertie visits Old Hager (Spencer Williams), a "Voodoo woman," to find out what is in store for her. The Voodoo woman's bleak prediction "of a bloody confrontation with a man who is angry with her" leaves Gertie even more frightened than she had been before. Viewers familiar with Williams's work would have expected to find him playing a part in the film (as he had done in others he directed), and his appearance in this part proves particularly amusing. In addition to providing a typical moment of comic relief, this scene investigates the impact of the African-derived religious traditions of many immigrants from the Caribbean on the black church. It is also possible that the voodoo traditions of Rinidad stand in for the conjure practices that southern migrants brought with them to the urban North. But here it is not simply the form of religious practice that Williams presents as problematic but its explicit commercialization. Old Hager is not a servant of the community but a businesswoman, representing a blending of religious and commercial culture that Williams rejects.

Dirty Gertie from Harlem, U.S.A.'s use of comedy makes it possible to take on the controversial issues of clergy and sexuality, the relationship between African Americans and Caribbean immigrants, conflicts between Christianity and folk traditions, in addition to the broader question of the impact of the nightclub on black communities in ways that might not have been possible had it employed a serious, dramatic framework. Although comedy deliberately works "against the demand of realism," it is also a genre that serves a useful "social and psychological function in that it is an arena, or provides an arena, where . . . tensions can be released in a safe manner."[27] *Dirty Gertie* is merely one of a number of race films of the 1930s and 1940s that took seriously and evaluated—even while employing comedic genres—the nature of black religious leadership. This and other films did not take for granted that black churches should function as the unquestioned conduit that produced leaders to whom both blacks and whites would look for guidance concerning black issues. In contrast to Williams's earlier religious melodramas, however, no character clearly represents Christian virtue, and the film does not identify a path for the future. Female sexuality, inextricably linked with the urban nightclub in this film, definitively represents sinfulness, and Williams punishes his main character without the aid of divine intervention in this case.

In the 1940 musical comedy *Sunday Sinners*, the female members of the congregation, with the exception of the members of the minister's family, are marked as those who present the greatest threat to the church community and whose various forms of contagion must be contained. *Sunday Sinners*, produced by Jack and Bert Goldberg, directed by Arthur Dreifuss, and featuring blues singer Mamie Smith, follows the same general story line as *Go Down, Death*, but Dreifuss takes an approach to the material that is quite different from Williams's typical portrayal of miraculous interventions that resolve the central conflict.[28] Moreover, while the film contains elements of a straightforward, sermonizing meditation on the evils of worldliness, it blurs many of the boundaries between church and world and refuses to embrace stark prohibitions against commercial entertainments. Where it is clear in Williams's work that he frequently uses film to promote a particular religious sensibility, *Sunday Sinners'* relationship to Christianity is ambiguous, and religious elements appear alongside stories that include gangsters, cabaret numbers, and comedy routines. The film's reliance on many of the conventions of the musical genre facilitates its conclusion, one that resolves the tensions between church and secular world without the kind of sacrifices of women's lives required in *Go Down, Death* or *Dirty Gertie* or even the serious injury of *The Blood of Jesus*.

The story in *Sunday Sinners* moves between Club Harlem and a black church, both located in a small town, and pits different constituencies within the church against one another and the church's members against "the café people." The story opens in Club Harlem, where Gene Aiken (Norman Astwood), its owner, positions himself largely with the church people from the outset, insisting to his wife and business partner, Corinne (Edna Mae Harris), that it is wrong for the town's young people to be in the club on a Sunday night. Corinne—who we later find out is having an affair with her chauffeur, consorts with gangsters, and is also willing to kill to gain complete control of the club—insists that business is business. In the church world, Rev. Hampton (Earl Cyndor), pastor of a Methodist church, sits with his family in their living room and discusses the problem of the town's young people spending Sunday nights dancing instead of at the church. Their home is modest but neat, all the family members are dressed conservatively, and the teenage children are attentive to their elders. Rev. Hampton, in formal, staid speech, asserts that he does not oppose dancing in general but simply cannot support the activity on Sunday nights. Rev. Hampton concludes that it is not the young people's fault but "the

condition itself. As long as these places are open, our youth will be tempted."
The family decides that the best approach will be for Rev. Hampton to direct his
next sermon at "those café people."

The film includes two long segments set in the church in which Rev. Hampton preaches, providing some of the most explicit commentary in any of these
race movies on the relationship of the church to the commercial arena of the
nightclub. The first, and longer of the two, begins with an external shot of a
large church and cuts to the interior, where we find the congregation listening
to Rev. Hampton and the choir sing. This introduction to the sermon immediately sets *Sunday Sinners* apart from films like Williams's religious melodramas
in that the choir sings a musical number written for the film rather than a traditional hymn. The minister begins his sermon:

> Today the forces for evil have struck up business at the city gates. And it
> is our Christian duty to cry out against these sinners. It has been said that
> without vision the people perish. There can be no greater vision than to
> fight against the forces that seek to lead our youth astray. They call them
> nightclubs, cafés. But as they are run in this town they are nothing more
> than palaces of sin. I ask that we pray that the café people come to the real-
> ization that the youth of any community needs religious guidance for
> good citizenship and that they, the café people, cease in their effort to
> tempt our youth from their Christian and Sabbath duties.

Rev. Hampton's sermon employs a formula found in many race movies, in
which he contrasts an idyllic rural environment with the sinful influences of
urban life. In this case, however, he does not present the city or its commercial
culture as inherently evil. His appeal to the proprietors of the cafés to recognize
the need to cultivate responsible citizenship in young people marks a significant
moment in the film and one that, as we will see shortly, distinguishes Rev.
Hampton from some of the fundamentalist members of his church. Thus, while
his argument is partly theological, it is also largely sociological, focusing on the
political and social needs of the community in the modern world. In contrast to
Rev. Hampton's sociological diagnosis of the city's lures, his discussion of the
merits of the rural notably does not focus on what it offers by way of forming
community, as do many race film discourses on the virtues of rural life. He provides instead a theological justification of the inherent worth of the countryside,
imploring his congregation to "visit God's café." "Go out into the open country
among the birds, the trees and the flowers. Breathe in the good fresh air and
come back with your mind refreshed," he tells the congregation.

Rev. Hampton's second sermon, also directed against "those café people,"
leads to the film's conclusion and the resolution of the tension between the

church and the nightclub. Where his first sermon merely encouraged church members to stay away from the corrupting environment of the nightclub, his second sermon enjoins them to become crusaders in a great holy battle. He emphasizes to the congregation that "at this very moment when our youngsters should be here listening to the word of God, that vile and corrupting gang has got them there in sin and degradation." Rev. Hampton continues, "We've stood just about enough. It's time for us to shed this humble cloak for one of righteous indignation. We should roll up our sleeves and with the good book in one hand, power and might will come to the other. With this hand David killed Goliath; with this hand Samson slew the Philistines; with this hand old Joshua fought the battle of Jericho." Rev. Hampton's sermon impels the congregation to join him on a march to the city and directly into Club Harlem and, in the end, Gene and Rev. Hampton strike a deal for a clean, wholesome place of amusement.

The film engages questions of class status and theological orientation as part of the discussion of urban versus rural and secular entertainments versus the world of the church, and it raises these questions in particularly gendered ways. Rev. Hampton's commitment to confronting "the café people" does not prove sufficient to overcome the criticism and scorn of the board members of his church. Two female board members and a male deacon confront him on a number of occasions, and in the film's presentation of these incidents we see brief discussions of class issues within the church community. The two unnamed "sisters" completely dominate the stuttering deacon in the exchanges. They harangue Rev. Hampton for allowing the members of the church to participate in a range of secular and commercial entertainments, most especially for permitting the men's club to play cards, for allowing a church club to conduct a raffle to raise funds, and for encouraging "devilish youngsters fighting and knocking each other around in their underwear." When the minister explains that he supports wholesome exercise and supervised entertainments for the young people, one of the women counters that the boys should be out working instead. The discussion continues, growing more heated, as Rev. Hampton underscores his sense of the relationship between church and citizenship:

Rev. Hampton: Those youngsters are the very foundation of our church, our race.

Sister #1: Race and Church are going to have a mighty weak foundation.

Sister #2: And we're going to take you in charge for your laxitiveness [*sic*].

Here the film associates these women's rigid theological approach to modern entertainments with their class status, marked as below that of Rev. Hampton and his family, both because of their fundamentalism and their lack of education.

The film ridicules these women for their beliefs and portrays them as inappropriate representatives of black religiosity because of their theological conservatism.

In addition to the class conflict between the women on the church board and the minister, the film sets out another class conflict between Club Harlem, an up-scale club with mild entertainments—the music is not marked as "black" and the dancing is "modest"—and the 7–11 club, a small juke joint run by Bootsie (Sydney Easton) and Mamie (Mamie Smith). Eli (Alex Lovejoy), Rev. Hampton's brother-in-law, is a regular at the 7–11, drinking to excess and constantly talking about just needing to "get a little capital" in order to get some scheme or other off the ground. This plot line contains within it a range of problematic stereotypes, most notably that of Chin (Al Young), a Chinese laundry owner who enters into one of Eli and Bootsie's schemes. Inspired by Rev. Hampton's charge to "visit God's café," the three go out into the country and discover a type of mud that they eventually use to make an expensive beauty product. Where, at the film's conclusion, Club Harlem is saved by the elimination of Corinne and her gangster friends from the scene, the 7–11 club and its regulars cannot be redeemed in the context of their own environment. In the end, it takes the success of Eli's scheme and new-found money to incorporate the men and their wives, somewhat uncomfortably, into the upscale world of Club Harlem.

Sunday Sinners stands in contrast to films like Spencer Williams's religious melodramas in its reliance on the structures of the Hollywood musical. Susan Hayward has noted that the musical is, almost by necessity, a self-referential genre that devotes a great deal of attention to justifying its own existence, as, for example, with the putting-on-a-show musical.[29] *Sunday Sinners* justifies its reliance on the structure of the musical by setting part of the story in a nightclub and, within that venue, focusing on the preparations for an amateur contest to choose the club's new featured act. The film's use of the strategies of the musical genre does not remain confined to the nightclub, however, and musical elements appear very clearly within the arena of the church. Recall that the song that introduces Rev. Hampton's first sermon is more like a musical number than a church hymn. It is important for the film's conclusion (a rapprochement between church and nightclub) that the musical also inhabits the space of the church. Rick Altman observes that "cause and effect are fairly tenuous in the musical and that it is less a case of chronology or psychological motivation than one of paralleling stories in a comparative mode."[30] This comparative analysis in musicals takes place, he argues, through a pairing of seemingly irreconcilable opposites which the musical ultimately resolves. As Hayward notes, "The musical therefore functions ideologically to resolve the fear of difference. In this way, it functions as a text that disguises one of society's paradoxes. By extension, of course, this means that it makes invisible the other sets of para-doxes that are inherent in society, thereby ensuring society's stability."[31] With the danger of Corinne, as the embodiment of the contamination that the secu-lar commercial sphere represents, contained, Rev. Hampton and Gene come to an agreement that permits room for the church and Club Harlem to coexist in peace, thus resolving what at first seemed to be an intractable conflict. Other tensions in evidence in this film do not get resolved, however, but merely masked by the resolution of tension between church and nightclub, including profound gender and class conflicts as well as different approaches to worship style. Nevertheless, the audience leaves assured that commitment to the church and enjoyment of secular entertainments can be reconciled, a decidedly differ-ent conclusion than that found in Williams's body of work.

One cannot help but notice that the attention devoted to constructing and reconstructing African American religious leadership in relation to urban com-mercial culture takes place in particularly gendered ways in many of the race movies that take up religious themes. Certainly, struggles over women's access to religious leadership have not been confined to black Christian contexts and predate the period in which these films were produced. The increasing urban-ization of African Americans in the early twentieth century and the religious changes that resulted from migration make the filmic representations of debates about the gendering of black church communities especially notewor-thy. The future of the ministry in black communities was of particular concern in these films, and time and again audiences were treated to models of minis-ters who were useful, productive race men or counterexamples of unscrupu-lous, uneducated, selfish preachers. Although many of these films place black women in central roles in their religious communities and present them as moral exemplars—as in the case of Sister Caroline—they also insist on the lim-its of black women's spiritual power. *Go Down, Death* gives evidence of a certain anxiety about the strong presence of women in black churches. Here and in his earlier film, *The Blood of Jesus*, Williams presents women as the most important moral agents in black church life and, in many ways, praises them. At the same time, this film seems to require them to step aside, mobilizing them as sacrifices for the greater good. Perhaps not surprisingly, even in stories in which women successfully defend their church communities against a corrupt minister, there is no sense that these women can ever make appropriate religious leaders. *Sunday Sinners'* marking of the church women as ignorant and fundamentalist bars them from any kind of leadership in the world of the film. Although coun-tering the relentlessly negative representations of African American religiosity in Hollywood films with a complex range of images, race movies nevertheless remain invested in the traditional institutional structures of black communities.

The films valorize black women's religious experiences in ways never done in mainstream American popular culture, and they recognize the reality that the black church no longer constitutes the dominant part of the black public sphere. They do not, however, take an approach that argues for the possibility of black women as religious leaders within the changing institution of the black church. The message of many of these films concerning the relationship between religion, gender, and black commercial culture positions women either as debilitating in their predominance in the sphere of the church or as representatives of immorality unleashed in their participation in commercial culture.

The body of surviving race movies produced from the 1910s through the 1940s includes films that focus on a range of themes and genres from historical dramas and murder mysteries to comedies and musicals. Religious melodramas and films whose stories were located in religious contexts represent a small subset of these films, but while Thomas Cripps is correct in pointing out the self-contained nature of the subgenre of black religious films, religious themes appear across the range of race films in ways that have not received sufficient attention.[32] As a result of this brief examination, it becomes apparent how important questions of religious sensibilities and practice were to the race movie project of describing, defining, proscribing, and projecting African American communal identity in the 1940s. It is also striking how much of the conversation about religion within this subset of race movies takes place through an exploration of conflict between the church and the nightclub. To a large extent, the nightclub—which appears as a stand-in for a range of entertainment and social venues in African American communities, from the juke joint, pub, and saloon to the dance hall and upscale nightclub—did pose a particular challenge to black churches in urban contexts. In addition, many black Christians saw the newest and most popular music and dance styles as lewd and sinful, and the films express some of this discomfort, and some, like *Sunday Sinners*, try to reconcile the two in ways that would recognize but limit the authority of the church.

Despite the attention in many of these films to the commercial entertainment world of the nightclub as well as to other urban commercial enterprises as a possible threat to the church, the films are not forthcoming about the race movie industry's potential complicity in the conflict they chart. African American film critics and other commentators on race movies generally argued for the likely benefits of community control of popular culture images, and many asserted their belief that the goal of producing movies should be the uplift of black communities. They also noted with consternation the degree to which many race film makers resorted to sensation in their films' stories and in the marketing of the movies.[33] In many ways, then, from the point of view of some black Christians, the movies posed as much of a danger to the moral integrity of black communities as any other segment of commercial culture in the period. Examining this arena of competing institutions and commercial enterprises reveals a rich discussion in film about how to manage the relationship between the church and other institutions in light of the interest of many African Americans in broadening the scope of black social and civil life as they moved into the latter part of the twentieth century.

Notes

I am grateful for the comments and assistance of students and faculty at the various institutions where I presented this work in progress. Parts of this work were also presented at the 1999 Berkshire Conference on the History of Women and the 2001 meeting of the American Historical Association.

1. The classical Hollywood cinema is defined by both stylistic markers and issues relating to production and exhibition. Bordwell, Staiger, and Thompson argue that the classical Hollywood system was in place from 1917 until 1960 and involved a particular style of narrative that emphasizes character and motivation, causation, and the creation of a coherent world in the use of space, composition, sound, and editing. The primary emphasis was on realism. In addition, the vertically integrated studio system in which studios controlled production, distribution, and exhibition of films prevailed. See David Bordwell, Kristin Thompson, and Janet Staiger, *The Classical Hollywood Cinema: Film Style and Mode of Production to 1960* (New York: Columbia University Press, 1985).
2. Jack Alicoate, ed., *The 1930 Film Daily Yearbook of Motion Pictures* (New York: Wid's Films and Film Folk, 1930), 794–795.
3. Film historians have estimated that in the period from 1912 to 1948 filmmakers produced more than 350 race movies. Prior to 1929, when sound film began to become the standard, many of the companies that produced race films were black-owned. The financial burden of sound production, along with the Great Depression, put many of these companies out of business. During the 1930s and 1940s, race movies came from white-owned production companies as well as from joint ventures between black and white producers and directors. Race movies declined in the late 1940s as film production became increasingly expensive and as Hollywood began to make greater use of African American actors and actresses. See G. William Jones, *Black Cinema Treasures Lost and Found* (Denton: University of North Texas Press, 1991); and Pearl Bowser, "From Harlem to Hollywood," Program Notes, American Museum of the Moving Image, 1990. On audiences for race movies in the silent film era, see Pearl Bowser and Louise Spence, *Writing Himself into History: Oscar Micheaux, His Silent Films, and His Audiences* (New Brunswick, N.J.: Rutgers University Press, 2000).
4. On race records, see Paul Oliver, *Songsters and Saints: Vocal Traditions on Race Records* (Cambridge: Cambridge University Press, 1984).

5. See Judith Weisenfeld, "For Rent: 'Cabin in the Sky': Race, Religion, and Representational Quagmires in American Film," *Semeia* 74 (1996): 147–165.

6. None of the available secondary sources provide any information on Williams's religious affiliation. His interest in explicitly Christian religious melodramas certainly supports a conclusion that he was a believing Christian. It also seems very possible that he was Roman Catholic, given his interest in St. Martin de Porres (and his plans to make a film called *Brother Martin, Servant of Jesus*) and his childhood in Louisiana, in addition to his frequent reliance on a theological world in which intermediary beings intercede with God on behalf of humans. For a discussion of Williams's plans for *Brother Martin*, for which only a trailer survives, see Arthur L. Terry, "Genre and Divine Causality in the Religious Films of Spencer Williams, Jr." (Ph.D. diss., Regent University, 1995), 162.

7. Clarence Taylor, *The Black Churches of Brooklyn* (New York: Columbia University Press, 1994), 69, 70.

8. On the black church as public sphere, see Evelyn Brooks Higginbotham, *Righteous Discontent: The Women's Movement in the Black Baptist Church, 1880–1920* (Cambridge: Harvard University Press, 1993), 1–18.

9. Williams directed *Tenderfeet* (Midnight Productions, 1928).

10. *The Bronze Buckaroo* (Hollywood Productions, 1938); *Two-Gun Man from Harlem* (Merit Pictures, 1938); *Harlem Rides the Range* (Hollywood Pictures, 1939); *Son of Ingagi* (Sack Amusement Enterprises, 1940). Williams's short story "House of Horror" served as the basis for the script for *Son of Ingagi*. John Kisch and Edward Mapp, eds., *A Separate Cinema: Fifty Years of Black Cast Posters* (New York: Noonday Press, 1992), 21.

11. *The Blood of Jesus* (1941); *Marching On!* (1943); *Of One Blood* (1944); *Go Down, Death* (1944); *The Girl in Room 20* (1946); *Dirty Gertie from Harlem, U.S.A.* (1946); *Beale Street Mama* (1946); *Juke Joint* (1947). Jones, *Black Cinema Treasures*, 31–34; *Amsterdam News*, March 6, 1929.

12. Thomas Cripps, *Black Film as Genre* (Bloomington: Indiana University Press, 1978), 86. Williams later appeared as Andrew Brown on the short-lived television series *Amos 'n' Andy* (1951–1953).

13. See Weisenfeld, "For Rent," and Terry, "Genre and Divine Causality," for discussions of *The Blood of Jesus*.

14. There is a precedent for Williams's approach to sacred drama in black church theater productions, such as Atlanta's Big Bethel African Methodist Episcopal Church's production of *Heaven Bound*, written in 1930 by two female members of the congregation. The play shows twenty-four pilgrims and their various journeys toward heaven or hell, with saints, angels, and the devil also appearing as major characters. Williams's costuming choices in *The Blood of Jesus* are quite similar to those in this play. See Gregory D. Coleman, *We're Heaven Bound! Portrait of a Black Sacred Drama* (Athens: University of Georgia Press, 1992).

15. Terry, "Genre and Divine Causality," 211.

16. Poster for *Go Down, Death!* in Kisch and Mapp, *Separate Cinema*, 23.

17. The credits list the actors' names but do not associate them with their characters. The cast for *Go Down, Death* includes Myra Hemmings, Samuel H. James, Eddie L. Houston, and Spencer Williams. The poem "Go Down, Death" is part of James Weldon

Johnson's 1927 collection *God's Trombones: Seven Negro Sermons in Verse* (New York: Viking Press, 1927).

18. All dialogue included in this essay represents my own transcriptions.

19. On Sallman's religious art see Colleen McDannell, *Material Christianity: Religion and Popular Culture in America* (New Haven, Conn.: Yale University Press, 1995); David Morgan, *Icons of American Protestantism: The Art of Warner Sallman* (New Haven: Yale University Press, 1996); and David Morgan, *Visual Piety: A History and Theory of Popular Religious Images* (Berkeley and Los Angeles: University of California Press, 1998).

20. The advertising for the film claims that the story was by James Weldon Johnson, the writer and National Association for the Advancement of Colored People (NAACP) activist who had died in 1938. Johnson's poem, "Go Down, Death," tells the story of the death of Sister Caroline in Yamacraw, and Rev. Moon's sermon follows the text exactly.

21. We see the gates of hell, the devil devouring bodies and images of people tormented in hell, all images from a silent film of Dante's *Inferno*.

22. Arthur L. Terry writes of Williams's work: "Even for work of their time, these films leave something to be desired aesthetically. They all suffer from jump cuts, poor editing, continuity problems, and uneven acting. Certainly a percentage of this is due to age and the restoration process of the prints, but many problems were inherent in the production. . . . For the most part, actors had to be taken from wherever they could be found, and there was little or no time (or money) to allow for rehearsal, blocking, rewrites, or retakes. . . . In a very real sense, we are seeing part of a process more than a finished product." Arthur L. Terry, "Run Chile Run: Critical Analyses of Three Films By Spencer Williams," *Sync: The Regent Journal of Film and Video* 1, no. 2 (spring 1994) <http://www.regent.edu/acad/schcom/rojc/terry.html> (July 1, 1998).

23. On film and melodrama, see Christine Gledhill, ed., *Home Is Where the Heart Is: Studies in Melodrama and the Woman's Film* (London: BFI Books, 1987).

24. Jane Gaines, "*The Scar of Shame*: Skin Color and Caste in Black Silent Melodrama," in *Representing Blackness: Issues in Film and Video*, ed. Valerie Smith (New Brunswick, N.J.: Rutgers University Press, 1997), 63–64, 69.

25. Christine Gledhill, "The Melodramatic Field: An Investigation," in Gledhill, *Home Is Where the Heart Is*, 33.

26. In many ways, *Dirty Gertie*'s story follows that of Somerset Maugham's story "Miss Thompson," produced as *Sadie Thompson* (Gloria Swanson Productions, 1928), directed by Raoul Walsh and starring Gloria Swanson, and again as *Rain* (United Artists, 1932), directed by Lewis Milestone and starring Walter Huston and Joan Crawford.

27. Susan Hayward, *Key Concepts in Cinema Studies* (London: Routledge, 1996), 55.

28. William Greaves, an actor in a number of race films, remembered the Goldberg brothers as important financial supporters of race films in their heyday. He argued that such partnerships came about because many American Jews in the 1940s, suffering from anti-Semitism and "the exclusion of Jewish businessmen and Jewish political figures throughout the whole length and breadth of this country," identified with African Americans and, in turn, felt accepted as business partners in film. Jones, *Black Cinema Treasures*, 163. Arthur Dreifuss was born in Frankfurt, Germany, in

1908. He directed a number of race movies at the beginning of his career, including *Mystery in Swing* (Aetna, 1940) and *Murder on Lenox Avenue* (Colonnade Pictures, 1941).

29. Hayward, *Key Concepts*, 241.
30. Ibid., 242.
31. Ibid., 244.
32. Cripps, *Black Film*, 86.
33. For a useful discussion of the range of responses to race movies, see Bowser and Spence, *Writing Himself into History*.

Nine

Kathryn Jay

"In Vogue with Mary"

How Catholic Girls Created an
Urban Market for Modesty

A 1954 fashion show held at a Catholic high school in El Paso, Texas, featured adolescent girls modeling recent fashions, with one important twist. As they walked down the runway in various "modern—even ultra modern" fashions, a classmate provided running commentary that encouraged audience members to think of each outfit adorning the Virgin Mary as she ran errands "in Nazareth's shopping center." The narrator assured her audience that if Mary were to pay a spiritual visit to the 1950s, she would be most comfortable in a "sack dress of beige linen, smartly set off with a navy blue suede belt with gold buckle."[1] Because Mary was an attractive, even beautiful woman, "many eyes were attracted to the beauty of this reserved, yet magnetic Jewess as she paid for her purchases over the counter of that Semitic super market." The "Blessed Lady" served as a role model who combined spiritual modesty with an enthusiasm for looking attractive and participating in consumer culture. For the girls emulating Mary in this fashion show, a "winsome dress of polished cotton, glittering with rhinestones" could be a demonstration of religious belief as well as a "smart buy" at the local department store. This perspective assured girls that they could be "in vogue with Mary," earning approval from the Church for their modesty and from their peers for their style. Indeed, female adolescent Catholic culture depended on this appropriation of consumer fashion: middle-class Catholic girls constructed an urban religious identity that dressed—and expressed—their piety in eye-catching ball gowns and "sack dresses of beige linen."

Texas high school girls who wanted to look like a fashionable "Blessed Lady" were part of a larger national movement that integrated sacred concerns and commercial culture. Between 1947 and 1963, thousands of urban Catholics joined an organization with the unwieldy—and decidedly unspiritual—moniker of Supply the Demand for the Supply. Known as SDS, the group conducted local "modesty crusades" that encouraged adolescent girls to approach local shopkeepers and department store owners, asking them to stock and sell modest yet stylish garments.[2] The group combined the idiom of modesty with continuing social activism to convince middle-class adolescent Catholic girls of their economic influence on the marketplace. Urban teenagers used the all-girl organization to negotiate between the demands of adolescent beauty culture and the teachings of their faith, to become cultural producers instead of merely passive consumers.[3] The message of SDS was often conservative, but the group's activities provided teenage girls with a sense of personal agency and nurtured the development of a spiritual identity that grew out of consumer-based youth culture.

Whether talking to store owners about prom gowns or competing in fashion shows or working on "fashion caravans" designed to spread the message of modesty, SDS became a small part of the fashion industry itself.[4] Adolescent girls in SDS learned the language of commercial beauty culture but spoke in a particular dialect that resonated among those in their peer group. The SDS message appealed to adolescent girls precisely because it imagined the Virgin Mary in the popular "sack dress" style, shopping for appealing clothes and accessories at the market. Members vehemently rejected many of the fashions popular in the 1940s and 1950s as dangerous to their faith, yet they remained eager to look stylish and to participate in urban youth culture. To facilitate this, the group imagined a space in which consumer products and religious belief merged. They worked to sell purity and chastity as well as a sense of positive Catholic identity, all woven into a demure bathing suit or modest formal dress. This essay argues that, for SDS members, urban commercial culture served as the key mediating space between the concomitant pressures of participating in urban youth culture and remaining a spiritually devout Catholic.

Modesty crusades were spiritually motivated, but they also need to be understood as a part of a burgeoning youth culture obsessed with fashion and style and centered on prosperity and the possibilities of consumerism. World War II and the increasing economic opportunities of wartime work helped to create a teen culture that emphasized "immense spending power, consumer ritual, and peer pressure to be in fashion."[5] Youth culture during the postwar period was "a series of decisions about personal appearance and entertainment," dependent on a vision of teenagers as a separate category, an isolated market with special needs and concerns.[6] Clothing and style were critical to postwar youth culture because "fashions and style expressed a variety of youth 'folk' subcultures, and sometimes challenged the hegemony of the dominant culture."[7] Style became "a manifestation or a symbol of difference," a way for teenagers to purchase a sense of identity.[8] SDS nurtured a sense of Catholic style within this emerging marketplace of identity, allowing teenagers to envision themselves as a separate—and very important—category within the Church and encouraging members to use fashion choices to help them define their own religious sense of self. Unlike the well-known images from the 1950s of teenagers wearing ducktails, dungarees, poodle skirts, and tight sweaters, SDS encouraged modest frocks, serving as a conservative counterpoint to the hegemony of a dominant youth culture focused on sexuality rather than religion. Nevertheless, the girls of SDS wanted to be invited to the prom. Religious belief did not preclude intense engagement with the fashions and styles of youth culture.

SDS girls focused on the spiritual reformation of fashion because the fashion industry focused on them. Advertisers in the fashion, beauty, and entertainment industries began to target teenage girls in the 1950s, with "sex appeal" their strongest selling point. The allure of Hollywood's "sweater girl" Lana Turner, for example, helped to sell 4.5 million "breast pads" in 1948 to girls and women hoping to achieve the same buxom look.[9] Magazines like *Seventeen* helped to create a "teenage market" for all kinds of consumable items but especially for clothing like "Pert and Pretty Teenage Hats, Hi-Campus Caper Sweaters, and Kickerino Boots," as well as an overwhelming variety of beauty products.[10] By 1952 the cosmetics industry had sold over $1 billion in beauty products, and teenage girls spent over $20 million on lipstick alone every year. According to historian Wini Breines, "white, middle-class girls in the 1950s learned to construct and imagine themselves almost exclusively through consumer goods and images in the media."[11] And it was an image that heavily emphasized the importance of appearance. Hygiene films shown in high school emphasized how crucial appearance was for high school girls. In *Body Care and Grooming* (1947), for example, the heroine wins a boyfriend after she gets new shoes and neater socks, while in *Habit Patterns* (1954), sloppy teenager Barbara sobs after being rejected by her peers because of her dressing habits.[12] This beauty-dominated youth culture—imposed from above and from within youth culture—became the standard against which personal experience was measured for adolescents, independent of class, race, ethnic, or religious differences. In a survey on the impact of fashion, one Catholic teenager emphasized the power of advertising to determine style, claiming that "if a mode of dress is advertised enough," girls would accept it even if they believed it was immoral.[13] This vision of popular culture's hegemonic control left adolescent girls seemingly powerless, subject to the tremendous influence of a consumer culture aimed squarely at them, and encouraged to scrutinize every aspect of their personal appearance. For high school girls, the pervasive message of the 1950s was that feminine success was defined by looks—the right makeup, the most fashionable dress, the smoothest skin, the most stylish haircut—not by intellectual abilities or religious values.

This made the bodies of Catholic girls a site of particular contestation in the 1950s. While the fashion industry emphasized the importance of external beauty, the language of the Church presented those same young women's bodies as markers of social decay. Immodestly dressed adolescents reflected the perceived moral failings of a nation, one that preferred Hollywood glamour to Church-based morality.[14] Many in the Catholic hierarchy created a rigid dichotomy between secular styles and religious belief, believing that when adolescent girls wore low-cut blouses and revealing skirts, they abandoned the tenets of their faith. There were other consequences as well. In an oft-cited pastoral letter on immodesty, Archbishop Albert Meyer of Milwaukee (later Cardinal of Chicago) argued that a lack of fashion decency dangerously challenged masculine authority in the home. For Meyer, "indecent" female bodies threatened family stability by undermining traditional gender roles, while modest female bodies symbolized women who accepted their "natural" roles as wives and mothers.[15] Clothing stood as a stark symbol of moral resolve. Like many, Meyer also maintained that Catholic men—both clergy and laity—had an ethical responsibility to criticize and control feminine fashions and female behavior. This was especially true of teen-age girls, whose dangerous bodies were held directly responsible for the spiritual downfall of teen-age boys. Adolescent girls sinned by wearing immodest clothing because they "seriously excite[d] the sexual urge of the average boy or man."[16] Immodesty was a temptation that few teenage boys could resist. Priests compared the impact of immodest clothing to the evils of Stalin and Hitler and the horrors of unleashed atomic energy, and young women who wore Hollywood-inspired fashions were termed "feminine germ-carriers."[17] As a result, Catholic girls who took their fashion cues from Hollywood and an international fashion industry seemed poised both to ignore their own religiously mandated roles as submissive wives and mothers and to undermine the weaker spiritual abilities of young men. As SDS members well realized, the clothes they wore mattered.

SDS needs to be understood as a part of this Catholic worldview. The group reflected a deep and ongoing tension between secular desires and spiritual obedience for Catholic girls in the 1950s. To understand how SDS articulated and managed this tension, this essay starts with a historical overview, examining the beginnings of this national movement in two midwestern cities in the late 1940s, with particular focus on an early citywide campaign in Cleveland.[18] From Cleveland, the organization spread to Chicago, where it found its strongest base in the 1950s. The essay explores how the Chicago SDS set national standards for the movement and found symbolic and practical local success in reshaping the language of youth fashion. After this historical background, the essay details how the group created a space in which attending dances, designing ball gowns, and organizing fashion shows merged the divergent concerns of Church and beauty culture. By negotiating between the moralistic demands of the Church, the advertising campaigns of the fashion industry, and a youth culture increasingly obsessed with appearance and style, Catholic girls in SDS created new meanings for their fashion choices. Modesty campaigns engaged popular culture within the boundaries of the urban marketplace—allowing girls to use their influence as consumers to mediate divergent claims on how their bodies should look and how they should behave. In adopting the industry's language and advertising tactics, SDS crafted new ways to experience and symbolize adolescent religious life. In SDS, behaving in a "Mary-like" manner and looking fashionable carried similar weight, as the group blurred the boundaries between the secular and the sacred in ways that resonated with the lived experiences of teens in the 1950s.

"Be a Cover Girl": The History of SDS

SDS began at a Cincinnati Catholic high school in 1947. Inspired by an article in the national Catholic teen magazine *Queen's Work* called "No Money for Indecency," young women at Seton Hall High School began to educate themselves about how the fashion marketplace worked. Members started by doing consciousness-raising among their peers. The girls made posters reading "Modesty is the Best Policy," "Don't be a deadbeat—be neat and sweet," "Keep It Under Cover," and "Be a Cover Girl"; sold doughnuts with the slogan "No Dough for Immodesty"; and held a mock burial ceremony for two-piece bathing suits.[19] In combining symbolic protest with basic economic principles about supply and demand, the Seton Hall crusade laid the groundwork for campaigns across the country. After their initial school-based campaign, SDS organized among all the high schools in the diocese of Cincinnati, with four thousand members by April 1948. Each new high school chapter was assigned a local department store to contact, with their goal to increase the variety and styles of one-piece bathing suits available for sale.[20] As part of this effort, the group sponsored a swimsuit design contest and sent the three winning designs to the Janzten Company, a bathing suit manufacturer.[21] They even succeeded in getting a public swimming pool operator to offer a free summer pass to the student who won the contest.[22] The girls' efforts to reform fashion became so well known that the archbishop of Cincinnati asked them to expand their efforts to include opposing offensive movies.[23] The archbishop's request for further activities by SDS reflected the kind of approval and endorsement that teen-age girls often received for their "fashion" efforts, but while he saw SDS as part of the Catholic opposition to Hollywood's commercial vision, he missed entirely the group's engagement with existing fashion trends and adolescent leisure opportunities.

SDS promoted a merger of morality and youth-based fun; instead of working to ban bathing suits, they intended to expand the selections so that they could be comfortable spending the summer at the pool.

SDS spread quickly from Cincinnati to Cleveland and other midwestern cities. In Cleveland, thirty-five girls from six Catholic high schools met in December 1948 to start a local chapter. After a kickoff style show featuring students modeling acceptable prom formals for their peers, the Cleveland SDS quickly moved their program into the community.[24] Their first efforts to talk with department store managers prompted ridicule and disbelief that adolescent girls would want more "modest" prom gowns. As a result, these public actions earned the girls a great deal of publicity within the Catholic community. A two-column headline blared "Girls Seeking Modest Gowns Tell of 'Insults' in Downtown Stores," and four pictures—including two "modeling" shots (one of a young woman in a prom gown, the other of a young woman in a "modest playsuit")—dominated the December 17 edition of the diocesan newspaper. Their determination in the face of marketplace opposition and public scorn earned the organization the local approval of the diocesan superintendent of schools, giving their student-run campaign important institutional support. The superintendent of Cleveland's parochial schools sent an open letter to the students and principals of the twenty-one high schools in the diocese, urging all seven thousand girls to join SDS and asking each school principal to support their efforts.[25] On one level, then, SDS efforts to convert store clerks and managers were read as a powerful expression of Catholic faith in the face of secular resistance and ridicule.[26]

At the same time, these citywide attempts at reform belie the idea of a closed "Catholic ghetto" in the 1950s, as adolescent girls moved outside their Catholic community to influence public values and "clean up" urban society. They talked to department store owners and salesclerks with a conviction that their voices mattered and that their message would resonant with non-Catholic girls. Mary Ellen Sloan of Lourdes Academy argued that "girls in public high schools will go along the same as Catholics" after SDS convinced them that modesty was important.[27] Like the Legion of Decency, through which Catholics regularly boycotted "indecent movies" in order to preserve society's moral values, SDS members maintained it was their right as consumers to provide all shoppers with an alternative to the mainstream fashion industry. In addition, while activism for modesty provided Catholic girls with a spiritually distinct identity, the arguments they made for modest fashions assumed that other local teenagers and many adults would eventually agree with them.

Though store managers found this initial SDS action amusing rather than threatening and clearly did not view Catholic girls as a consumer power, the teenagers of SDS were quite certain of their goals and of their potential strength in the fashion marketplace. As one SDS member explained: "We didn't go in to argue. We don't want to antagonize the stores. But we want them to realize what we want. And we won't buy anything else." Told by a salesclerk that "strapless gowns were the style now," another SDS participant replied that "styles are a matter of opinion and opinions change. But this is a matter of principle and principles don't change."[28] Sixty-one girls promised to make their own prom gowns rather than buy them off the rack, carefully pointing out that, at an estimated $30 per gown, the stores stood to lose at least $1,830 in profits. SDS members had quickly mastered the language of the marketplace. When they spoke to other teenagers or to other Catholics, SDS emphasized the spiritual need for modesty and the threat some fashions posed to local community values. When talking to store owners, members stressed the bottom line—their revenue-producing abilities as teenage girls. By the end of 1948, the movement had already begun to frame the meaning of their activism as both moral suasion and economic commonsense, a merger of religious and market values that became increasingly powerful as SDS grew.

The widespread negative publicity surrounding the initial store canvass pushed department store owners to reconsider their position and to propose a meeting with the leaders of the organization.[29] By mid January 1949, at a city-wide rally of SDS members, Cleveland store owners had changed their public tune. At the rally, attended by approximately four hundred girls and representatives of all the major stores in Cleveland, SDS demanded "clothes that comply with Christian principles and conscience" and "an end to Paris-dictated fashions and a determined stand to show the world this generation is not a bunch of 'milk-sops.'"[30] The reference to "Paris-dictated fashions" indicates a persistent thread of SDS rhetoric, that European designers and degraded European standards threatened the morality of American women. On a local level, this was an effective technique for finding common ground with store owners, since it shifted blame away from the shopkeepers and assumed shared local values that had been subverted by "mass culture" and other external evils. Indeed, newspaper stories noted that department store representatives "were unanimous in their willingness to co-operate with the girls," often blaming "outsiders" for the kinds of dresses they stocked. One store's clothing buyer gave SDS students a strapless formal and asked them to remodel it so that it would be acceptable. Another promised to listen to Catholic girls' requests and order what they wanted. By joining their voices in organized protest, SDS members had forced department stores to take their consumer desires seriously.

Both store representatives and SDS students acknowledged that the problem was larger than the offering of local stores—that sometimes stores sold "immodest" clothing because it was the only style made available by national chains—yet SDS members remained confident in their ability to use consumer power to win the fashion battle.[31] And why not? Even if very little actual change came from this Cleveland SDS campaign, it must have been a heady feeling for teen-age girls to hear major department store managers promising to answer their demands. It would have been equally exciting to find their high school efforts regularly on the front page of the Catholic newspaper, applauded by important religious figures in the diocese. Cleveland's high school girls succeeded by appropriating the language of commercial culture and applying it to questions of moral behavior, creating a space for adolescent female agency in two institutions—the Church and the marketplace—dominated by adult men. At the same time, they helped other adolescents make sense of the bewildering array of consumer choices available to them, offering fashion parameters that promised teen-age girls that they could be in style with their Church and their peers.

SDS had equal symbolic—and occasionally practical—success in other cities, with its strongest chapter emerging in Chicago. SDS emerged from a student convention sponsored by Chicago's Inter-Student Catholic Action (CISCA) where "various problems such as movies, drinking, dating, clean speech and modesty" were being discussed. CISCA, which promoted ongoing apostolic and social actions around issues of racial injustice, housing, and indecent literature, was the major site of Catholic activism for teenagers in the archdiocese and became the national home for SDS, producing pamphlets and outlines that teenagers in other cities could order.[32] As a part of CISCA, SDS established a "Fashion Board" composed of girls from high schools around the archdiocese who met regularly to set policies and plan strategy. Their mission was to help other teenage girls find ways to combine fashionable styles and spiritual awareness. Like other emerging lay Catholic Action groups of the 1950s, SDS used the popular approach of "like helping like" encouraged by Pope Pius XI's 1931 encyclical, *Quadragesimo Anno*.[33] In their outreach to teenagers, SDS was part of a move away from a completely priest-centered model of Catholic activism. Instead, "like to like" activism encouraged individuals to focus on the spiritual problems that most concerned their social group—workers tackled labor issues, married couples approached questions affecting the family, and teenagers tried to resolve the seeming conflict between spirituality and youth culture. Catholic Action asked lay Catholics to "accept the responsibility of re-christianizing their family life, work and social life."[34] The rhetoric of Catholic Action assumed that the "like to like" approach would be effective for two reasons: first, people would be working on issues about which they were experts, and second, others would listen to their message because they shared similar struggles and concerns. Its practical effect was to give greater spiritual agency to the girls of SDS, making them standard-bearers on both teenage fashion and teenage modesty.

Under the direction of Rev. Francis Lawlor, Chicago girls created the most far-reaching and successful program to convince store owners to stock modest fashions for sale. Fashion Board members argued that it was a "known fact" that "designers and manufactors [*sic*] will produce only the kind of clothing for which there a great or a steady demand," so their goals centered equally on creating a demand for modesty and finding a regular supply.[35] In 1951 they approached department store owner Morris Sachs and asked him to stock "modest formals," promising to mobilize Catholics girls to buy them from his stores. Sachs, who realized a promising merchandising opportunity when he saw it, agreed and also offered $1,000 for prizes in a citywide design contest for modest fashions run by SDS. In a 1952 photograph featured on the front page of the Chicago archdiocesan newspaper, the middle-aged businessman sits grinning at a desk covered with sketches of prom gowns. Surrounded by seven nicely dressed teenage girls, Sachs points to one gown sketch, with the layout of an advertisement offering "modest" prom formals just peeking out from under the pile of sketches on the desk.[36] After Sachs bought more than twenty-five hundred SDS-approved dresses for his stores in 1952, another retailer "approached the SDS campaigners and literally begged their approval for his stores. Within a month, he had stocked $20,000 worth of prom gowns which he had ordered on the basis of selections made by the SDS Fashion Board."[37] Other SDS groups followed Chicago's lead; similar efforts to persuade stores to "stock modesty" emerged in New Orleans, St. Louis and Dubuque, Iowa.[38] By 1955, a New York City–based group had convinced sixteen stores in the area to carry SDS-approved styles.[39] All these stories reveal the complexities of the urban marketplace: An adolescent fascination with ball gowns and other markers of beauty culture allowed local store owners the opportunity to capture the Catholic high school prom formal market, to use religious belief as a marketing tool. At the same time, the girls of SDS appropriated consumer items important to secular youth culture and repackaged them as a demonstration of religious identity.

Using the slogan "Fight for your Right to be Modest," the Chicago group published the first set of "standards of dress" for the SDS crusade in 1951.[40] In 1956 they sent a copy of their standards to every Catholic high school in the country.[41] What did SDS girls object to in clothing? Prom formals and two-piece bathing suits attracted the most attention, but the standards also discouraged bare midriffs, strapless swimsuits, and short shorts. They argued that transparent fabrics should not be worn unless "undergarments provide the required coverage" and that sweaters, knit dresses, and wool jerseys "should be of the proper size so as not to unduly and immodestly emphasize the definitely dangerous parts of the body." SDS also set standards for length and coverage, proclaiming that the top of women's clothing should "not be lower, in front, than the line where cleavage begins."[42] Though more detailed and prescriptive—two pages of guidelines broken down by dress category—Chicago standards were similar to a 1948 pledge in Cleveland. There, girls promised not to wear "immodest bathing suits, strapless and low-cut formals and dresses, tight sweaters and shorts and such clothes that might lead myself or others into sin."[43] The contours of modest fashion were fairly clear across time and place. SDS focused its energy on the "definitely dangerous" parts of the body but left room in the standards for personal style and individual tastes.

In Rochester, New York, SDS members sent department store managers a letter detailing the "requirements" of modest formals, including covered shoulders and moderate necklines. They added that jackets and stoles "added to cover the bare shoulders" did not make a strapless dress acceptable.[44] Still, as approximations rather than "sharp lines indicating to the half-inch" where sinful behavior began, SDS standards gave teenage girls and department store managers alike room for interpretations of modesty. And because, as one approving clergy member noted, they "were far from prudish," SDS standards helped religious advisers offer specific instructions to their teenage parishioners with the conviction that students might listen and be convinced.[45] By focusing so clearly on strapless formals and two-piece bathing suits and by refraining from "measuring modesty by a yardstick," SDS created standards that made demonstrating religious conviction through clothing choices relatively painless.[46]

As a result, instead of focusing on hemlines, SDS worked to convince Catholic girls that modesty could be fashionable. In the same pamphlet in which Chicago's SDS group published the group's national standards, they explained the crux of their campaign. They demanded "modest clothing that is both beautiful and stylish. All who cooperate in this effort are asked to insist on these same points so that SDS may everywhere be recognized as being synonymous with 1) beauty, 2) style, and 3) modesty."[47] The relationship between these broader guidelines and the Sachs department stores' advertising decisions are clear. Sachs placed multiple advertisements in the Chicago archdiocesan newspaper, the *New World*, featuring "a charming collection of S.D.S. approved summer formals." Because SDS had made inroads into many Catholic parochial schools, Sachs assumed that modesty, especially when combined with a gown described as a "dance frock with the charm of a Southern belle," would sell well.[48] And despite Sachs's assertion at the bottom of each advertisement that his stores were "the only stores in Chicago with formals that have been approved by the members of the S.D.S. fashion board of CISCA," other department stores in Chicago followed Sachs's lead, also advertising SDS-approved formals in the *New World*. A May 1952 advertisement for the Wm. A. Lewis department stores, whose slogan was "where the models buy their clothes," featured sketches of two young women in flowing prom gowns "worn by the prettiest girls at the prom." The advertisement promised: "'You don't have to be strapless to be in fashion.' That's what you said, and we agree. Just see the bewitching gowns in our breathtaking collection of S.D.S. approved formals. They're lovelier than you've ever imagined . . . so disarmingly feminine he can't help but fall in love."[49] As the advertisements for both department stores made clear, Catholic girls did not need to sacrifice their attractiveness to boys in order to dress modestly. SDS-approved fashions were "pretty," "breathtaking," "charming," and "bewitching," all adjectives that mattered to adolescent girls eager to be popular on the teenage dating scene. SDS allowed Catholic girls to claim spiritual purity and still attend the prom.

"Formals in Focus": Catholic Youth Culture

Although girls earned widespread media coverage when they approached store owners, fashion shows and formal dances were probably the most popular SDS feature, allowing girls to feel spiritually modest when enjoying participation in the cultural staples of 1950s youth culture. In Cincinnati, for example, SDS sponsored a 1948 citywide formal dance called the Star-Dust Special, where girls were elected "queen and attendants based on personality and modesty."[50] The constant focus on dances and formal gowns demonstrates again that SDS was not opposed to either commercial culture or urban youth culture. SDS expected that members would go to the prom and other school-sponsored dances and would be willing to spend money to get dressed up for big event. They simply wanted more options when choosing their gowns. One of the main reasons that SDS enjoyed success was because its message encouraged young women to create a body image that combined spiritual awareness with fashion sense. SDS members used events popular among high school students to publicize their crusade, suggesting that local chapters write "parodies of popular songs," hold slogan contests, host radio programs, sponsor dances, and, if possible, televise an SDS fashion show.[51] A 1957 formal dance in Milwaukee called the Lourdes Ball, sponsored by students involved in a year-long campaign for modest dress for young women, featured high school couples dressed in their finest. Pictures of the young couples emphasize the relationship between modesty crusades and the kind of dress-up style found in high schools around the country. Many of the young women look like princesses, with floor-length taffeta skirts, white gloves, and tiaras in their hair.[52] SDS encouraged young women to attend proms and other formal dances and to take a proactive role in teen culture.

Another part of the effort to partake in the teen culture of appearance were SDS-run fashion shows. The Chicago SDS organization held yearly fashion shows called "Formals in Focus"; photographs of the winners modeling their designs appeared yearly in the Catholic newspaper.[53] Although the Church adamantly opposed beauty contests, fashion shows emerged as a key activity for Catholic girls and women alike, an opportunity to model formal dresses and casual wear with Church approval. In Peoria, Illinois, for example, more than a thousand people attended an SDS fashion show.[54] These very popular "modest fashion shows" provided a spiritual alternative to what Boston Archbishop Richard Cushing called the "immoral business of beauty contests," even as they featured young women parading about on stage. Perhaps this was because SDS fashion shows aimed at showing off fashion designs for an audience of other women, rather than hoping for masculine approval. Or perhaps it was because despite their emphasis on appearance and attractiveness, the rhetoric that surrounded SDS fashion shows was closer to being what Cushing called "representative of American life [and] of the ideals of American womanhood."[55] In a 1954 SDS fashion show at Vincentian Academy in Albany, New York, four girls modeled their prize-winning gowns for an audience of high school girls "to demonstrate that modesty and attractiveness are not incompatible."[56] In Minneapolis, a "Create Your Own" contest for girls featured sixty-three girls who designed, made, and modeled formals to "increase the social pressure for decency in dress."[57] And more than twenty-five hundred young women attended Chicago's SDS's seventh annual fashion show in 1958 featuring "modest spring styles . . . ranging from beachwear to formal wear."[58] By engaging the adolescent fashion imagination, SDS shows and contests made modesty material—girls could literally embody Christian purity by designing and modeling an elaborate gown or demure pantsuit.

Fashion shows were also popular because they were public displays of middle-class tastefulness. While "female modesty" stood as a code phrase for patriarchal control for many men within the Church, in high schools modesty was also a symbol of "proper" middle-class behavior. In many ways, the standards and goals of SDS functioned in much the same way that historian William Graebner describes the "Dress Right" code working in Buffalo, New York. Formulated by high school students under close adult supervision, "Dress Right" standards were ostensibly about creating self-respect and preventing juvenile delinquency among teenagers. While "Dress Right" did help to ensure a certain level of uniformity among Buffalo teenagers, the high school dress code also enforced class distinctions, separating working-class youths in jeans and gang jackets from middle-class adolescents in pressed pants or skirt and sweater sets. Like the "Dress Right" campaign, SDS reform efforts were partially about setting class standards.[59] This is particularly apparent in the group's objections to wearing blue jeans in public, dressing in a "sloppy" manner, or wearing tight shirts and sweaters. Group members equated modest fashion with "good taste" and refinement, and photographs of SDS girls in self-designed clothing reveals a style far removed from the tight sweaters and skirts marked as working class in the 1950s.

"Modesty Is Needed for Protection":
Keeping Catholic Boys in Line

These class concerns also need to be understood in the context of gendered expectations about the relationship between dress and sexuality. Dressing "modestly" might be about looking middle class, but a middle-class appearance offered important visual protection against the advances of adolescent boys. In a 1960 survey of over twelve hundred boys in two large midwestern cities, teenagers overwhelming equated "immodest clothing" with "immodest behavior." One high school boy argued that "when a boy sees a girl in a tight sweater or jeans or a low-cut bathing suit, he tends to think she is not decent or modest because of her dress. Therefore, a boy would seek the girl that is indecent in dress to fulfill his evil desires." Another added that "the way a girl dresses means everything. For I (and many other guys) think sloppy, sexy, dirty clothes make a guy think the girl is also dirty or trampish."[60] In a different survey of almost a thousand boys, a teenager blamed his own lack of sexual purity on the way adolescent women dressed, especially since he felt they took their cues from movies. He argued that "some girls are careless the way they dress. They try to be sexy like Hollywood glamour girls, and by wearing tight skirts and sweaters they tempt boys to commit impure acts with them."[61] Because clothing provided such a clear signal for boys, girls who chose to buy and wear the fashions of the 1950s risked a wide range of male response, from censorship to possible sexual assault. The rhetoric of immodest clothing placed an enormous value on the consumer choices made by Catholic girls. Looking middle class by wearing "modest" clothing was one defense against the "evil desires" of young men.

Catholic boys who blamed their behavior on female temptation reflected the attitudes held by many members of the Catholic clergy. A 1957 editorial in *America*, the premier Catholic weekly magazine, written after two adolescent women had been raped and killed, agreed with a New Jersey prosecutor who proclaimed that "girls are inviting sex attacks by parading around 'in tight pants and tight sweaters, and hanging around ice cream parlors late at night.'" Many in the clergy believed that girls, spurred by the styles they saw in movies, in magazines, and on television, regularly wore immodest clothing that inflamed adolescent male desires and sometimes led to violence. Urban situations and commercial culture combined to make teenager girls dangerous to themselves and to others. Explaining that young girls were "by nature" eager to "attract attention," the editorial argued that it was "sometimes a dangerous kind of attention" and that boys were "faced with constant sexual temptations—merely by the act of walking down the street."[62] Female sexuality on display threatened men and boys with the occasion of sin, encouraging them to treat women as sexual objects and inflaming their desires to a fever pitch. Even within mainstream Catholic rhetoric, "sex attacks" were the almost inevitable outcome of female immodesty.

As a result, most of the chastisement and sexual burden fell upon adolescent girls. Broader postwar trends in youth culture held true for Catholic adolescents, so that "a double standard survived that perpetuated differences in the meaning of sexual experience."[63] Catholics warned that if a girl "wears a low-cut dress, clings tightly . . . on the darkened dance floor, asks to be taken for a ride along the lake, and snuggles up to the driver, she knows what to expect. . . . Whereas, if she dresses, dances, talks decently and keeps the evening lively, [the boy] will fall into line and things will work out okay. It's a pretty dumb girl who can't handle a 'fast fellow.'"[64] SDS generally accepted the perception that female adolescents needed to act (and look) smart to keep young men's sexual desires in check.[65] An SDS leader in Chicago argued that while girls themselves might feel comfortable in strapless clothes, "how does she feel when passing men, young and old alike, stop and leer at her? . . . Modesty is needed for protection just as a fence is needed to keep the wolf from the flock."[66] By discounting women's own fashion desires while equating men with "wolves," she reinforced the assumption that displays of open masculine sexuality were acceptable, or at least irrepressible, and that Catholic women had a moral responsibility to make fashion concessions in order to restrain male desire. Church outreach to teenagers taught that the male adolescent sex drive was "as automatic as turning on a light switch and seeing the lamp light up," and as a result, teenage boys necessarily depended on their girlfriends "to set sensible, but realistic boundaries."[67] To contain the "forceful" desires of young men, Catholic girls had to dress and behave in a manner that reminded their dates that "every time he is out with a girl . . . the Virgin Mary is in the next seat."[68] Striking a delicate balance between appearing "desirable" and appearing "in control" was the uncertain fashion line that teenage girls had to walk. In this context, SDS's call for attractive modesty made sense.

"Mary for a Model": Getting Help to Maintain Modesty

SDS members used the traditions of their faith to help themselves maintain their modesty and to keep young men from temptation. Their crusades were part of the pledge culture of postwar Catholicism, where Catholics made public promises to follow the teachings of the Church. For example, all Catholics stood once a year during Mass to take a pledge of decency, this one promising that they would not attend motion pictures rated as "objectionable" by the Legion of Decency. In the pledge, Catholics condemned "indecent and immoral motion pictures," agreed to do their part to "strengthen public opinion" against those movies, and acknowledged their obligation to stay away from movies that were "dangerous to moral life."[69] Because of this national pledge, every church-going Catholic was aware of the Legion of Decency and its weekly movie-rating system, and even if many chose to ignore its prescriptions, the pledge legitimized Church authority over popular culture and provided a clear sense of what the Church considered acceptable. SDS pledges were part of this larger tradition. Their pledges for modesty, like the Legion of Decency pledge, were not binding, meaning that they set moral guidelines, not religious obligations. Nevertheless, the SDS pledge made the connection between religious prescriptions and public behavior explicit and acknowledged that spirituality and consumption were intimately connected.

Pledges—and the attendant promise to take a stronger interest in religious activities—sometimes preceded activism in the community. In 1948 the Cleveland teenagers who started SDS in the city made a pledge campaign their first activity, urging students to take a "modesty pledge" and receive a "specially designed modesty shield" during school-time assemblies.[70] They also agreed that "little good [could] come of their efforts unless they first fortified themselves with Masses, Communions, Rosaries and Christ-like lives."[71] By 1951, Chicago's SDS Fashion Board had published a nationally distributed "pledge of modesty" where girls promised a "Mary-like modesty in dress and action" that would set a positive example for others.[72] In a cultural system where pledges were commonplace, these were understood by teenagers as important spiritual aids to good behavior, a promise to God to try and follow the modest path. Regular attendance and other religious devotions at Mass clarified some of the complexities of being an urban teenager and provided SDS members a sense of direction in their negotiations with the demands of a beauty-dominated youth culture. Pledges used the language of religion to make sense of the possibilities of the marketplace.

As the Chicago Fashion Board's pledge makes clear, the Virgin Mary was a vital role model as well, and not just on dates. The rhetoric of SDS often depended on Marian devotion to explain the need for modesty, as members committed themselves to a vision of dress and behavior based on the Virgin Mary, arguing that secular society "had someone other than Mary for a model."[73] Seventeen-year-old Milwaukee SDS member Mary Ann Dearing emphasized the need for girls to model their dressing habits after the Virgin Mary, asking whether Mary would "walk down Broadway in the clothes that we venture out in today."[74] And the New York City SDS group's slogan was "Dare to be different for our Lady's sake."[75] Marian devotion was particularly popular in combination with SDS fashion shows. Dressed in elaborate taffeta formal wear, SDS members in Chicago started their 1952 fashion show by proceeding up the center of the room in single file, where each paused and placed flowers at the foot of a statue of the Virgin Mary.[76] In a play performed at Sacred Heart High School in Pittsburgh, a group of young girls met together in four acts to talk and compare outfits. Each girl walked forward to model her outfit in every scene, and the play had the Virgin Mary appear to one character and offer support for her fashion choices. In the first scene, the girl asks for the Virgin's approval, noting that all the girls at Sacred Heart were trying hard to please Mary, looking for Mary-like clothes in all their purchases.[77]

When clergy members talked about the Virgin Mary, they presented her to young people as the antithesis of commercial youth culture; Marian devotion was supposed to replace a fixation on consumer goods and style with a passion for the spiritual life.[78] This was not the way SDS members understood Mary's role in their lives. Adolescent girls envisioned Mary as an integral part of urban teenage life, not in opposition to it. As a guest editor for a teen column explained, after a girl dressed for a date, she whispered a quick prayer to Mary, asking "make him act like St. Joseph did and, incidentally, let us have a good time."[79] In their calls to be more "Mary-like," SDS teenagers brought the Virgin into their lives and made her part of their concerns about being stylish and popular, as well as depending on her for spiritual guidance and as a way to resist pressures to act immodestly. They called on Christ's mother for assistance when they faced uncertain dating situations and imagined Mary walking down city streets, just as they did. Like the El Paso fashion show in 1954 where girls envisioned Mary in a stylish "sack dress" with coordinating accessories, the rhetoric of SDS promised young women the opportunity to be "in vogue with Mary." The movement assured young women that the Virgin Mary, far from abhorring all modern fashions, would want to dress beautifully and would enjoy shopping for clothes at the local department store. Their Marian devotion merged the joys of youth beauty culture with a modest spirituality, mediating the pressures of urban adolescent life by reconciling consumerism and religious belief in the figure of Christ's mother.

Conclusion

The Catholic SDS faded away in the 1960s to be replaced by a new SDS, one that featured a different cultural style among youth and different concerns about American society. The enormous changes brought by Vatican II made modesty crusades seem old-fashioned and outdated within the Church. And new fashions like the miniskirt made worrying about strapless prom gowns seem silly. By 1963 even some Catholic magazines that had long supported SDS crusades were beginning to question their worth, arguing that "tape measure morality" only led to confusion among youth.[80] Still, sixteen years after SDS emerged in Cincinnati, members continued their fight for modesty. Just as in that first protest in 1947, the focus was on bathing suits, and the approach was symbolic protest. In Chicago, twenty-eight girls in polka-dotted bloomer-style bathing suits from the 1890s and sixteen boys in swimming trunks that resembled long underwear demonstrated along the Lake Shore beach.[81] They carried signs with slogans like: "Let's put an end to the bikini trend," "You have to be teeny to wear a bikini," and "If people dress as they think, some people think very little." The group's spokesperson, Roseann Nelmark, argued that the group wore outmoded swimming suits to demonstrate the problem with extremes. To SDS members, the overdressing required by the standards of the 1890s was no sillier than the "underdressing" that the 1960s' bikini represented. Nelmark admitted that "we might look silly to some people," but she maintained that symbolic protest could be effective in swaying public opinion.[82] The 1963 protest, which advocated a one-piece suit for women as the wise consumer alternative to the bikini, continued the long-standing argument that female bodies symbolized the moral standards of a country. Nelmark claimed that "the moral fiber of a nation is reflected in its women—and we want our American women to have a high moral standard and to show it in the clothes they wear."[83] The fashion shows and dances, the pressure on store merchants, may have largely disappeared, but to the end, SDS made forceful symbolic displays about the importance of the teenage female body.

As SDS members from 1948 to 1963 realized, female bodies carried multiple symbolic meanings in both secular and Catholic society, representing at different moments the moral decay of the nation, the blossoming power of youth culture, the undermining of the family, the spiritual purity of the Virgin Mary, or an irresistible temptation to adolescent boys. Much like the prom gowns they worked to reform, girls' bodies were literally on constant display. The language of SDS encouraged young women to think of themselves as constantly under supervision, subject to masculine authority and approval, responsible for restraining masculine sexual desires while striving to look both beautiful and spiritually modest. But while SDS members accepted that they would be watched and judged, they combined the divergent messages they heard to carve out a site of authority for themselves based on personal appearance. As one young woman explained, it was the duty of Catholic girls to "set a Christian example in modest dress" because it would allow them "to control fashion tomorrow."[84] As consumers advocating for their right to modesty in an ever-expanding market, they believed wholeheartedly that it was their religious obligation to take part in the business of fashion. SDS provided a way for high school girls across the United States to flex their consumer muscles while following the Church's teachings about modesty in dress. Their ongoing efforts to combine up-to-date styles with modesty meant that teenagers could demonstrate their Catholicism by buying modestly, wearing an exhibition of their faith on their bodies. The social activism and "modest" fun that SDS provided its members helped to create a sense of religious identity that joined religious devotion to commercial desires, ironically making modest prom dresses a clear marker of spiritual commitment.

By appropriating and refashioning the language of the commercial marketplace, SDS gave Catholic girls the agency to negotiate the often fraught boundary between youth culture and the Church. In a decade that stressed the public consumption of the female figure and emphasized the connection between female sexuality and consumer goods, foregoing strapless dresses, low-cut necklines, and two-piece bathing suits offered young Catholic women a telling way to demonstrate their faith. The SDS emphasis on fashion worked precisely because fashion was so important to the image of 1950s' femininity. In SDS, girls made a statement about the importance of religion and "traditional" values in their lives. As one SDS member argued, "Have a good time in a strapless dress? I couldn't."[85] Still, SDS members wanted to "have a good time." They paid close attention to current styles and the demands of the youthful trends. Appearance mattered. In a culture where female success was largely defined by stylish hair, trendy clothing, and beautiful makeup, regular fashion shows and dances gave girls a chance to create and show off their modest good taste, to be a part of a beauty-dominated youth culture. As a consumer-based alternative to Lana Turner sweaters and Hollywood glamour girls, SDS created a space for its members to design their own prom gowns, to participate in well-attended fashion shows, and to show off their spiritual modesty at high school dances. A stylish prom dress could be used both to "look good" and to "be good," to reflect a desire to take part in middle-class secular culture and to be proudly and spiritually Catholic. In their outreach to department store owners and in setting new standards for Catholic beauty, SDS members artfully combined the secular and sacred and thus transformed themselves into active cultural producers in the marketplace of fashion.

Notes

1. All quotes from the El Paso fashion show in this paragraph come from Sister Robert Marie, S.L., "In Vogue with Mary," *Catholic Educator*, June 1954, 536.
2. The Catholics version of SDS was not related to the later, and more famous, Students for a Democratic Society, though both sought to empower their members to change society and believed that young people should be leaders in social activism.
3. Angela McRobbie's work on British teenager girls' culture, especially *Feminism and Female Youth Culture* (Boston: Unwin Hyman, 1991), is useful for theorizing the relation between adolescents as cultural producers of their own subcultures and as consumers of mainstream commercial culture. See also Mary Celeste Kearney, "Producing Girls," in *Delinquents and Debutantes: Twentieth-Century American Girls' Cultures*, ed. Sherrie A. Inness (New York: New York University Press, 1998), 285–310; and Vickie L. Ruiz, "The Flapper and the Chaperone: Cultural Constructions of Identity and Heterosexual Politics among Adolescent Mexican American Women, 1920–1950," in Inness, *Delinquents and Debutantes*, 199–225.
4. Karal Ann Marling, *As Seen on TV: The Visual Culture of Everday Life in the 1950s* (Cambridge: Harvard University Press, 1994), 9–49, explores the importance of women's clothes as revealed by Mamie Eisenhower's "new look" and the outrage over the "sack dress." See also Linda Arthur, ed., *Religion, Dress and the Body* (New York: Oxford University Press, 1999), which explores the complex relationship between clothing, gender identity, and religious belief.
5. By 1944 adolescent spending power was estimated at $750 million of largely discretionary income. See Michael C. C. Adams, *The Best War Ever: America and World War II* (Baltimore: Johns Hopkins University Press, 1994), 126–127; John Modell, *From Youth to Adulthood in the United States, 1920–1975* (Berkeley and Los Angeles: University of California Press, 1989), 213–262; Thomas Hine, *The Rise and Fall of the American Teenager* (New York: Avon Books, 1999), 225–248; and William Graebner, *Coming of Age in Buffalo: Youth and Authority in the Postwar Era* (Philadelphia: University of Pennsylvania Press, 1990).
6. Hine, *Rise and Fall*, 226.
7. Graebner, *Coming of Age*, 43.
8. Marling, *As Seen on TV*, 169–175.
9. Marjorie Rosen, *Popcorn Venus* (New York: Avon Books, 1973), 282.
10. Grace Paladino, *Teenagers: An American History* (New York: Basic Books, 1996), 103–105. See Kelly Schrum, "Teens Means Business: Teenage Girls Culture and 'Seventeen' Magazine, 1944–1950," in Inness, *Delinquents and Debutantes*, 134–163, for the development of *Seventeen* magazine as a major marketplace for teenager culture.
11. Wini Breines, *Young White, and Miserable: Growing Up Female in the Fifties* (Boston: Beacon Press, 1992), 95, 106. See also Susan Douglas, *Where the Girls Are: Growing Up Female with the Mass Media* (New York: Random House, 1994), especially 25–27 and 97–121.
12. Ken Smith, *Mental Hygiene: Classroom Films, 1945–1970* (New York: Blast Books, 1999), 38–39.
13. "How Can Teens of Today Control the Modesty of Tomorrow's Dress?" *Extension*, May 1954, 29.
14. The Church generally agreed with liberal critics of the 1950s who claimed that the popular media had become a form of subtle mind control, suppressing an individual

sense of identity and fostering an unhealthy conformity. See Richard H. Pells, *The Liberal Mind in a Conservative Age: Intellectuals in the 1940s and 1950s* (New York: Harper and Row, 1985), 227; and Philip Gleason, "The Crisis of Americanization," in *Catholicism in America*, ed. Philip Gleason (New York: Harper and Row, 1970), 143.

15. Archives of the Archdiocese of Chicago (AAC), Meyer Papers, Box 2778, Pastoral Letter, December 28, 1955.

16. Sylvester Juergens, S.M., "It's a Sin to Be a 'Baby Doll,'" *Our Lady's Digest*, May 1957, 7–8.

17. E. F. Miller, "On Low–Cut Dresses," *Liguorian*, June 1952, 329; Marian Library, University of Dayton, Clipping File, 1630, *Divine Love*, July-September 1957.

18. SDS was truly a national urban movement. In addition to El Paso, Cincinnati, Cleveland, and Chicago, references to SDS activities appear in New York City; Boston; Washington, D.C.; New Orleans; St. Louis; Milwaukee; Minneapolis; Baltimore; Albuquerque; Akron, Ohio; Dubuque, Iowa; Kansas City, Missouri; Scranton, Pennsylvania; Newark, New Jersey; and Albany, Syracuse, and Rochester, New York.

19. Cincinnati Catholic girls were part of a larger American outrage over the new fashion innovation of the bikini. Created in France in 1946, the bikini caused storms of protest—even in Hollywood—throughout the 1940s and early 1950s. Jennifer Chaik, *The Face of Fashion: Cultural Studies in Fashion* (New York: Routledge, 1994), 147–149.

20. Hildegard Stiglmaier, Sally Pepple, and Karen Keller, "S.D.S. Sparks a War on Immodesty," *Catholic Home Journal*, January 1950, 8–9.

21. Ann Tansey, "Call Letters S.D.S.," *Information*, February 1958, 17.

22. David Bowen, "Cold Shoulders for Bare Shoulders," *Catholic Digest*, May 1949, 3.

23. Ann Tansey, "S.D.S.—Modern Davids," *Ave Maria*, July 4, 1953, 17.

24. "Six Schools to Wage Fight on Immodesty," *Catholic Universe Bulletin*, December 3, 1948, 16.

25. "Modesty Leaders Win New Support in Drive," *Catholic Universe Bulletin*, February. 25, 1949, 13.

26. "Girls Seeking Modest Gowns Tell of 'Insults' in Downtown Stores," *Catholic Universe Bulletin*, December 17, 1948, 1. For example, store clerks insulted nuns, calling them "penguins." The girls who canvassed the stores admitted that "the treatment was pretty rough . . . ranging from cold to indifferent politeness to the outright brush-off."

27. "Stores Pledge Aid to Girls in Drive to Make Modesty Fashionable," *Catholic Universe Bulletin*, January 14, 1949, 1, 16. By March 1949, when crusaders began to turn their attention to summer fashions, three public schools in Cleveland sent representatives to a citywide meeting. "Modesty Rally Eyes Summer Fashions," *Catholic Universe Bulletin*, March 25, 1949, 13.

28. "Girls Seeking Modest Gowns," 16.

29. "School Head Enlists 7,000 Girls in Crusade for Modest Clothing," *Catholic Universe Bulletin*, December 24, 1948, 1, 4.

30. "Stores Pledge Aid," 1, 16.

31. Ibid., 16.

32. AAC, Meyer Papers, CBC Correspondence, Box 43785.03, Folder "Correspondence CISCA," "The CISCA Organization."

33. The encyclical defined Catholic Action as "the participation of the laity in the apostolic mission of the hierarchy." For the history of Catholic Action groups in the

United States, see Dennis Robb, "Specialized Catholic Action in the United States, 1936–1949: Ideology, Leadership and Organization" (Ph.D. diss., University of Minnesota, 1972).

34. AAC, Meyer Papers, Box 2789, Fred J. Mann, C.SS.R., "Content and Techniques of Cana Conference Program," September 1948, 14.

35. "S.D.S. Crusade for Modesty," n.d., 1. Archives of the University of Notre Dame (UNDA), PMRH, 67/118,

36. AAC, *New World* Photographs Collection, Folder: CISCA, May 1952.

37. Paula Starck, "SDS . . . What? Why?," *Voice of St. Jude*, August 1952, 8; Tansey, "Call Letters," 17.

38. "Modish and Modest," *America*, October 6, 1951; "Teen-agers Turn the Tide," *America*, May 7, 1955.

39. See "Morality and Good Tastes in Apparel," *America*, July 2, 1955, 342.

40. "What about Modesty," n.d., 7. UNDA, PMRH, 67/118.

41. Archives of the Catholic University of America (ACUA), NWCW/USCC, Youth Department, Box 52, *Youth*, November 1956, 13.

42. "What about Modesty," 5–6.

43. "Six Schools to Wage Fight," 16.

44. "Modesty Demanded," *Catholic Mind*, July 1952, 438.

45. "Confused Consciences or Confused Confessors?," *Homiletic and Pastoral Review*, March 1959, 525–526.

46. In a letter to the *Homiletic and Pastoral Review*, May 1959, 800–802, Chicago's SDS religious adviser, Francis X. Lawlor, attributed the group's success to creating "general principles" rather than explicit guidelines.

47. "What about Modesty," 2–3.

48. Quarter-page advertisement for Morris B. Sachs stores, *New World*, May 9, 1952, 7. See also advertisements in the *New World*, May 2, 1952, 3, and April 25, 1952, 11.

49. Quarter-page advertisement for Wm. A. Lewis stores, *New World*, May 9, 1952, 3.

50. Bowen, "Cold Shoulders," 3.

51. "What about Modesty," 7.

52. Archives of the Archdiocese of Milwaukee, SUMA Papers, MC 94, Box 8, photographs from the Lourdes Ball, 1957.

53. AAC, *New World* Photographs Collection, Folder: CISCA, 1952–1960.

54. ACUA, NCWC/USCC, Family Life Bureau, Box 48I, *Family Apostolate*, winter 1955–56, 6.

55. AAC, Meyer Papers, Box 2781, Portfolio 7, Drawer 4, clipping "Let Your Voice be Heard Archbishop Tells Women."

56. "Gowns, Modest and Modish," *Albany Evangelist*, April 30, 1954, 6.

57. ACUA, NCWC/USCC, Youth Department, Box 52, *Youth*, September, 1954. In Indianapolis, the Junior Catholic Youth Organization sponsored a similar show called "Styles in Rhythm," in which contestants designed, made, and modeled dresses made according to SDS standards. *Youth*, January 1955, 9.

58. ACUA, NCWC/USCC, Youth Department, Box 53, *Youth*, January 1958, 12–13.

59. Graebner, *Coming of Age*, 99–103.

60. Hugh J. O'Connell, "What Boys Think of Girls' Dresses," *Liguorian*, September 1960, 7–12.

61. Quoted in Lawrence A. Killelea, F.S.C.H., "Attitudes of Catholic High School Students as to What Constitute Their Failures in Christian Living" (master's thesis, Catholic University of America, 1957), 26.

62. "Background for Sex Crimes," *America*, July 6, 1957, 377.

63. John D'Emilio and Estelle Freedman, *Intimate Matters: A History of Sexuality in America* (New York: Harper and Row, 1989), 262. See also Beth L. Bailey, *From Front Porch to Back Seat: Courtship in Twentieth-Century America* (Baltimore: Johns Hopkins University Press, 1988), especially 87–96.

64. Rev. Raymond Wahl, *Everybody's Going Steady* (St. Louis: The Queen's Work, 1954).

65. In a survey of four Catholic high schools, 265 of the 300 students surveyed agreed that "physical passion is aroused more easily in boys than in girls," and 234 of the 300 agreed that "girls are more responsible for keeping a courtship pure than are boys." See Sister Mary Eleanore Edelbeck, O.P., "An Investigation of the Attitudes of Catholic High School Seniors Concerning Marriage and Family Living" (master's thesis, Catholic University of America, 1953), 13.

66. "Chicago SDS Girls Give Their Answers: Why Be Modest?," *Voice of St. Jude*, August 1952, 32.

67. Archives of the Archdiocese of Hartford, Knott Collection, Director's Outline, Tri-Une Conference for Eleventh and Twelfth Graders, n.d., 16.

68. Michael F. Bradley, F.S.C.H., "Some Senior Catholic High School Boys' Appraisal of Love and Sex and Love" (master's thesis, Catholic University of America, 1957), 34.

69. AAC, Meyer Papers, Box 2778, Drawer 2, "Pledge of the Legion of Decency."

70. "Six Schools to Wage Fight," 16.

71. "Modesty Rally," 13.

72. "A Pledge and a Prayer," *Catholic School Journal*, October 1956, 245.

73. "Chicago SDS Girls Give Their Answers," 32.

74. "How Can Teens of Today Control the Modesty?," 29.

75. "Morality and Good Tastes," 342.

76. Starck, "SDS . . . What? Why?," 7.

77. Diane Herbele, "Queen Mary, Teen Mary," *Catholic School Journal*, October 1956, 252–254.

78. Devotion to the Virgin Mary was critical to American Catholic culture before Vatican II. For background on Marian devotion in the United States, see especially Robert A. Orsi, *The Madonna of 115th Street: Faith and Devotion in Italian Harlem, 1880–1950* (New Haven, Conn.: Yale University Press, 1985); John T. McGreevy, "Bronx Miracle," *American Quarterly* 52, no. 3 (September 2000): 405–443; and Thomas A. Kselman and Steven Avella, "Marian Piety and the Cold War in the United States," *Catholic Historical Review* 72, no. 3 (July 1986): 403–424.

79. Rita Fowler, "Teendom: A Youth Religion," *Extension*, May 1954, 29.

80. Rev. Leon McKenzie, "Editorial: Modesty Crusades," *Ave Maria*, March 23, 1963, 18

81. One sign of change was the inclusion of teenage boys in the 1963 protest. None of the SDS actions of the 1950s included boys, unless they were commenting on what they thought was appropriate for women to wear.

82. "Crusaders Protest Beach Dress," *Chicago New World*, August 2, 1963, 16.

83. Ibid.

84. "How Can Teens of Today Control the Modesty?," 29.

85. "Six Schools to Wage Fight," 16.

Ten

Melani McAlister

Nation Time

*Black Islam and African American
Cultural Politics, 1955–1970*

---

raise up christ nigger
Christ was black . . .
    Shango budda black
    hermes rasis black
    moses krishna
    black . . .
and we are the same, all the blackness from one black
    allah. . .
—Amiri Baraka, *"It's Nation Time,"* 1970

"I'm not an American; I'm a black man "
—Muhammad Ali, 1964

Two events, separated by just over a year, in two very different spheres of cultural activity, marked the extraordinary influence of Islam in the African American community in the 1960s. Two prominent African American men, one an athlete, the other a poet and a playwright, took highly visible and conscious steps away from their old identities and affiliations and began instead to articulate a black consciousness and politics based on the teachings of Islam. These two public transformations—rituals of self-identification and self-naming—developed out of a fateful convergence that in the 1960s made U.S. urban areas home to a potent combination of shifting religious affiliations, artistic populism, anticolonial politics, and black radicalism. The convergence of these forces made transnational politics salient to "domestic" identities, which were in turn rooted in urban areas increasingly affected by a global flow of people, capital, and ideas. As international politics and urban culture intersected in the 1960s, it became clear that claims about the Middle East, as a site of contemporary politics and of reclaimed histories, had become a type of cultural capital and a rich resource within African American communities.[1]

On February 25, 1964, the twenty-three-year-old fighter Cassius Clay defeated Sonny Liston and took the world heavyweight boxing title, the most lucrative individual prize in professional sports. On the day after his triumph, Clay—who had already become one of the most well known and controversial figures in the boxing world—announced at a press conference that he was a Muslim.[2] Until that day, Clay had been known as a playful, rather apolitical youngster with a fondness for pink Cadillacs, extravagant bragging, and comic poetry.[3] But in the months before the fight, rumors of his association with the Nation of Islam (NOI) had circulated widely, and he had been seen frequently in the company of Malcolm X, whom he had invited to his training camp in Miami.[4] A few weeks after the victory, Elijah Muhammad, the leader of the NOI, bestowed on Clay his Muslim name: Muhammad Ali. Clay's victory and subsequent announcement were widely reported; his association with the NOI was often viewed with skepticism or anger. In the spring of 1964, when Malcolm X left the NOI, Ali stayed, and he quickly became the most famous Black Muslim in the country and one of the NOI's most prominent spokespersons.[5] Just a few months later, Ali embarked on a tour of Africa and the Middle East; when he returned, he announced to the press: "I'm not an American; I'm a black man."[6]

In 1966 Ali's status as political figure took a new direction when he refused his induction into the U.S. Army, saying, "I'm a member of the Black Muslims, and we don't go to no wars unless they're declared by Allah himself. I don't have no personal quarrel with those Viet Congs."[7] That refusal—that risky stand on behalf of the politics of his religious belief—transformed Ali's image: vilified in the mainstream media, he became one of the most visible and influential antiwar figures in the country. In the words of poet Sonia Sanchez, he was "a cultural resource for everyone in that time," a man whose refusal to fight in Vietnam became an emblem of the far-reaching influence of the black nationalist critique of American nationalism and U.S. foreign policy.[8]

A little over a year after Muhammad Ali's highly public conversion, in 1965 the poet and playwright LeRoi Jones left his literary circles in Greenwich Village to move uptown to Harlem, where he founded the Black Arts Repertory Theatre/School (BARTS). In Harlem, Jones turned his back on his earlier ties with Beat poetry and even his more recent success with plays on race relations (*Dutchman* had won an Obie in 1964).[9] He turned instead toward the task of building a community theater and developing the themes and writing styles that would launch the Black Arts movement. During his time at BARTS, Jones wrote *A Black Mass*, a one-act play that presented in dramatic form the NOI's central myth: the story of Yakub, the evil scientist who "invented" white people.

Then, in 1968 Jones also changed his name to Ameer (later to Amiri) Baraka. He studied Sunni Islam under the tutelage of Hajj Heesham Jaaber, who had been affiliated with Malcolm X near the end of his life.[10] By then, Baraka, whom his contemporaries considered to be "the most promising black writer" in the nation, was also the best-known representative of the Black Arts movement, a champion of black cultural nationalism, a significant theorist of the reemergence of a committed art, and an articulate critic of U.S. imperialism. Baraka would turn away from Islam and toward Maoism in the 1970s.[11] But from at least 1965 until 1973, Baraka and others saw Islam as a significant cultural resource, an authentically black religion that would be central to the requisite development of an alternative black culture and a liberated spirituality. Significantly, Baraka also envisioned that this black culture would be a popular culture, one that would function much like the cultural commodities that already circulated broadly in African American communities. As Baraka later wrote, he and his colleagues wanted "[a]n art that would reach the people, that would take them higher, ready them for war and victory, as popular as the Impressions or the Miracles or Marvin Gaye. That was our vision and its image keep us stepping, heads high and backs straight."[12] Knowing full well the power of popular culture, they wanted an art and a religion that would be as meaningful as Motown.[13]

Between 1955 and 1970, some African Americans, many from urban communities in the North and West, developed a cultural politics that made Islam into a symbol and site for a reconstituted black identity. In recent years, scholars in religious studies have amply documented the remarkable diversity of Muslim practice among African Americans, from orthodox Sunni Islam to the less traditional doctrines of the NOI.[14] But in the general historical scholarship, the larger political and cultural influence of Islam as a religious/cultural/political nexus has been remarkably neglected. In the 1960s this influence was significant. By the early 1960s one need not have entered a Muslim temple or read a NOI newspaper to know that black Islam had moved far beyond the sectarian curiosity it had been just ten years earlier. In urban areas around the country, in a cultural field that ranged from poetry and plays to highly charged sports matches, from local community theaters to the boxing ring, Islam was a significant presence.

This essay will argue that as African American Islam staked its claim in urban communities, it played an important role in a larger shift in the politics of black liberation. In important ways, that role was forged in and through the production of culture, including but not limited to commercial culture. From blues and jazz records to cheaply reproduced sheaves of poetry to magazines and newspapers published by African Americans, commercialized cultural forms were integral to a black public sphere that urban migration was making increasingly vibrant. Within that sphere, Islam—and the NOI in particular—played a central role in refigurations of black radical politics, challenging the hegemony of black Christianity and the politics of integration associated with it while highlighting the importance of a genuinely black cultural expression. It was the beginning of a larger transformation, which by the late 1960s would bring black Islam, populist culture, Arab nationalism, and African American radicalism into a powerful historical alliance.

To examine this transformation, I will focus on three critical sites: the religious teachings and daily practices of the NOI itself; the influence that the NOI and other Muslim sects had on cultural producers, especially the young men and women who would become the heart of the Black Arts movement; and the impact of both religion and art on the anticolonial radicalism of a new generation of African Americans. Connected to all of these was the changing life of cities in the 1950s and 1960s, where, with the migration of African Americans from the South in the 1920s, there emerged a different type of black community, one that was less attached to traditional community institutions and, importantly, all but untouched by the southern-focused civil rights activities of the late 1940s and 1950s. In these cities, an expanding popular and commercial culture opened up opportunities for African Americans to express their experiences and to speak to each other.

This process of political and cultural change involved the development of what Michael Shapiro has called "moral geographies," cultural and political practices that work together to mark states as well as regions, cultural groupings, and ethnic or racial territories. Moral geographies shape human understandings of the world cognitively, emotionally, and politically; they consist of "a set of silent ethical assertions" that mark connection and separation.[15] This essay explores the impact of the religious practices and cultural poetics of African American Islam in the construction of a new moral geography that became important in many urban areas by the early 1960s (Chicago, Detroit, New York, Los Angeles, and Washington, D.C., among others) and that influenced even those who were not Muslims. Islam, like Christianity, has traditionally turned to the Middle East as a "holy land," making salient not only its ancient histories but also the contemporary political events in the region. In the 1950s and 1960s this religiously infused transnationalism gained a broader currency: African Americans in this period constructed significant cultural, political, and historical links between their contemporary situation and the Arab world. This moral geography imagined a community very different from dominant constructions of "America." Despite the fact that what emerged from this mapping has often been called (even by its adherents) "black nationalism," the community it envisioned provided an alternative to—and in some sense a fundamental critique of—the nation-state.[16]

In the early to mid-1960s the NOI brought its interpretation of Islam to prominence in the African American community and defined Islam as the religion of black American militancy. For African Americans disaffected with the Christian church—those frustrated by the commitment of black Christians to solidarity with whites or angered by the continuing violence by white Christians against nonviolent civil rights activists—Islam offered an alternative. Islam, its adherents argued, provided the basis for a black nationalist consciousness that was separate from the civil rights goals of integration into a white-dominated and oppressive nation. Islam offered a set of values and beliefs that were at once spiritual, political, and cultural. As LeRoi Jones described it, Islam offered "what the Black man needs, a reconstruction . . . a total way of life that he can involve himself with that is post-American, in a sense."[17] The NOI in particular provided both an alternative religious affiliation and a countercitizenship, an identity that challenged black incorporation into the dominant discourse of Judeo-Christian Americanness.

The Nation emerged as a significant social and political force in the black community in the late 1950s after a period of disarray and declining membership in the 1940s. When Malcolm X was released from prison in 1952, he quickly came to play a major role in the organization's expansion, founding new temples or reinvigorating older ones in cities all over the country. In these cities—Chicago, New York, Pittsburgh, Los Angeles, Atlanta, Baltimore, Washington, D.C., and Hartford, Connecticut, among others—the NOI temples often established themselves as urban institutions, running schools and restaurants, selling newspapers, and providing community services, as well holding as religious meetings.[18] By December 1959 the Nation had fifty temples in twenty-two states; the number of members in the organization is difficult to estimate but by 1962 was probably in the range of fifty thousand to one hundred thousand, with many more supporters. In 1962 *Muhammed Speaks*, the major NOI newspaper, founded by Malcolm X, had the largest circulation of any black paper in the country.[19]

The NOI was an avowedly "black nationalist" organization, but its vision of black nationalism cannot be fully understood separate from either its explicitly religious content or its insistently transnational dimensions. The religious and the transnational aspects are, in fact, intimately related: though the NOI was unorthodox Islam, Elijah Muhammad had, since the 1930s, consistently affirmed the significance of its connection to other Muslim communities around the globe, particularly those in the Middle East. The Nation challenged the assumption that African Americans were simply or primarily a subset of all Americans; its political program never posited black nationalism as a self-contained subnationalism, even when Elijah Muhammad or Malcolm X made claims for the right to control specific tracts of land within the United States. Instead, the NOI built on the fact that Islam was a major world religion with a strong transnational orientation; Muslim governments and communities often forged ties across borders, politically and culturally as well as religiously.[20] Drawing on this global vision, the NOI developed a model of community that linked African Americans both to Africa and to "Asia" (by Asia, Elijah Muhammad seemed to mean primarily what is usually called the Middle East and the Indian subcontinent).[21]

By the time the NOI began to reach a larger audience in the 1950s, it was able to draw on several decades of black anticolonialist activity, led by intellectuals and activists from W.E.B. Du Bois to Paul Robeson to Walter White, which had envisioned African Americans as part of a pan-African diaspora.[22] At the same time, the Nation's theological politics departed from that earlier activism's primary focus on Africa, opting for a more expansive transnationalism that included much of the nonwhite world (Latin America is an exception). Like the pan-Africanist intellectual and cultural movements of the 1930s and 1940s, however, Elijah Muhammad described the connections between African Americans and colonized peoples through a language of naturalized race; he simply claimed both Africa and the Middle East as black heritage, insisting that the Arabian peninsula and the Nile valley were the historic home of what he called the "Afro-Asiatic black man" now living in America.

The significance of this religiously influenced political and racial refashioning was profound. In the NOI temples being rapidly established in urban areas in the late 1950s and early 1960s, ministers brought a message of worldwide black Islam to thousands of African American converts.[23] A few of the cities where the Nation was growing were also home to small but visible Muslim immigrant populations. In Detroit and nearby Dearborn, Arab immigrants had been a significant minority since the 1920s, when Syrians and Lebanese had arrived to work in the auto industry (alongside the African Americans who were pouring in from the South). It was there that W. D. Fard, claiming to be of Middle Eastern origin (but in fact probably born in New Zealand of a white mother and an Indian father whose family came from the area that eventually became Pakistan), had made his first ministry and founded the NOI in 1930. Fard had earlier been involved in the Moorish Science Temple, one of the small Muslim-influenced groups that proliferated in African American communities in the 1920s. The founder of the Moorish Science Temple, in turn, had been influenced by a Muslim missionary from the Ahmadiyya movement in India, though he ultimately taught that African Americans had originally hailed from Morocco.[24] But for most adherents, their connections with the Muslim world did not stem from these cross-cultural contacts; instead, the links were emotional and metaphorical. The presence of Muslims in urban areas might have been the spark, but it was the perceived failure of Christianity in those same areas that was the kindling.

Lectures in NOI temples generally, often harshly, indicted the traditional Christianity of the African American church and argued that African Americans should recognize their true heritage as the descendants of the Muslim prophet Muhammed. The Nation taught that Islam was the "natural religion of the black man," which had been stripped from the Africans who were sold into slavery and taught their masters' Christianity. Arabic was the original language of black people, not only because many of the Africans who were taken into slavery and carried to the New World spoke Arabic but also because "the so-called Negroes" in America were descendants of the original Arabic-speaking peoples to whom Islam was revealed.[25] As the religious service began, the minister greeted his parishioners with the Arabic greeting, "As-salaam-alaikum" (Peace be with you), and the members responded, "Wa-Alaikum as-salaam" (And also with you). At the Islamic schools set up by the Nation, Arabic lessons were an integral part of the curriculum: Arabic language instruction was said to began at the age of three.[26]

The Nation's theology included an alternative genealogy for black Americans—understood to be descendants of the original inhabitants of Asia in general and Mecca in particular. As Elijah Muhammad wrote in his 1965 treatise, *Message to the Blackman in America*: "It is Allah's (God's) will and purpose that we shall know ourselves. . . . He has declared that we are descendants of the Asian black nation and the tribe of Shabazz . . . the first to discover the best part of our planet to live on. The rich Nile Valley of Egypt and the present seat of the Holy City, Mecca, Arabia."[27]

The NOI's assertion that all black people were by nature Muslims was part of its critique of black Christianity—a critique that was at once theological, political, and historical. NOI meetings often had a display, drawn on a chalkboard, featuring two flags: on one side of the board, a U.S. flag with a cross beside it and underneath it the caption "Slavery, Suffering, and Death"; on the other side, a flag bearing the Crescent and underneath it the words "Islam: Freedom, Justice, and Equality." Beneath both was the question: "Which one will survive the War of Armageddon?"[28] Elijah Muhammad's message to African Americans focused on pride and transformation. The Christianity of their slave masters had functioned to continue their spiritual enslavement, he argued, but Islam, which built upon the teachings of the Bible but succeeded them with additional revelations, would provide the key for understanding old teachings in the way they were intended rather than through the perversions of white Christianity. In this way NOI teaching revised, without discarding, important aspects of Christian symbolism that were salient in the black community.[29] At the same time, this teaching also carried with it a racial, political, and moral geography: it pitted (black) Islam against (white) Christianity in a worldwide and historic struggle.

The NOI tapped into a larger set of concerns, as Christianity began to be challenged within the black community as inadequate to the spiritual and political needs of African Americans. In 1962 James Baldwin explored his own Christian heritage, the failures of the church, and the concomitant appeal of the NOI in what was perhaps his most famous essay, "Letter from a Region in My Mind," published in the *New Yorker*. The Nation had recently begun to gain broad public attention within and outside of the African American press. For Baldwin, the appeal of Islam lay precisely in its challenge to the Christianity's Eurocentric heritage and its links with imperialism:

> The Christian church itself—again, as distinguished from some of its ministers—sanctified and rejoiced in the conquests of the flag, and encouraged, if it did not formulate, the belief that conquest, and the resulting relative well-being of the Western population, was proof of the favor of God. God had come a long way from the desert—but then so had Allah, though in a very different direction. God, going north, and rising on the wings of power, had become white, and Allah, out of power, had become—for all practical purposes anyway—black.[30]

If the Christian Bible had provided for many civil rights activists metaphors to evoke the hope of liberation, Christianity was also increasingly becoming identified with the European powers who invoked it to justify their international expansion.

This political and religious mapping of the world was directly opposed to contemporary black Christian understandings that focused on Israel (both ancient and modern) as a strong source of religious and political identification. Black Christianity had traditionally presented African American history as a not-yet-completed retelling of the Hebrew story, a potential site for the reentry of God into history on the side of a people.[31] By the late 1950s, the Christian-dominated civil rights movement was making highly effective use of the exodus as a figure for African American liberation. The alliance between African Americans and Jews in the early civil rights movement, though grounded in the active Jewish participation in the movement, was almost certainly strengthened by a strong metaphorical affiliation between the narrative of ancient Hebrew liberation from bondage and the purposeful imagining of African American liberation from discrimination in the United States. The exodus trope was a link, one articulated in churches and meetings, in songs and in sermons, as well as in the writings of African American intellectuals and activists, from Martin Luther King Jr. to James Baldwin to Joseph Lowrey.[32]

The link that black Christians felt with the Hebrew story extended into contemporary international politics. The establishment of modern-day Israel in 1948 was a source of enthusiasm and even inspiration for many African Americans. In 1947 Walter White, the executive director of the National Association for the Advancement of Colored People (NAACP), had played a crucial role in lobbying African nations to vote for the United Nations's resolution partitioning Palestine into Jewish and Arab areas. Ralph Bunche, the U.N. secretary for peacekeeping, was active in negotiating the end to the Arab-Israeli war in 1948 on terms generally considered favorable to Israel. And in 1948 the NAACP passed a resolution stating that "the valiant struggle of the people of Israel for independence serves as an inspiration to all persecuted people throughout the world."[33]

Martin Luther King Jr. exemplified the move that connected biblical history with contemporary politics. He believed that civil rights was part of an international transformation in power relations. He saw the rise of anticolonialism and the rise of civil rights activity not only as parallel sets of events but as a connected force, with the two movements affecting and influencing each other in direct ways—everywhere, the enslaved people were rising up against Pharaoh and demanding to be free.[34] The success of the new nationalisms, particularly in Africa, Egypt, and India, provided a living model for the kind of successful struggle that King envisioned in the United States. Within this frame, Israel—as one of the "new nations" seeking freedom and national rights—was a symbol, one made all the more powerful by the biblical story of exile and return and by the ways in which this rhetoric had played a central role in the successful transformation of the Zionist movement into the Israeli state.[35]

The NOI's vision of a worldwide Islamic alliance confronting white Christianity challenged the black Christian sanctification of ancient Israel and offered an alternative sacred geography with Mecca as its center. Significantly, Elijah Muhammad taught that the stories told in the Christian Bible were prophesies rather than histories and that, as prophesy, they spoke of the contemporary experiences of African Americans rather than the historical experiences of the ancient Hebrews: "Before the coming of Allah (God), we being blind, deaf, and dumb, had mistaken the true meanings of these parables as referring to the Jews. Now, thanks to Almighty God, Allah . . . who has opened my blinded eyes, and unstopped my ears, loosened the knot in my tongue, and has made us to understand these Bible parables are referring to us, the so-called Negroes and our slave masters."[36] Within this paradigm, Jews were not those whose ancient history was the prototype for contemporary liberation, as was the case for King and other civil rights leaders, but those whose putative status as "the chosen people" usurped the position of the black people in relation to God. This scriptural interpretation did a complex cultural work for the Nation: obviously, it carries the kernels of the NOI's anti-Semitism, which would become more and more pronounced over the decade. And surely this metaphorical removal of Jews from the stories of the Old Testament had particular salience in terms of the domestic tensions that were already rife in urban areas between African Americans and Jews.[37] But the specifically religious content works affirmatively as well by mobilizing, appropriating, and refashioning an honored tradition to claim as one's own, as earlier Christianity had done with Judaism or as the Romans did with Greek mythology.

This mixture of denigration and affirmative appropriation was also apparent in the Nation's attitude toward modern-day Israel. Like earlier black nationalist movements, the NOI saw in the success of Zionism an example and motivation for black nationalism.[38] Malcolm X often referred to Israel respectfully in his speeches and interviews, even as he insisted on the rightness of the Palestinian cause, as in this remarkably ambiguous passage from his autobiography:

> If Hitler *had* conquered the world, as he meant to—that is a shuddery thought for every Jew alive today.
> The Jew will never forget that lesson. . . . [T]he British acquiesced and helped them to wrest Palestine away from the Arabs, the rightful owners, and then the Jews set up Israel, their own country—the one thing that every race of man in the world respects, and understands.[39]

This grudging respect did not translate into emotional identification with Zionism's success, as it did within much black Christian discourse, but it did further establish the complex meanings the Middle East held for the NOI and its members. If, as nationalists, they respected and even hoped to emulate Jewish nationalism, they nonetheless saw the Arab struggle with Israel as a parallel to the NOI's struggle for national self-determination in the United States, where the Nation claimed the right to "separate" from the rest of the United States by taking control of three or four states in the South for black people. Both the Arab (largely Muslim) population in Israel/Palestine and the black ("originally Muslim") population in the United States were in a struggle over land: control over that land was essential to nationalism and political rights.

The NOI identified with colonized nations politically, from the standpoint of a "colored" nation oppressed by whites, but it also drew very specifically on cultural and religious identifications with Arab nations, which were understood to be also racial and historical. In December 1957 Malcolm X organized a meeting on colonial and neocolonial issues that included representatives from the governments of Egypt, the Sudan, Ghana, Iraq, and Morocco. That meeting, hosted by the NOI, sent a cable from Elijah Muhammad to Egyptian president Gamal

Abdul Nasser, who was hosting the Afro-Asian People's Solidarity Conference in Cairo. In it, Elijah Muhammad, describing himself as the "Spiritual Head of the Nation of Islam in the West," addressed Nasser and the other national leaders as brothers, as coreligionists, and as peers:

> As-Salaam-Alikum. Your long lost Muslim brothers here in America pray that Allah's divine presence will be felt at this historic African-Asian Conference, and give unity to our efforts for peace and brotherhood.
>
> Freedom, justice, and equality for all Africans and Asians is of far-reaching importance, not only to you of the East, but also to over 17,000,000 of your long-lost brothers of African-Asian descent here in the West. . . . May our sincere desire for universal peace which is being manifested at this great conference by all Africans and Asians, bring about the unity and brotherhood among all our people which we all so eagerly desire.[40]

The cable, and Nasser's friendly reply, circulated widely within the Nation; these contacts later facilitated Malcolm X's trip to Egypt in 1959, where he laid the groundwork for Elijah Muhammad's visit to Mecca in 1960.[41]

The NOI made explicit the link between a shared heritage and shared origin: a myth of commonality remapped the dominant imaginative geography that separated the Middle East from Africa, instead uniting Africa and northwest Asia (the Middle East) into one geographical space deemed "black Asiatic-African." The vision of one black culture meant that blackness was no longer simply a synonym for Africans and people of recent African descent but a literal linking together of large groups of non-Europeans—the "Asians and Africans" connected, in Malcolm X's words, by history and "by blood."[42]

Elijah Muhammad's genealogical and political views circulated widely in the early 1960s, both within and beyond the African American community. Mainstream media heavily reported on their "discovery" of the Black Muslim phenomenon in multiple television specials and interviews (often with Malcolm X), in paperback "reports," and in newspaper and magazine articles.[43] The NOI was extensively discussed in the public discourse surrounding *The Autobiography of Malcolm X*, which was published in 1965, just months after he was assassinated.[44] The organization was also covered in magazines with primarily black audiences, including *Negro Digest*, *Sepia*, and *Jet*.[45] In addition, the NOI made a concentrated effort to construct its own, alternative public sphere based on a system of widely disseminated newspapers and large public meetings. From 1959 to 1961 the organization published five different newspapers and magazines; one of these, *Muhammed Speaks*, launched in May 1960, became extraordinarily successful, garnering a circulation of over six hundred thousand by

1961.[46] NOI members also produced plays and songs: Louis Farrakhan (known as Louis X in this period) produced two plays in the early 1960s: *Orgena* ("a Negro," spelled backward) and *The Trial*, both of which were performed for Muslim audiences at rallies and meetings. Farrakhan, who had been a Calypso singer before converting, also wrote and recorded several songs, including "White Man's Heaven Is Black Man's Hell" and "Look at My Chains!"[47]

As cultural source and resource, then, the NOI functioned through diverse sites. As a religious and political organization, it took culture and media representation quite seriously, but it also existed and had an impact in many spaces/locations that Elijah Muhammed did not directly control and thus had significant influence well beyond its membership. One site for this diffusion of Islamic sensibility beyond the bounds of the organization was the remarkable infusion of NOI mythology into the cultural products of the emerging Black Arts movement, which would then influence the direction of black liberation politics as the 1960s drew to a close. The signs of the Nation were frequently incorporated into the productions of a new generation of young writers, who took the symbols and myths of this African American–Islamic sect as part of the raw material for the production of a new, black, postnational culture.

When LeRoi Jones left Greenwich Village to found Harlem's Black Arts Repertory Theater/School in 1965, Malcolm X had just been killed, and young African American intellectuals and activists found themselves and their communities in upheaval—in shock, torn by heated debates over the split between Malcolm X and Elijah Muhammad and by questions of who was responsible for the assassination. Then *The Autobiography of Malcolm X* was released; it became an immediate best-seller, creating a sensation within the circles of young, increasingly radicalized men and women who had listened to Malcolm X's speeches and were now riveted by the story of his life.[48] It was in this context, coming to terms with the death of the country's most important spokesperson for black radicalism, that Jones/Baraka set out to form a community-based popular theater and to invent a form and language that would reach a broad African American audience with a message of black (post)nationalism.

Though BARTS was short-lived (it collapsed within a year), its founding was an inspiration to a new generation of poets and playwrights. Black theater and poetry burst onto the national scene—a flowering of African American cultural production unlike anything since the Harlem Renaissance. African American poets and writers began to produce prolifically, and they quickly found new venues for their work as several new publishing houses devoted specifically to black literature were born, including Dudley Randall's Broadside Press, Chicago's Third World Press, and Washington's Drum and Spear Press. In addition, new or revamped literary magazines and academic journals chronicled the scene, including *Umbra, Black Scholar, Journal of Black Poetry, Liberator, Black Books Bulletin, Black Theatre*, and, most importantly, *Negro Digest/Black World*.[49] Baraka himself was also a model; his transformation from a highly literary poet into a radical artist committed to straightforward poetic language and generally short, accessible plays inspired the young writers who were publishing and performing in his wake (and quite consciously in his debt): Ed Bullins, Sonia Sanchez, Marvin X, Ben Caldwell, and Nikki Giovanni, among others.

Perhaps the most striking aspect was the development of a radical, independent theater movement. Within a year of the founding of BARTS, small, community theater groups were being formed in several major cities, including Detroit, New Orleans, San Francisco, Detroit, Chicago, Los Angeles, and Washington, D.C. These new community theaters were distinctly urban institutions; linked with bookstores and community organizations, they produced plays and held poetry readings not only in traditional theaters but also in schools, at local meetings, and in the streets.[50] In April 1966 *Negro Digest* produced its first of several annual issues on the black theater; later that year, a San Francisco–based group, which included Baraka (who was then a visiting professor at San Francisco State), performed at the annual convention of the Congress of Racial Equality (CORE).[51] By 1967 the new black theater was being widely discussed as a major development in the arts of the decade—so much so that when Harold Cruse published *The Crisis of the Black Intellectual*, he ended the book with two chapters on African Americans and the theater, analyzing the significance of BARTS and declaring that "there can be a cultural method of revolutionizing the society in which the theater functions as an institution." A year later, the nation's most important drama journal, *TDR (The Drama Review)*, published a special issue on black theater.[52]

Poetry and plays were the favored genres of the Black Arts movement, despite the fact that both had, up until this point, appealed to a very narrow audience. Both forms were, in Pierre Bourdieu's terms, subfields of highly restricted production, and both carried the cultural capital (and the distance from popular culture) that came with their elite position.[53] But the short poem and the one-act play are often more accessible to new or nontraditional writers, precisely because they are short, and Black Arts movement artists tried with some success to broaden the audience for both genres. Writing in a self-consciously vernacular language, in free verse and street talk, and distributing work in small pamphlets, magazines, paperback anthologies, and public performance, they aimed for a style and a format that were accessible and relevant to people who might otherwise be uninterested in or intimidated by "art." Like earlier avant-garde movements, they wanted to eradicate the separation of "art" from "life."[54] Ed Bullins, a playwright who began writing during this period and who went on to become one of the most prolific and most-produced playwrights of the late 1960s and early 1970s, argued (as many in the movement did) that black theater and poetry were effectively transforming both the genres and their audiences:

> Black literature has been available for years, but it has been circulating in a closed circle. . . . It hasn't been getting down to the people. But now in the theatre, we can go right into the Black community and have a litera-ture for the people . . . for the great masses of Black people. I think this is the reason that more Black plays are being written and seen, and the reason that more Black theatres are springing up. Through the efforts of certain Black artists, people are beginning to realize the importance of Black theatre.[55]

Theater would provide a different kind of avenue, because it could be pre-sented in more accessible forms, to those for whom reading a novel or even a poem might seem daunting.

The mix was potent—cultural capital combined with a new, populist approach and a broader audience. It gave art and artists a highly visible role in the African American community overall, and among younger radicals in par-ticular, and it allowed for the dissemination and generalization of radical politi-cal and cultural perspectives. Thus already by 1966, the influence of black arts was strong enough that the new chair of the Student Non-Violent Coordinating Committee (SNCC), Stokely Carmichael (Kwame Ture), asserted that poetry writing and, by extension, poetry reading were threatening to overtake other kinds of political work. In a speech reprinted in the Chicago SNCC newsletter, he complained: "We have to say, 'Don't play jive and start writing poems after Malcolm is shot.' We have to move from the point where the man left off and stop writing poems."[56]

The genuine popularity and broad reach of these new works is only part of the story, however. No matter how many performances they gave in local ven-ues or how many inexpensive editions they distributed, these poets and play-wrights never had the kind of direct reach enjoyed by major political or religious groups, including the NOI itself, with its distribution network of magazines and newspapers. Nor did they have the popularity of the Miracles or Marvin Gaye, despite Baraka's early hopes and his admiration for the cultural and polit-ical role of music.[57] This limitation on the reach of the Black Arts movement can be attributed at least in part to its ambivalent relationship to the commercial-ization of culture. Though Black Arts movement artists wanted to produce a genuinely popular culture, one with the large, cross-class audience that popular black music had achieved, they were also rightfully suspicious of the process of commodification. Initially, they often tried to avoid circulating their plays and poems in commodity form, offering instead free performances in community buildings or low-cost editions sold on city streets. Artists and activists thus maintained a certain amount of control over their productions, and the movement itself had a democratic element: young and untried artists could have their plays performed in a local community center, where there were no investors to please. But in this model, there was little money to be made and thus little incentive for the kind of corporate involvement that would have been necessary for the large-scale distribution that an institution like Motown could achieve. Commercialized culture has been so important to religious institutions and religious practices precisely because of the remarkable *mobility* of commodities, including cultural commodities—Marvin Gaye reached audiences who might never have heard of Amiri Baraka and who might not have the community resources, or interest, to produce even the simplest of plays.

Yet the irony here is that the limits of the Black Arts movement's popularity were also part of its cultural power. These anticommodity cultural products could have such an impact precisely because of the prestige that art, even popularized art, carried. And the prestige of art—the sense that it *matters* as something more than mere entertainment—is often in inverse proportion to its popularity. Freedom from commercial culture, for art no less than religion, has often been seen as a sign of its purity. Thus the noncommercial approach of the Black Arts movement conferred status within the African American community as well as notoriety for the new artists in the mainstream (white-dominated) media.

The Black Arts movement defined political struggle as cultural struggle; this cultural transformation, in turn, required a new spirituality. In literary circles, Islamic symbolism and mythology were incorporated into the self-conscious construction of a new black aesthetic and a revolutionary black culture. As literary critic Addison Gayle put it, "the historic practice of bowing to other men's gods and definitions has produced a crisis of the highest magnitude, and brought us, culturally, to the limits of racial armageddon."[58] The aim was to establish a basis for political nationalism through the production of a set of cultural and spiritual values "in tune with black people." Artists and theorists of the movement called upon those seeking black power to understand the significance of culture. "The socio-political must be a righteous extension of the cultural," Baraka argued. "A cultural base, a black base, is the completeness the black power movement must have. We must understand that we are replacing a dying [white] culture, and we must be prepared to do this, and be absolutely conscious of what we are replacing it with."[59] The attempt to construct a new black culture was deeply intertwined with the search for religious alternatives to mainstream Christianity, a search that included not only Islam but also renewed interest in the signs and symbols of pre-Islamic and traditional African religions (such as the Yoruba religion) and the study of ancient Egypt. Baraka and others often enthusiastically combined these influences in an eclectic, sometimes deliberately mystical, mix.

Baraka's short play *A Black Mass* exemplifies the cross-fertilization and appropriation that linked Islam and the Black Arts movement in the self-conscious production of a black mythology. The play told the story of how white people had come to be born in an originally black world. It explained the current plight of black people, while reversing the traditional associations of Eurocentric Christianity, making "whiteness" the category associated with evil and thus in need of explanation.[60] Baraka wrote the play in 1965 while he was at BARTS; it was first performed in Newark in May 1966.[61]

When Baraka wrote *A Black Mass*, he was not a member of the NOI and did not even identify as a Muslim, though he would affiliate with orthodox Sunni Islam a few years later. Baraka would always mix Islam with his support of Kawaida, Ron Karenga's syncretic doctrine based on traditional African religions.[62] His fascination with the story of Yakub, however, and his general interest in the myths of the NOI were not idiosyncratic. Thus, though *A Black Mass* was not produced as often as some of Baraka's more explicit social commentary, Black Arts critics admired it. The editor and essayist Larry Neal, who was also Baraka's friend and colleague, described it as Baraka's "most important play" because "it is informed by a mythology that is wholly the creation of the Afro-American sensibility." Another commentator writing in *Negro Digest* called it "Jones' most accomplished play to date."[63] The play was an early, explicit statement of the ways in which, even after the death of Malcolm X and even with suspicions about Elijah Muhammad's role in his murder, the beliefs of the NOI were often presented *as* black culture, influencing and infusing a new black sensibility even for those who were not NOI adherents. In this sense, *A Black Mass* was both symptomatic and anticipatory of what would happen in the sphere of black cultural production over the next few years.

The play was a revision and a condensation of Elijah Muhammad's version of the Yakub story, which explained the creation of white people from Earth's original black inhabitants as the product of generations of genetic breeding.[64] In *A Black Mass*, Yakub, now called Jacoub, is introduced as one of three "Black Magicians" who together symbolize the black origin of all religions: according to the stage directions, they wear a skullcap, a fez, and an African fila.[65] The play's title alludes to the necessity of black revisions of religious ritual, and the play itself is designed to revise and rewrite implicitly white-centered origin myths—not incidentally, it also defines and explains the theological problem of evil as represented in white people.

Baraka turns the Nation's myth into a reinterpretation of the Faust story and a simultaneous meditation on the role and function of art. Jacoub is a complex figure: his desire to "find out everything" makes him in some ways more attractive and accessible than the other magicians, who insist that "we already know everything" and that creation or innovation is impossible and dangerous. But the play's condemnation of Jacoub is apparent not only in the fact that he is trying to create "whiteness" (surely the moral weight of that choice needed no further amplification for the primarily black audience to which the play was addressed) but also in his insistence that "creation is its own end"; this art-for-art's-sake view was precisely the aesthetic philosophy that Baraka and other leaders of the early Black Arts movement were determined to challenge and, if possible, eradicate.[66] The point was underscored by the fact that the play relied heavily on music composed and played by the avant-garde jazz artist Sun-Ra, as Baraka enacted his own argument that black music should be the model for the new black literary culture.[67]

At the opening of the play, Jacoub is determined to pursue knowledge narcissistically, to create for the sake of creating. Jacoub decides to make his own creature—"a super-natural being. A being who will not respond to the world of humanity." Castigated by the other magicians, Jacoub nonetheless proceeds with his experiment; as he does so, the natural world is disturbed by raging seas and thundering skies that have a Lear-like portentousness. Three women run in from outside, upset and frightened; they wail and moan, serving as a chorus and as representatives of "the people" who will be destroyed by Jacoub's creation. Ignoring the portents, Jacoub pours his solutions together: there is an explosion, and out leaps a cold, white creature in a lizard-devil mask. The creature vomits and screams, "slobberlaughing" its way through the audience. Jacoub insists that he can teach the beast to talk, but it has only two words, incessantly repeated: "Me!" and "White."

The beast immediately tries to attack the women and soon bites one of them, who is quickly transformed into another monster. With this "bite-caress" of the woman, Baraka brings sexuality to the forefront: the depraved and dangerous (and decidedly unsexy) red-caped beast infects the women first, using its lust to spread its "white madness."[68] At the end of the play, the infected woman and the beast become hideous Adam and Eve substitutes: The two of them attack and kill the other women and the rest of the magicians, including Jacoub. With his dying breath, Jacoub condemns the two beasts to the caves of the north. These two creatures will reproduce and eventually will create the white race that comes to dominate and enslave the rest of the world.

If the play allegorically represents the rape of black women by white men, it also constructs "Woman" as the first and most susceptible conduit for the spread of "whiteness," reproducing the tendency of many nationalist ideologies to make women's bodies the sites of both nationalist reproduction and potential cultural impurity. *A Black Mass* describes white people as the spawn of monsters, a crime against the natural order, but distorted (black) reproduction is the unspoken but crucial undercurrent.[69]

At the end of *A Black Mass*, a final voice-over issues a call to racial struggle, now framed in mythical and theological terms: "And so Brothers and Sisters, these beasts are still loose in the world. Still they spit their hideous cries. There are beasts in our world, Brothers and Sisters. . . . Let us find them and slay them. . . . Let us declare Holy War. The Jihad. Or we cannot deserve to live. Izm-el-Azam. Ism-el-Azam. Izm-el-Azam. Izm-el-Azam." The call for a jihad becomes a religious and moral response to the problem of evil, the answer of the present to the history presented in the play. The language of Islamic militancy is mobilized for black militancy; religious struggle and racial struggle are made one.

The influence of Islam and Islamic symbolism went well beyond Baraka's work; it was highly visible in the Black Arts movement in general, acknowledged, and often supported, even by those who did not share its religious presumptions. Members of both the NOI and orthodox African American Sunni Muslim groups were active in political and cultural organizations all over the country. Baraka's own interest in Islam continued to manifest itself in poetry and essays for the rest of the decade.[70] By the time Baraka and Larry Neal published the field-defining anthology *Black Fire* in 1968 and Ed Bullins edited the collection *New Plays for the Black Theatre* a year later, they were able to canonize a body of work, produced and written in the previous several years, in which the influence of Islam was highly visible. Many of the plays, poetry, and essays either were direct translations of NOI ideology (such as Salimu's "Growing into Blackness," which instructs young women on the proper Islamic way to support their men) or simply presumed working familiarity with Islam on the part of the audience. The prominence of Muslim-derived names is also significant in both collections; many poems and plays are by writers who have changed their names to, among others, Yusef Iman, Yusef Rahman, Ahmed Legraham Alhamisi, Salimu, and Marvin X.[71] When Baraka published his own collection of plays that same year, he introduced it with a poem that claimed the political power of the literary renaissance:

> This is an introduction to a book of plays
> i am prophesying the death of white people in this land

> i am prophesying the triumph of black life in this land and over
>   all the world
> we are building publishing houses, and newspapers, and armies
>   and factories
> we will change the world before your eyes,
>   izm-el-azam,
>   yes, say it
>   say it
>   sweet nigger
>   i believe in black allah
>   governor of creation
>   Lord of the Worlds
>   As Salaam Alikum[72]

Looking at the cultural products and newspaper accounts of the period, it is clear that the NOI provided one significant touchstone for a larger project—that of re-visioning history and geography in order to construct a moral and spiritual basis for contemporary affiliations and identities. As Larry Neal described it: "The Old Spirituality is generalized. It seeks to recognize Universal Humanity. The New Spirituality is specific. It begins by seeing the world from the concise point-of-view of the colonized."[73] In *A Black Mass*, Baraka offered a religiously infused narrative as empowering myth, as a culture specific to black people. Within this project, Islamic affiliations often functioned as both site and source for those black identities, linking African Americans to the Arab and Muslim Middle East in ways both literal and metaphoric.

As black nationalism gained prominence in the late 1960s, some writers and thinkers in the Black Arts movement began to offer challenges to the cultural politics of Christianity and Islam, expressing a desire to transcend both. Islam had always been only one of several religious resources available in this period, though a particularly prominent one. Groups like Ron Karenga's US drew on a syncretistic mix of various African traditions, updated and revised. Baraka himself supplemented his Islam with Yoruba symbols and beliefs and also began in the period after 1967 to add ancient Egyptian motifs. The unofficial leader of this new syncretism was the young writer Ishmael Reed. In several novels, in his collected poems, and in interviews and essays, Reed presented himself as an iconoclast, both formally and spiritually. His extraordinary 1972 novel, *Mumbo Jumbo*, challenged the connection to a black Islam and instead constructed a historical, religious, and cultural matrix that privileged Caribbean voodoo (or, as Reed called it referring to the U.S. terminology,

"HooDoo") as the authentic African American religion. He linked these traditional religions directly back to the myths and gods of ancient Egypt, which he saw as a model for a liberated black sensibility.

Mumbo Jumbo's pantheistic moral geography represented the culmination of a generation of rethinking the spiritual heritage and the international links that might underlay a new black religious-cultural politics. It was also, in some sense, the end of a journey. Fascination with and claims for ancient Egypt would continue throughout the 1970s and into the 1980s and 1990s, and of course African American Islam would remain a dynamic, if diminished, force in the black community, but by the middle 1970s hope had faded that African Americans would develop a fully realized and widely shared political-cultural-religious new order.[74]

Yet the moment itself is important, and careful attention to the world and worldviews of African American urban activists and artists reveals several key issues for thinking about the cultural politics of religious movements. The first is simply a reminder that scholarship must bring together analysis of the political, cultural, and religious spheres, because these are interconnected so often in lived experience. And in this particular period of the 1960s, African American activists and intellectuals made conscious attempts to link these arenas, in new ways, for the benefit of a community in transition. The second is that we must not be too quick to frame African American religious culture as outside of commodity culture, an alternative to the secular world of black popular music, art, and dance. As other scholars have shown, it is not only that such clean lines of division were blurred in practice but that for many African Americans they were not even an ideal.[75] In the case of the African American intellectuals and artists discussed here, there was often concern about the commodification of art, but religious beliefs and practices mattered because they were not separate spheres. Instead, they would be part of a transformation that, like music and art—and through music and art—would be part of remaking the world.

This recognition of interconnected developments can help transform our understanding of political relations as well. For example, careful attention to the politics of Islam speaks to the history of black and Jewish relations, particularly in urban areas where both the NOI and the Black Arts movement were strong. African American support for Palestinians or Arabs in the Arab-Israeli conflict, long considered to be an expression of black anti-Semitism, has a more complicated genealogy. Attention to the development of black Islam and its role in the radicalization of African American culture and politics helps us reframe the questions we ask about that moment and about the history of black-Jewish and black-Arab relations overall. This alternative analysis avoids the common conflation of black-Jewish relations within the United States (and the concomitant issues of racism and anti-Semitism) with the meanings and significance of the Middle East for African Americans.[76]

Of course, anti-Semitism was present in the black community and the Black Arts movement, sometimes virulently. And it is not sufficient to say, as James Baldwin once did, that blacks were anti-Semitic because they were antiwhite.[77] However, these anti-Semitic expressions do not explain the pro-Arab feelings of many African Americans in this period, since it would have been quite possible for them to be both anti-Jewish and anti-Arab. The pull toward Arab culture was something far more than an outgrowth of anti-Semitism; it connected to the complex religious affiliations that also linked African American identity with the Arab and Islamic Middle East.

Finally, revisiting black cultural and religious productions makes clear that to describe these productions as simply nationalist is to miss the complicated transnational moral geographies that animated African American identities in this period. Religious connections became bound up with both urban politics and international affiliations and simultaneously became a way of constructing a range of differences within black communities. African American Muslims often distinguished themselves from black Christians by highlighting their separatism and claiming an uncompromising radicalism, and these claims were then mapped onto a whole range of distinctions: urban versus rural; masculine resistance versus feminized nonviolence; black origins versus white influence. In this, the ongoing realities of the Arab-Israeli conflict became powerful political rhetoric for describing and maintaining "domestic" boundaries.

These religious and cultural connections were also part of a forceful redefinition of race that virtually made anticolonial activity into a marker of blackness. Though black Christians and civil rights activists had claimed ties to anticolonial movements around the world, NOI and those influenced by it upped the ante, insisting that African Americans were literally connected, "by blood," to Africans, to Arabs, and even to Asians. This vision was also a critique, as when Addison Gayle exhorted African American artists to turn their back on nationalist identities: "To be an American writer is to be an American, and for black people, there should no longer be any honor attached to either position."[78]

Thus African American cultural production in the era of black liberation challenged the very notion of a national identity in highly public and influential ways. That is one reason it matters. Of course, transnational identities are not magically unproblematic: the black cultural radicalism of the 1960s often framed black identity in terms that were ahistorical, masculinist, and anti-Semitic. This is its irony, its limit, and its loss. But the intervention was significant: a transformed domestic politics, a remapping of the urban cultural landscape, an alternative moral geography (and a new imagined community) that did not begin and end with either America or Africa. Often centered in constructions of spirituality and religious belief, this African American narrative of countercitizenship remade black urban identities, using art and a revamped spirituality, by transforming the map of the world into a politics of the heart.

Notes

This essay draws from chapter 2 of my book, *Epic Encounters: Culture, Media, and U.S. Interests in the Middle East, 1945–2000* (Berkeley and Los Angeles: University of California Press, 2001). That material is used here with permission. I would like to thank friends and colleagues who have read various versions of these arguments, particularly Carl Conetta, Ruth Feldstein, and Uta Poiger. Thanks also to Gail Bederman, Krista Comer, Jane Gerhard, Ted German, R. Marie Griffith, William Hart, James A. Miller, Teresa Murphy, Kirsten Swinth, Robert Vitalis, Priscilla Wald, Diane Winston, Stacy Wolf, two anonymous reviewers and the editors of the Crossroads series at the University of California Press, especially George Lipsitz and Peggy Pascoe. I would also like to thank Robert Wuthnow and the Center for the Study of Religion at Princeton University for affording me the opportunity to research and write for a year.

1. Arjun Appadurai has theorized this flow in "Difference and Disjuncture in the Global Cultural Economy," in *Modernity at Large: Cultural Dimensions of Globalization* (Minneapolis: University of Minnesota Press, 1996).

2. On the day after the fight, Clay announced that he "believed in Allah"; at a press conference the following day, he clarified his membership in the Nation of Islam. See Thomas Hauser, *Muhammad Ali: His Life and Times* (New York: Simon & Schuster, 1991), 81–84; John McDermott, "Champ 23: A Man-Child Taken In By the Muslims," *Life*, March 6, 1964, 38–39; Huston Horn, "The First Days in the New Life of the Champion of the World," *Sports Illustrated*, March 9, 1964, 26ff; and "Prizefighting: With Mouth and Magic," *Time*, March 6, 1964, 66–69.

3. See "Cassius Marcellus Clay," *Time*, March 22, 1963, 78–81; Pete Hamill "Young Cassius Has a Mean & Sonny Look," *New York Post*, March 8, 1963; Howard Tuckner, "'Man, It's Great to Be Great,'" *New York Times*, December 9, 1962; and "C. Marcellus Clay Esq." *Sports Illustrated*, June 10, 1963, 19–25.

4. Malcolm X with Alex Haley, *The Autobiography of Malcolm X* (1954; reprint, New York: Ballantine Books, 1992), 349–356; Bruce Perry, *Malcolm: The Life of a Man Who Changed Black America* (Barrytown, N.Y.: Stanton Hill Press, 1991), 245–250; Stan Koven, "The Muslim Dinner and Cassius Clay," *New York Post*, January 23, 1964; William Braden, "Muslims Claim the Credit for Clay's Victory," *New York Post*, February 2, 1964; "Cassius X," *Newsweek*, March 16, 1964.

5. Ted Poston, "Clay in Malcolm X's Corner in Black Muslim Fight," *New York Post*, March 3, 1964; J. Cannon, "The Muslims' Prize," *Journal American*, February 23, 1965; "Cassius Clay Says He Is Not 'Scared' of Killing Reprisal," *New York Times*, February 24, 1965; Milton Gross, "The Men Around Cassius Clay," *New York Post*, May 28, 1965; "FBI Probes Muhammad and Clay," *New York Post*, February 28, 1966.

6. Robert Lipsyte, "Cassius Clay, Cassius X, Muhammad Ali," *New York Times Magazine*, October 25, 1964, 29ff. See also Alex Haley's *Playboy* interview with Ali in October 1964, reprinted in Murray Fisher, ed., *Alex Haley: The Playboy Interviews* (New York: Ballantine Books, 1993), 46–79.

7. Bill Jaus, "Cassius: I'm Still Unfit," *New York Post*, February 21, 1966. See also Henry Hampton and Steve Fayer, *Voices of Freedom: An Oral History of the Civil Rights Movement from the 1950s through the 1980s* (New York: Bantam Books, 1990), 321–334; and Hauser, *Muhammad Ali*, 142–201.

8. Sanchez is quoted in Hampton and Fayer, *Voices of Freedom*, 328.

9. For a very useful discussion of Baraka's early work, see James A. Miller, "Amiri Baraka," in *The Beats: Literary Bohemians in Postwar America: Dictionary of Literary Biography*, vol. 16, part 1, ed. Ann Charters (Detroit: Gayle Research, 1983), 3–24.

10. Baraka describes writing the play in *The Autobiography of LeRoi Jones/Amiri Baraka* (New York: Freundlich Books, 1984), 210; his affiliation with Sunni Islam is discussed on pp. 267–269. Baraka says that Jaaber "buried Malcolm X," but Peter Goldman mentions only Sheikh Ahmed Hassoun, the Sudanese cleric who had returned with Malcolm X from Mecca, in *The Death and Life of Malcolm X* (Urbana: University of Illinois Press, 1979), 302.

11. The designation of Baraka came from a poll of thirty-eight prominent black writers published in the January 1968 issue of *Negro Digest*. The writers also voted Baraka "the most important living black poet" and "the most important black playwright." Werner Sollors, *Amiri Baraka/LeRoi Jones: Quest for a Populist Modernism* (New York: Columbia University Press, 1978), 264 n.6. On Baraka's transformation to Maoism, see his *Autobiography*, 308–314.

12. Baraka, *Autobiography*, 204.

13. On Motown as a powerful political force, despite its apparently apolitical lyrics and crossover appeal, see Suzanne Smith, *Dancing in the Street: Motown and the Cultural Politics of Detroit* (Cambridge: Harvard University Press, 2000).

14. On the Nation of Islam in the 1960s, see Mathias Gardell, *In the Name of Elijah Muhammad: Louis Farrakhan and the Nation of Islam* (Durham, N.C.: Duke University Press, 1996); C. Eric Lincoln, *The Black Muslims in America*, rev. ed. (New York: Eerdmans, 1993); and Karl Evanzz, *The Messenger: The Rise and Fall of Elijah Muhammad* (New York: Pantheon Books, 1999). See also Aminah Beverly McCloud, *African American Islam* (New York: Routledge, 1995).

15. Michael Shapiro, "Moral Geographies and the Ethics of Post-Sovereignty," *Public Culture* 6, no. 3 (1994): 479–502, 482. Edward Said, in *Orientalism* (New York: Vintage, 1979), uses the phrase "imaginative geography" to a similar effect.

16. Here I am also, of course, engaging with the issues raised by Benedict Anderson, *Imagined Communities: Reflections on the Origin and Spread of Nationalism* (New York: Verso, 1991).

17. Marvin X and Faruk, "Islam and Black Art: An Interview with LeRoi Jones," *Negro Digest* 18 (January 1969): 4–10ff; reprinted in Jeff Decker, ed., *The Black Arts Movement: Dictionary of Literary Biography Documentary Series*, vol. 8 (Detroit: Gayle Research, 1991). Jones used the phrase "post-American" earlier as well, in his essay "What the Arts Need Now," *Negro Digest* (April 1967): 5–6.

18. In several of these cities, temples had already been established by W. D. Fard or Elijah Muhammad, and Malcolm X worked to reinvigorate membership. In other places, he set up new temples. For a list of active temples in the period 1958–1959, see Evanzz, *Messenger*, 453–462.

19. Gardell, *In the Name of Elijah Muhammad*, 65; E. U. Essien-Udom, *Black Nationalism: A Search for an Identity in America* (New York: Dell, 1964), 84.

20. John Voll, *Islam: Continuity and Change in the Modern World* (Syracuse, N.Y.: Syracuse University Press, 1994).

21. Perhaps Elijah Muhammad was also incorporating some reference here to Asia Minor, which comprises most of modern Turkey.

22. Penny M. Von Eschen's *Race Against Empire: Black Americans and Anticolonialism, 1937–1957* (Ithaca, N.Y.: Cornell University Press, 1996) is an excellent study of the internationalism of African American politics in the period, focused primarily on Africa.

23. Until Elijah Muhammad's death in 1975, the NOI generally used the term "temples"; after Wallace D. Muhammad took over leadership and began a transformation of the organization into the American Muslim Mission, with a more orthodox doctrine, the term "mosques" was used. Eventually, followers simply joined whatever local mosque was in their community, and the organization dissolved. The original NOI was revived by Louis Farrakhan in 1978. Gardell, *In the Name of Elijah Muhammad*, 99–135.

24. The best and most detailed history of Fard's life is in Evanzz, *Messenger*, 398–417.

25. On Muslim slaves and early Muslim communities in the United States, see Richard Turner, *Islam in the African-American Experience* (Bloomington: Indiana University Press, 1997). There is some indication, however, that Muslim Africans were *less* likely than others to be taken and sold as slaves; see Monroe Berger, "The Black Muslims," *Horizon* (winter 1966): 49–64.

26. Lincoln, *Black Muslims*, 120.

27. Elijah Muhammad, *Message to the Blackman* (Chicago: Muhammad Mosque of Islam No. 2, 1965), 31.

28. Described by Malcolm X, *Autobiography*, 224–225; also in Perry, *Malcolm X*, 142.

29. On the theological difference between the NOI and both Christianity and orthodox Islam, see Gardell, *In the Name of Elijah Muhammad*, 144–186.

30. James Baldwin, *The Fire Next Time* (New York: Dell, 1977), 46.

31. Jonathan Kaufman describes the exodus metaphor as a primary link between black and Jewish history in *Broken Alliance: The Turbulent Times between Blacks and Jews in America*, rev. ed. (1988; reprint, New York: Charles Scribner's Sons, 1995), 35. See also Lawrence Levine, *Black Culture and Black Consciousness: Afro-American Folk Thought from Slavery to Freedom* (New York: Oxford University Press, 1977); and Albert Raboteau, *Slave Religion: The "Invisible Institution" in the Antebellum South* (New York: Oxford University Press, 1978).

32. Lowrey makes the link while being interviewed by Howell Raines in Howell Raines, *My Soul Is Rested: Movement Days in the Deep South Remembered* (New York: Penguin Books, 1983). For one example of Martin Luther King Jr.'s use of the trope, see his last speech, "I See the Promised Land," given on April 3, 1968, at the Mason Temple in Memphis and reprinted in *A Testament of Hope: The Essential Writings and Speeches of Martin Luther King, Jr.*, ed. James Washington (San Francisco: Harper Collins\HarperSanFrancisco, 1986), 279–286.

33. Robert Weisbord and Richard Kazarian Jr., *Israel in the Black American Perspective* (Westport, Conn.: Greenwood Press, 1985), 20–22.

34. See David Garrow, *Bearing the Cross: Martin Luther King and the Southern Christian Leadership Conference* (1961; reprint, New York: Vintage Books, 1988), 110–115; and M. L. King, "My Trip to the Land of Gandhi," in *A Testament of Hope*, 23–30.

35. Jonathan Boyarin argues persuasively that the influence of the exodus trope also worked in the other direction: the civil rights connotations of exodus played a role in the increasing tendency to use that rhetoric to represent Israel. "Reading Exodus into History," *New Literary History* 23, no. 3 (summer 1992): 540.

36. Muhammad, *Message to the Blackman*, 95–96.

37. Of the many that explore this history, perhaps the best single source is Jack Salzman, ed., with Adina Black and Gretchen Sullivan Sorin, *Bridges and Boundaries: African Americans and American Jews* (New York: George Braziller in association with the Jewish Museum, 1992). On the prewar period, see Hasia Diner, *In the Almost Promised Land: American Jews and Blacks, 1915–1935* (Baltimore: Johns Hopkins University Press, 1992).

38. Paul Gilroy explores the link with Zionism in *The Black Atlantic: Modernity and Double-Consciousness* (Cambridge: Harvard University Press, 1993); see also Hollis Lynch, *Edward Wilmont Blyden: Pan-Negro Patriot, 1832–1912* (New York: Oxford University Press, 1967).

39. Malcolm X, *Autobiography*, 320.

40. Brenda Gayle Plummer, *Rising Wind: Black Americans and U.S. Foreign Policy* (Chapel Hill: University of North Carolina Press, 1996), 261. Also quoted in Lincoln, *Black Muslims*, 225.

41. Perry, *Malcolm X*, 205–206. Evanzz also traces the complex history of this trip in *Messenger*, 193–195: Nasser originally invited Elijah Muhammad for a visit that could have ended with a hajj to Mecca, but the FBI successfully delayed Elijah Muhammad's passport so that Malcolm X visited Egypt instead but did not make the pilgrimage.

42. Speech at Boston University, February 15, 1960, quoted in Lincoln, *Black Muslims*, 169.

43. The television special "The Hate that Hate Produced," produced by Mike Wallace and Louis Lomax, aired in 1959. Already in 1959 and 1960, the Black Muslim movement had been covered in articles in *Time* ("Black Supremacists," August 10, 1959), *Newsweek* ("The Way of Cults," May 7, 1956), *New York Times* ("Rise in Racial Extremism," January 25, 1960), *Christian Century* ("Despair Serves Purposes of Bizarre Cult," August 10, 1960), and *Reader's Digest* (Alex Haley, "Mr. Muhammad Speaks," March 1960). The first book-length study, C. Eric Lincoln's scholarly *The Black Muslims in America*, was published in 1961; a year later, James Baldwin's "Letter from a Region in My Mind" came out in the *New Yorker*, and E. U. Essien-Udom published *Black Nationalism*. Louis Lomax's popular account of the NOI, *When the Word Was Given*, came out in 1963, and in that same year Malcolm X was interviewed by *Playboy* (May 1963), while Alfred Black and Alex Haley published a long article in the *Saturday Evening Post* ("Black Merchants of Hate," January 26, 1963). Some of this coverage is discussed in the third edition of Lincoln's *Black Muslims*, 174–176. Evanzz, *Messenger*, 193–198, discusses the impact of the Mike Wallace special within the Nation.

44. The book was excerpted in the *Saturday Evening Post*, September 12, 1964, before its official publication. It was widely reviewed; see, for example, I. F. Stone's review, "The Pilgrimage of Malcolm X," in the *New York Review*, November 11, 1965.

45. *Negro Digest* ran several articles on the Black Muslims in the early 1960s, including an essay by Elijah Muhammad called "What the Black Muslims Believe," November

1963, 3–6. *Jet* covered the impact of Muslim identity on the career of Cassius Clay: Bobbie E. Barbee, "Will Link with Malcolm X Harm Clay's Career?" March 26, 1964, 50–57. Coverage in the black press was often ambivalent: when Malcolm X was killed, *Sepia*'s headline was "The Violent End of Malcolm X: He Taught Violence, He Died Violently," May 1965.

46. Lincoln, *Black Muslims*, 128. On the black public sphere, see The Black Public Sphere Collective, ed., *The Black Public Sphere* (Chicago: University of Chicago Press, 1995), in particular Manthia Diawara, "Malcolm X and the Black Public Sphere."

47. Lincoln, *Black Muslims*, 108.

48. Baraka, *Autobiography*, 203. For a contemporary discussion of the response, see Lawrence P. Neal, "Malcolm and the Conscience of Black America," *Liberator* (February 1966) 6, no. 2, 10–11. Mance Williams discusses the impact of Malcolm X's autobiography on the Free Southern Theater company in *Black Theatre in the 1960s and 1970s: A Historical-Critical Analysis of the Movement* (Westport, Conn.: Greenwood Press, 1985), 62.

49. On the publishing scene, see Komozi Woodard, *A Nation within a Nation: Amiri Baraka (LeRoi Jones) and Black Power Politics* (Chapel Hill: University of North Carolina Press, 1999), 65–68; and Henry Louis Gates and Nellie McKay, eds., *The Norton Anthology of African American Literature* (New York: Norton, 1997), 1791–1806.

50. See Ed Bullins, "A Short Statement on Street Theatre," *TDR* (summer 1968), 93.

51. Baraka, *Autobiography*, 249.

52. Harold Cruse, "Intellectuals and the Theater of the 1960s," in *Crisis of the Negro Intellectual: A Historical Analysis of the Failure of Black Leadership* (1969; reprint, New York: Quill, 1984), 531. See also the penultimate chapter of the book, "The Harlem Black Arts Theater." *TDR*'s special issue on black theatre was summer 1968.

53. Pierre Bourdieu, *The Field of Cultural Production: Essays on Art and Literature* (New York: Columbia University Press, 1993).

54. Peter Burger, *Theory of the Avant-Garde* (Minneapolis: University of Minnesota Press, 1984).

55. Interview with Ed Bullins, *New Plays from the Black Theatre*, ed. Ed Bullins (New York: Bantam Books, 1969), vii.

56. Stokely Carmichael, "We Are Going to Use the Term 'Black Power' and We Are Going to Define It Because Black Power Speaks to Us," in *Black Nationalism in America*, ed. J. Bracey, August Meier, and E. Rudwick (Indianapolis: Bobbs-Merrill, 1970), 472. Carmichael is also quoted by Philip B. Harper, *Are We Not Men? Masculine Anxiety and the Problem of African-American Identity* (New York: Oxford University Press, 1996), 51.

57. See Baraka as LeRoi Jones, *Blues People: Negro Music in White America* (New York: W. W. Morrow, 1963).

58. Addison Gayle, "Cultural Strangulation: Black Literature and the White Aesthetic," in *The Black Aesthetic*, ed. Addison Gayle (New York: Anchor Books, 1972), 46.

59. Amiri Baraka, "The Need for a Cultural Base to Civil Rites and Black Power Movements," in *Raise, Race, Rays, Raze: Essays since 1965* (New York: Random House, 1971), 43–46. On the broad diffusion of cultural nationalism, see William Van Deburg, *A New Day in Babylon: The Black Power Movement and American Culture, 1965–1975* (Chicago: University of Chicago Press, 1992).

60. Lincoln, *Black Muslims*, 72.

61. The play was then published in the little magazine the *Liberator* the following month and in 1969 collected in Baraka's *Four Black Revolutionary Plays* (London: Marion Boyars, 1998). Publication history from Decker, *Black Arts Movement*, 120–121. The following discussion quotes from the text of *Four Black Revolutionary Plays*. Page numbers in parentheses. Quoted by permission of Maron Boyars Publishers. Available in the United States from Consortium Book Sales, St. Paul, MN (ISBN 0-7145-3005-0).

62. For example, see Baraka's pamphlet, "7 Principles of US Maulana Karenga & the Need for a Black Value System," later reprinted in Baraka, *Raise, Race, Rays, Raze.*

63. Larry Neal, "The Black Arts Movement," in *Visions of a Liberated Future: Black Arts Movement Writings*, ed. Michael Schwartz (New York: Thunder's Mouth Press, 1989), 73; K. William Kgositsile, "Towards Our Theater: A Definitive Act," *Negro Digest* (April 1967): 15.

64. Elijah Muhammad explained the story of Yakub frequently, including in *Message to the Blackman*, 117–119. This myth was dropped from NOI theology after Wallace D. Muhammad took over leadership of the community after Elijah Muhammad's death in 1975. See McCloud, *African American Islam*, 72–88.

65. The transformation of the name of the villain Yakub into a name (and a spelling) that looks more like Jacob may have anti-Semitic overtones, though this is not explicit elsewhere in the play.

66. Larry Neal interprets the play as a critique of the Western aesthetic in "The Black Arts Movement."

67. Mance Williams, *Black Theatre*, 23.

68. Wernor Sollars discusses Baraka's various literary references in *Amiri Baraka/LeRoi Jones: The Quest for a "Populist Modernism"* (New York: Columbia University Press, 1978), 211.

69. There have been several other important studies of the masculinist bias of much of the Black Arts movement, including Joyce Hope Scott, "From Foreground to Margin: Female Configuration and Masculine Self-Representation in Black Nationalist Fiction," in *Nationalisms and Sexualities*, ed. Andrew Parker et al. (New York: Routledge, 1992). On cultural and gender conservatism in African American political movements, see E. Frances White, "Africa on My Mind: Gender, Counterdiscourse, and African American Nationalism," in *Words of Fire*, ed. Beverly Guy-Sheftall (New York: New Press, 1995).

70. For example, Amiri Baraka, "From: The Book of Life," written after the Newark riots in 1967 and collected in *Raise, Race, Rays, Raze.*

71. Larry Neal and LeRoi Jones, eds. *Black Fire: An Anthology of Afro-American Writing* (New York: William & Morrow, 1968). Essays with Islamic themes in the anthology include David Llorens, "The Fellah, the Chosen Ones, The Guardian," and Nathan Hare, "Brainwashing of Black Men's Minds." In the Ed Bullins anthology, *New Plays from Black Theatre* (New York: Bantam Books, 1969), other examples of NOI-influenced plays are *El Hajj Malik: A Play about Malcolm X*," by N. R. Davidson Jr., and *The Black Bird (Al Tair Aswad)* by Marvin X. See also Dudley Randall and M. Borroughs, eds., *For Malcolm: Poems on the Life and Death of Malcolm X* (Detroit: Broadside Press, 1969).

72. Baraka, *Four Black Revolutionary Plays*, vii–viii. Quoted with permission from Marion Boyars. *Four Black Revolutionary Plays* is available from Consortium Books Sales, Saint Paul, Minn., ISBN 0 7145 3005–0.

73. Neal, "Black Arts Movement," 77.

74. On Reed, see Reginald Martin, *Ishmael Reed and the New Black Aesthetic Critics* (New York: St. Martin's, 1988). The varied meanings of ancient Egypt are detailed in Melani McAlister, "A Common Heritage of Mankind: Race and Nation in the King Tut Exhibit," *Representations* 54 (spring 1996): 80–102.

75. Michael Eric Dyson, *Between God and Gangsta Rap: Bearing Witness to Black Culture* (New York: Oxford University Press, 1996).

76. Cornel West points out the significance of the principle of Palestinian rights in "On Black-Jewish Relations," in *Black and Jews: Alliances and Arguments*, ed. Paul Berman (New York: Dell, 1995), 144–153. Alice Walker makes a similar point in "To the Editors of Ms. Magazine," in *In Search of Our Mother's Gardens* (San Diego, Calif.: Harcourt Brace Jovanovich, 1983), 347–354. I discuss the political developments in more detail in *Epic Encounters*.

77. James Baldwin, "Negroes Are Anti-Semitic because They Are Anti-White," in *The Price of the Ticket: Collected Non-Fiction, 1948–1985* (1967; reprint, New York: St. Martin's/Marek, 1985).

78. Addison Gayle, "Introduction," in Gayle, *Black Aesthetic*, xxiii.

Eleven

Etan Diamond

Beyond Borscht

*The Kosher Lifestyle and the Religious
Consumerism of Suburban Orthodox Jews*

In the May 1952 issue of *Commentary* magazine, reporter Morris Freedman wrote an extended essay on the phenomenon of Barton's Chocolates. Established in the late 1930s by Stephen Klein, a European Jewish immigrant, Barton's almost single-handedly created a market for gourmet chocolates. Its boutiques—not stores—were "all show window, frivolously decked with tinsel and ribbon," and designed to give customers "pleasure" from entering the premises. When entering a Barton's boutique, they found an assortment of some of the finest chocolates available presented in elegant style. The goal, Klein explained, was "to make each piece of candy attractive. All the pieces should look good. You should keep wanting to eat more and not get tired." For the reporter Freedman, however, Barton's success lay not so much in its ability to make chocolate a luxury item but doing so while having all of Barton's chocolates manufactured and sold under the strict supervision of the Orthodox Union (OU), the kosher certifying agency of the Union of Orthodox Jewish Congregations of America. Such certification meant that every piece of Barton's chocolate—down to the chocolate Santa Clauses and Easter bunnies—could be eaten by Orthodox Jews who observed the religious dietary laws known as kashruth. Although Jews who observed these laws were the minority of Barton's customers, Stephen Klein recognized the value of gourmet kosher chocolate. Orthodox Jewish business owners, for example, could give chocolate as a gift to clients without feeling uncomfortable about giving nonkosher food. For Orthodox Jews, or for those who were guests of Orthodox Jews, a box of Barton's had also become "one of the habitual choices for the ritual gift picked up on the way to dinner at a friend's home, or for one's week-end suburban hostess, or for the weekly gathering of the *mishpocha* (family)." Kosher chocolate could even bridge the generations, since "a child may be supplied with a box to present to grandpa because it is *kosher* chocolate; grandpa, for his part, may bring a box to grandson because it is kosher *chocolate*."[1]

To Freedman, Barton's chocolates represented a "classic example of how Orthodoxy can be subtly attractive to the modern world," where "increased substance and status has found expression [among Orthodox Jews] as often in elegance of cuisine and dining ritual as in the greater modishness of matters pertaining to the synagogue."[2] This religious materialism Freedman described was a key component to the suburban Orthodox Jewish experience in the post–World War II period and today represents a strong challenge to the contemporary assumptions about the study of religion and suburbanization. In the postwar period, most social scientists assumed that the movement into suburbia and exposure to its consumerist culture would inevitably lead to a decline in religious traditionalism.[3] Few questioned the belief that the allure of consumerist culture would pull adherents away from traditional religious practices. Orthodox Judaism in particular, with its range of religiously restrictive practices, was seen as incapable of withstanding Jewish socioeconomic upward mobility.[4] Yet such assumptions failed to recognize the reality that the expansion of a consumerist culture actually made it easier to maintain traditional Jewish practices. This essay explores this expansion, as manifested in the emergence of the "kosher lifestyle," a religious-materialist orientation among suburban Orthodox Jews that originated in specific religious dietary laws but quickly expanded to encompass other consumerist activities, such as going to restaurants, listening to music, and traveling. Through the kosher lifestyle, suburban Orthodox Jews wrapped the veneer of secular consumerist styles—expensive wines, elegant restaurants, exotic vacations—around a strict adherence to religiously traditional rituals. Thus, rather than shed their religious traditionalism upon contact with secular suburban commercial culture, Orthodox Jews used that commercial culture to facilitate, strengthen, and even expand their traditionalist religious behaviors.

One of the places where the suburban kosher lifestyle developed most strongly was Toronto, a city with a long history of Orthodox Jewish suburbanization. Beginning in the early 1950s, Toronto's Orthodox Jews joined their nonobservant counterparts in moving from the downtown neighborhood of Kensington to newer neighborhoods about five miles to the north along Bathurst Street in the suburban municipality of North York. Over the next half century, the community continued to expand northward along Bathurst, creating a string of suburban Orthodox Jewish neighborhoods that, by the 1990s, stretched for more than ten miles. Although always a minority within Toronto's Jewish community, Orthodox Jews made up for their small size by creating a highly visible religious landscape along Bathurst that included synagogues, elementary and high schools, and, most relevant to this essay, a range of kosher groceries, butcher shops, bakeries, and restaurants. Toronto's extensive infrastructure dedicated to the kosher lifestyle was replicated across the United States and Canada in the metropolitan peripheries of dozens of North American cities. In places such as Teaneck, New Jersey; Brookline, Massachusetts; Silver Spring, Maryland; Oak Park, Michigan; Beverly Hills, California; and elsewhere, Orthodox Jews embraced the kosher lifestyle to express their upwardly mobile tastes within a religiously permissible framework.

Before embarking on this inquiry into the religious consumerism of suburban Orthodox Jews, however, it is important to clarify a number of issues about the concept of kashruth, or of "keeping kosher," which is among the most fundamental—but also misunderstood—parts of the Orthodox Jewish subculture. To start, kosher food is *not* food that is blessed by a rabbi. Rather, the laws of kashruth involve categories of foods that are and are not permissible according to Orthodox Jewish halakah, both as written explicitly in the Torah and as interpreted by rabbinical authorities. For example, permitted animals include only domestic and wild animals that chew their cud and have completely cloven hooves (for example, cow, goat, sheep, and deer). Animals with only one or neither of these characteristics are forbidden. All domesticated fowl are permitted, while all birds of prey are forbidden. One can eat fish that have both scales and fins (for example, tuna, salmon, and halibut) but not scavenger fish, shellfish, and other seafood.

In addition to the mere permissibility of animal or bird, kashruth is also determined by the way an animal is slaughtered. One must slaughter a kosher animal or bird (but not fish) in a ritually proper manner that involves cutting an animal's throat at a specific point using a specific type of knife. Common methods of killing, such as stunning or shooting, render even a permitted animal unfit for consumption. Once a ritually permitted animal is ritually slaughtered, its meat must be soaked, salted, drained, and rinsed of blood within a prescribed period of time. The entire slaughtering-salting-rinsing-packaging process must be supervised and approved by knowledgeable individuals who understand the extensive laws of kashruth. Any food that is not considered kosher is referred to as being *treyf*. Technical questions about kashruth apply to prepared and packaged foods as well, since the food prohibitions extend to animal by-products and derivatives. Because the thousands of additives, preservatives, flavorings, colorings, and production agents that are part of modern food technology are sometimes derived from nonkosher sources, these, too, must be specifically certified as kosher. Finally, the laws of kashruth also prohibit mixing dairy and meat products or even foods derived from dairy or meat sources.

The complexity of contemporary food production means that individuals can rarely ascertain the kashruth of any specific item on their own. Instead, large national kashruth organizations, such as the OU and the Organized Kashruth Laboratories (OK), supervise the production of national food brands. These large-scale supervisory organizations certify both that the food products contain permissible ingredients and that there was no mixture of dairy and meat ingredients. Many local Jewish communities also maintain their own kashruth supervisory organizations for local products, butchers, and kosher restaurants. To convey to consumers the status of a product, certifying agencies often place a small logo or marking on the product's label.[5]

That the laws of kashruth have so much technical detail is due to the development of modern food technology. The historical observance of kashruth presented far fewer problems for Jews of earlier generations. In the rural shtetls of Europe, Jewish families generally oversaw the entire production of their own food. Individuals slaughtered their own meat and poultry in the ritually proper manner or enlisted the services of the local *shohet* (ritual slaughterer). There was little concern about the kashruth of meat slaughtered by someone else, both because of the interpersonal familiarity of the shtetl and because the community could enforce strict religious standards. Moreover, because commercial food production was unknown, individuals who produced their own food could be sure of its kashruth.

In the urban neighborhoods of North American cities, the laws of kashruth were among the first rituals to be abandoned by immigrant Jews. Freed from the shtetl's communal pressures, immigrant Jews chose to eat what foods they wanted, when they wanted, and where they wanted. For those who chose to maintain the dietary rituals, several factors made the observance of kashruth difficult. For one thing, most Jewish immigrants lacked the space to raise their own animals; a tenement apartment, after all, made a poor barnyard. As a result, the personal supervision over the slaughtering process that was common in Europe was transferred to a third party. But whereas relying on someone else to do the slaughtering might have been acceptable in a small village, a person in a large, urban community did not know everyone and did not necessarily have immediate knowledge of a slaughterer's reliability. In addition, North American Jewish communities lacked the enforcement capabilities that European shtetl communities had; the religious freedom of the United States and Canada meant that no religious communal organization body could legally demand that all slaughterers be subject to rabbinical supervision.

In the absence of communal regulation, many butchers and meat merchants seized the opportunity to defraud the Jewish community. Most common, butchers sold lower-priced nonkosher meat as kosher meat, thus deceiving customers and obtaining an extra profit. "Kosher" butchers hung fake certificates attesting to the religious permissibility of the product. Some intentionally mis-led customers by using deceptive window signs. In Hebrew, the words *basar kasher* (kosher meat) are almost visually identical to the nonsense phrase *basar basar* (meat meat). Store owners who put the latter sign in a store window tech-nically told the truth—they *were* selling meat, after all—even though, in reality, many customers misread the signs and assumed the meat sold inside was kosher.[6] No standards of supervision or certification existed for manufactured goods either. Some manufacturers placed their own unsubstantiated claims for kashruth on the label, while others "cited personal endorsement by figures whose rabbinical status and personal qualifications may or may not have been identifiable."[7]

Standardization began to appear in the early 1920s, when the Union of Ortho-dox Jewish Congregations established the OU as a joint rabbinical-lay program of kashruth supervision to oversee local slaughtering and meat processing as well as commercial food manufacturing. The first company to place the trade-marked symbol—the letter "u" inside the letter "O," now known as the OU—on its label was the H. J. Heinz Company, which produced OU-supervised vege-tarian beans in 1923.[8] In some cities, groups of rabbis cooperated to ensure that properly slaughtered meat and poultry were available. In the 1930s, for example, a group of Orthodox Jewish rabbis in St. Louis formed the Va'ad Hoeir (city council) to provide a centralized kashruth certification service for local butchers. More common, however, was the situation in prewar Toronto, where Rabbis David Ochs, Myer Gruenwald, and Abraham Price each pro-vided his own supervision for specific butchers and stores. Because each rabbi had his own community of followers who trusted only their rabbi, this frag-mentation of supervision created divisiveness and even open conflict in the larger Orthodox Jewish community. Those Orthodox Jews who did not specif-ically follow one of these rabbis had little guidance in questions of kashruth, prompting a sense of frustration at the "petty politics" among those involved in the kosher food industry. In the words of one local businessman, it was personal "pride and prejudice" that kept Toronto's rabbis from getting "their house in order."[9]

Toronto's fragmented state of kashruth supervision began to change in the late 1940s, when a group of Orthodox Jewish communal leaders, together with several rabbis who were not formerly involved in kashruth supervision, formed the Division of Orthodox Synagogues as a branch of the Canadian Jewish Con-gress's Central Region (later known as the Council of Orthodox Rabbis, or COR). Over the next decade, the Orthodox Division slowly worked to create a comprehensive plan for the communal supervision of kashruth. Rabbis Gedalia

Felder and Nachman Shemen were selected as the Kashruth Council's chair and secretary-director, respectively. With the support of the other rabbis in Toronto's Orthodox Jewish community, the Kashruth Council took control of the inspection and certification of the city's butcher shops, slaughterhouses, and food stores. As announced in 1958, any store that was certified "kosher" would be given a sign to hang on the premises, and any packaged food approved by the council would have a small "COR" logo placed on the label. The new council also recognized the certification of those rabbis who already maintained their own separate supervision programs.[10]

Although the professionalization and expansion of kashruth supervision did not begin as a suburban phenomenon, it was important for the development of a suburban Orthodox Jewish community. First, these supervisory organizations helped to reinforce a developing consumerist identity among suburbanizing Orthodox Jews. When a series of incidents involving butchers who misrepresented the kashruth of their products occurred in the early 1960s, angry community leaders appealed directly to the kosher consumers rather than to the butchers and store owners who were at fault. A 1961 editorial in the *Canadian Jewish News* declared that there was "a need to reeducate the Jewish public regarding the laws and obligation and importance of kashruth." The following year another editorial urged consumers to take matters into their own hands and buy meat only from "reputable" dealers who dealt with Toronto's Kashruth Council. "It is up to the housewife" to win the "battle for *kashruth*," the editorial concluded.[11]

The emergence of centralized kashruth programs also eased the burdens of maintaining a kosher kitchen at a time when the management of the family's food consumption was the primary responsibility of suburban middle-class women. As one analysis of postwar suburbia explained, women were "responsible for buying supplies, for the smooth functioning of complicated mechanical gadgets which assist her to put the finishing touches to processed and semiprocessed foods; and above all, for the maintenance of proper nutritional standards as laid down by dieticians."[12] Even as the changing realities of middle-class life compelled Orthodox Jewish women to enter the workforce, the responsibilities of food preparation and the religious imperatives of the kosher dietary laws remained in place. Thus working Orthodox Jewish women were a ready and willing market for any developments that offered more convenient ways to obtain and prepare kosher food for their families.[13]

These developments included the rapid increase in the number of kosher food products available. In 1926, for example, the Union of Orthodox Jewish Congregations placed its OU label on products made by fewer than a dozen companies. By 1956 this total had increased to almost two hundred producers and over a thousand different individual products. Only seven years later, the

OU supervised more than two thousand products made by over 430 compa-nies.[14] Half a century later, the OU, the OK, and dozens of other supervisory agencies certified over nine thousand companies producing sixty thousand products, including some of the most popular and classic brand names, such as Oreo cookies and M&M candies.[15] With this expansion, Orthodox Jewish home-makers seeking to stock their pantries were no longer confined to the foods commonly associated with Eastern European immigrants, such as borscht, matzo balls, chopped liver, or anything with garlic and onions.[16] Kosher con-sumers could even choose kosher versions of nonpermissible foods; food tech-nologists produced soybean-based "Protose meats" that were meant to taste like ham, bacon, and other nonkosher beef products but were entirely acceptable. Again, it must be stressed that kashruth prohibitions are based on technical and legal categories of food. Although some might find the idea of eating fake ham as contrary to the spirit of the kashruth laws—and some might even argue that eating such foods violates the religious principle of not imitating non-Jewish behaviors—there is nothing ritually improper about these imitation foods. Fake bacon was perhaps an extreme example, but it reflected the extent to which kosher food had been transformed from a minor ethnic concern to a major com-mercialized industry.

Changes in the experience of kosher consumption extended out of the kitchen to the experience of shopping as well. Historically, kosher food was pur-chased in the traditional manner at small, corner grocery stores. Butchers would display their kosher meats and prepared foods in large refrigerator cases and assemble orders for customers individually. The few ready-to-buy prod-ucts were also specially assembled for the customer. As the general corner gro-ceries evolved to the large supermarket, the kosher store modernized as well.[17] At first, stores offered ready-to-eat take-out foods for customers wanting a break from cooking. "Why Waste Your Precious FUN TIME working over a hot stove?" asked a 1962 advertisement for Toronto's Rubenstein's Kosher Poultry Products, when Rubenstein's could provide "ALL YOUR FOOD ready pre-pared." Later, stores such as Stroli's in suburban Toronto, which claimed to be the city's first "self-service" kosher grocery store, allowed shoppers to fill their own baskets from several aisles of kosher products. Stroli's opening had fol-lowed on the heels of the opening of a kosher meat counter in the Steinberg's supermarket at the corner of Bathurst Street and Sheppard Avenue. Looking like the regular nonkosher meat counter, the kosher meat counter was super-vised by the COR and was closed on Saturdays and Jewish holidays. Because more grocery products bore kosher symbols, the Steinberg's kosher meat counter enabled shoppers to bypass the specialized kosher food stores alto-gether if they so chose.[18]

By the late 1960s Toronto's suburban Orthodox Jewish community had a variety of kosher shopping options, with over twenty-five different kosher establishments ranging from the large supermarket meat counters to smaller butcher shops and take-out storefronts.[19] The availability of kosher meat in regular grocery stores did not put the smaller, specialized kosher stores out of business. The market for kosher products in Toronto grew sufficiently large and diverse to support a range of store types. Many Jews simply preferred to shop in the all-Jewish environment, while some wanted to support Jewish entrepreneurs and others did not want to buy kosher food from a place that was open on the Sabbath (even if it was owned by non-Jews). In all probability, the presence of large and small stores that sold kosher meat and food helped Toronto's kosher consumers because it promoted competition, ensured a large range of products, and prevented any single store from having a monopoly position.

For suburban middle-class Orthodox Jewish consumers, then, the professionalization and standardization of kashruth meant that they could participate in the same consumerist trends as their nonkosher-consuming neighbors without abandoning their religious obligations. The COR or OU logos on food labels or in storefronts served as a religious equivalent to the Good Housekeeping Seal, communicating to consumers that a certain store or product was "approved." These instantly recognizable signs of kashruth meant that a consumer need not worry about a product's religious permissibility and could decide to purchase it based on other factors, such as taste, nutritional value, or convenience. Furthermore, the availability of such items as kosher television dinners and instant cake mixes gave the kosher homemaker the same flexibility as other suburban domestic managers. As one reporter explained in 1965, "The observant Jewish homemaker also wants preprocessed foods and she too can afford them." Like her non-Orthodox Jewish counterpart, an Orthodox Jewish housewife, not wanting to work over a stove and countertop all day, could now put together a meal for her family using ready-made and instant products without worrying about the permissibility of the ingredients contained inside.[20]

The Kosher Lifestyle

From the professionalization and commercialization of the kashruth industry, it was a short step to the creation of a broader kosher lifestyle that encompassed more than the basic staples of a kosher kitchen. Socioeconomic upward mobility was providing increasing amounts of disposable income for Orthodox Jews to expand their tastes for religious consumption. One example of this process was the growth of "gourmet" kosher foods such as Barton's Chocolates. Similarly, the kosher wine industry exploded in the mid-1980s with the introduction of wines that were not of the syrupy sweet Concord grape variety. In 1984 Israel's Golan Heights Winery marketed a kosher sauvignon blanc wine under the Yarden label. Kosher consumers took to the Yarden wine and to the other Golan and Gamla products issued by Golan. By the end of the decade, French, Italian, and Californian wineries had moved into the kosher wine market with consistently high-quality wines of all types. By the 1990s kosher wines were winning international wine competitions, and consumers responded. In 1989 over 180,000 cases of kosher wines were sold in the United States; by 1994 this number had more than doubled to over 365,000 cases.[21] Like the kosher food industry, kosher wine makers had their eyes on both the Jewish and non-Jewish consumers. Most of the new gourmet kosher wines had very non-Jewish-looking designs, with the kosher certification symbol often placed in tiny print in a corner of the label. Even the traditional sweet wines were repackaged. In a classic example of consumer-oriented marketing, Kesser Wines noted that its sweet Concord grape wine was made on "the western end of Long Island," a description that evokes far more romantic images than "Brooklyn."

For many Orthodox Jews, however, the major affirmation of material success and the key transformation of the kosher lifestyle came with the kosher restaurant and the experience of "eating out." In pre–World War II immigrant Jewish neighborhoods, restaurants often had more of an ethnic flavor than a religious one. Many "Jewish" restaurants served traditional eastern European fare such as stuffed cabbage and a delicatessen provided a Jewish atmosphere for socializing. Often the food served was not explicitly *un*kosher, but neither was it supervised by any rabbinical authority; a restaurant might have served stuffed cabbage with kosher meat while also offering bagels and cream cheese, thus violating kashruth prohibitions against serving dairy and meat food together. These establishments conducted their own supervision, and customers relied on the knowledge and honesty of owners not to use forbidden ingredients.

By the late 1950s, however, the changes in the kosher food experience inside the Orthodox Jewish home began to influence Orthodox Jewish eating habits outside the home. Increasingly, this community wanted religiously acceptable places to eat that also befit their newfound status as upwardly mobile consumers. In 1961, advertisements for Toronto's first kosher restaurant in the suburban neighborhoods reflected this religious consumption need. Named Sova, Hebrew for satisfaction, this "elegant" restaurant was touted as a "rendezvous of the elite," with food that was "lauded by gourmets." An Orthodox Jewish community leader expressed a similar sentiment, declaring that Sova filled the Orthodox Jewish community's "aspiration" for a "modern, deluxe, strictly kosher restaurant."[22] Over time, more kosher restaurants joined Sova and tapped into a market of religious consumption. By the late 1970s Toronto's kosher consumers had over fifteen restaurants from which to choose. By 1999 there were more than thirty.

Together with the growing numbers of bakeries, butcher shops, and take-out food stores, Toronto's new kosher restaurants testified to the socioeconomic maturation of the suburban Orthodox Jewish community. As eating out had become an everyday part of suburban consumerist society, Orthodox Jews no longer found religious dietary restrictions an impediment to participating in this trend. For businesspeople, kosher restaurants offered a religiously preferable alternative to eating cold salads in a nonkosher eatery. For homemakers, kosher restaurants provided another option in the growing array of alternatives for domestic religious consumption. The expanding kosher restaurant market also reflected a growing sophistication and awareness among suburban Orthodox Jews of their consumer power. Even though they desired such kosher dining establishments, the suburban Orthodox Jewish community by no means acted as unthinking automatons who supported every restaurant just because it was kosher. During a brief period of time during the mid-1970s, for example, several kosher restaurants in Toronto opened and closed in quick succession. Reviewers in the local Jewish press explained that most of these failures stemmed from a poor sense of consumer relations. For example, the Kosher Pizza House, "not the most attractive place," was "seedy" and "decrepit," with a "decor [that] is totally uninspiring." Hagalil Restaurant, a short-lived establishment that sold Israeli and Chinese food, dished "out pedestrian fare that will wilt taste buds." These restaurants failed because they "tended to relax their quality control in the mistaken belief that observant Jews, as a captive group, have no other options." In reality, suburban Orthodox Jewish consumers had a very powerful option: to "stay at home and cook" rather than support unappealing restaurants simply for the sake of having kosher eateries.[23]

By the 1980s the kosher restaurant industry had stabilized and grew at a steadier rate than it had during the decade before. A wider range of menu styles appeared, such as kosher Chinese, Moroccan, and Yemenite restaurants, and those that opened generally lasted longer than had their predecessors. Kosher pizza shops also sprouted, as Toronto joined with other Jewish communities in the Orthodox Jewish affinity for permissible versions of the stereotypical North American fast food. In fact, to many Orthodox Jews, being able to stop in at a pizza parlor and pick up a slice or two of greasy kosher pizza epitomized the kosher consumerist lifestyle. As Edward Shapiro has argued, the popularity of such religiously acceptable suburban eateries "disclosed an impulse toward cultural amalgamation as the Orthodox strove to combine the best of the Jewish and outside world." In Shapiro's estimation, "the consumption of [kosher] haute cuisine . . . was in itself a secular act."[24] But perhaps the exact opposite is a better interpretation: kosher consumerism was a *religious* act. After all, what was striking about the development of the kosher lifestyle was that it was a *kosher* lifestyle. The suburban Orthodox Jewish community might have developed food habits and restaurant tastes drawn from the secular suburban world, but these habits and tastes remained adaptations nonetheless. The creation of a kosher lifestyle and broader styles of religious consumption reflected Orthodox Jews' desires not to assimilate or to shed their religious practices but to maintain their religious observances.

Having expanded its consumption activities to kosher restaurants, the suburban Orthodox Jewish community soon turned to other outlets for its new-found kosher lifestyle, including hotels, resorts, and vacation tours that provided kosher foods to patrons. Kosher hotels were already a part of Orthodox Jewish culture in some parts of North America. Outside of New York City, for example, a number of hotels operated along the Atlantic shore and in the Catskill Mountains, serving kosher food and maintaining a generally religious atmosphere for observant Jewish guests.[25] Starting in the 1960s and 1970s and booming in the 1980s and 1990s, a new form of kosher hotels appeared. This model involved entrepreneurs temporarily taking over nonkosher hotels and resorts and providing kosher services for a limited period of time, often during the Passover holiday. Passover was a particularly popular (and profitable) time for the kosher hotel business because of the holiday's comprehensive food restrictions.[26] Staying in a kosher for Passover hotel and receiving three meals a day (plus endless dessert buffets, tearooms, and snack bars) for an entire week proved attractive to families—especially housewives who were familiar with the extensive housecleaning and food preparation associated with the holiday.[27] Although Miami Beach housed many of the original kosher for Passover hotels, others opened in Hawaii, the Caribbean, Israel, and elsewhere around the world; for the 2001 Passover holiday, more than fifty thousand hotel rooms were available for kosher for Passover vacations worldwide.[28] Although many hotels catered to families, the kosher vacation industry also began to focus on the market of unmarried people, and hotels and tours touted the opportunities to meet potential spouses within a "kosher" environment. One could now take an Alaskan cruise, a tour of Europe, or even an African safari with a full-service menu of kosher food.[29]

Colin Campbell once characterized modern consumption as an "insatiability which arises out of a basic inexhaustibility of wants themselves."[30] This was equally true for the kosher lifestyle; the expansion of religious consumption developed a momentum of its own as middle-class and upper-middle-class suburban Orthodox Jews developed new tastes to match their socioeconomic standing. Thus from restaurants and hotels, religious consumerism moved to other nonfood areas. Orthodox Jewish clothing styles, for example, changed. Specialized boutiques opened in many cities selling stylish hats and wigs to Orthodox Jewish women who were required by religious halakah to cover their hair. Among centrist Orthodox Jewish youth, the yarmulke, the head covering worn by Orthodox Jewish males, became a fashion statement. Colorful and intricately designed yarmulkes were prized by teenagers for their stylish presentation, while leather yarmulkes with cartoon characters or favorite sports team logos painted on were popular with younger boys. This commercialization of yarmulke fashions permitted an Orthodox Jewish boy to fulfill his obligation to cover his head while remaining connected to the secular world of pop culture.[31]

In many communities, the development of the kosher lifestyle led to the creation of specialized Yellow Pages targeted at suburban Orthodox Jewish consumers. In the early 1990s the *Smart Shopper's Guide* in Toronto began publishing a quarterly directory of businesses and services oriented to the city's Orthodox Jewish community. The guide included advertisements for kosher caterers and Jewish bands, wig and hat stores, sterling silver importers, and kosher restaurants. Many of the advertisements explicitly appealed to the consumerist tendencies of Toronto's Orthodox Jews. "Need to outfit your cottage?" asked an advertisement for Royal Linen, in a direct acknowledgment that Toronto's Orthodox Jews were as likely as other Canadians to own a summer vacation home. Another advertisement suggested that although Orthodox Jews have a custom to immerse new dishes and utensils in a special *mikveh* (ritual bath), they might also be willing to pay someone else to perform this ritual. The owners of Dunkin' Dishes—a name that cleverly played off the more prominent chain of doughnut stores—offered to "toivel [immerse] your dishes so you don't have to."[32] The success of publications like the *Smart Shopper's Guide* led others to undertake even larger projects, such as the *Toronto Community Directory*, first published in 1994. The directory featured "a residential listing of the Orthodox Jewish community, as well as a listing of the many professional, commercial, and retail establishments which flourish in our midst." The 1995 directory made even more explicit its target market, explaining that the listed businesses included "only Shomer Shabbos businesses." As if to emphasize the inward focus of this marketing plan, the directory urged readers to "Support Your Community, No One Else Will."[33]

Religious consumerism also infiltrated the world of Jewish music and media. The growth of folk and other alternative forms of music received a Jewish twist in the early 1960s by Rabbi Shlomo Carlebach, who almost single-handedly created a new form of Jewish music that combined traditional Hasidic melodies with modern musical styles. Carlebach's infectious tunes proved most popular with Jewish youth, and by the 1970s Jewish teenagers began to copy Carlebach's styles. In Toronto, for example, the Shma Yisroel (Listen, Israel) band began in 1974 among a group of students at the Community Hebrew Academy. Although looking very much like a typical teenage "garage band," Shma Yisroel was as apt to play Carlebach's popular wedding song, "Od Yishama," as to bang out Led Zeppelin's "Stairway to Heaven." Carlebach-influenced music grew in popularity in the next three decades in both North America and Israel. Tapes and compact discs recorded by artists such as Mordechai Ben-David and Avraham Fried and groups such as the Miami Boys Choir took Carlebach's style and expanded and redefined it for a digital age. Recordings of such *simha* (lit., happiness, refers here to a celebration, often connected to the life cycle, such as a wedding) music were as professional as any secular recording, and the live shows were equally slick and well presented. In Toronto and in other cities, *simha* music radio shows appeared in the 1990s, replete with advertisements from kosher butchers and Jewish bookstores, providing yet another testimony to the market of Orthodox Jewish consumers.

None of these developments could have happened had the Orthodox Jewish market not been both economically able and religiously interested in supporting such kosher lifestyle activities. The economic ability stemmed from changes in the occupational trajectories of Orthodox Jews, moving from independent businesspeople and self-employed professionals in the 1950s into the financial and technological corporate world in the 1990s. In the 1950s working for oneself avoided exposure to potentially anti-Semitic work environments, which was not uncommon in a Protestant-dominated corporate culture. Self-employment also permitted one to create a work schedule that did not conflict with the Orthodox Jewish observances of the Sabbath and Jewish holidays. To help Orthodox Jews circumvent possible clashes between work and religion, a 1952 article in the national Orthodox Jewish magazine, *Jewish Life*, titled "Careers for the Sabbath Observer," suggested careers such as architecture, optometry, engineering, social work, and teaching, all of which offered scheduling flexibility. For example, because optometrists regulated their own hours and rarely faced emergencies, "the *Shomer Shabboth* (Sabbath Observant Jew) should encounter few difficulties" in this career path. Of course, finding a religiously compatible career choice was only half of the equation, since like their non-Orthodox counterparts throughout middle-class suburban society, Orthodox Jews wanted jobs that offered economic growth potential. Thus the *Jewish Life* article on careers noted that in 1952 skilled architects could earn an annual income of $15,000 to $25,000 and optometrists from $4,000 to $20,000 (depending on location and practice).[34] The message was clear: being a religiously observant Jew need not interfere with socioeconomic upward mobility.[35]

By the 1980s and 1990s the diversification of corporate America meant that Orthodox Jews were increasingly found in companies once closed to them. The economic boom on Wall Street and the explosion of the high-tech industry made the Orthodox Jewish executive who earned in the high six figures not uncommon. Along with this newfound presence in the corporate world, Orthodox Jews found their religious traditionalism far less controversial or even detrimental. The popularity of flextime meant that an Orthodox Jew who had to leave early on Friday to be home before the Sabbath could easily make up the hours on another day of the week. Even taking off a day for a Jewish holiday became far less troublesome. And the availability of kosher food, whether in restaurants or the grocery store, made business lunches and other corporate functions more manageable for workers wanting to maintain their kosher diet.

From the religious side of things, the expansion of the kosher lifestyle is not only a reflection of the suburban Orthodox Jewish community's success in transmitting a core religious practice from generation to generation but also a reflection of the increasing stringency of Orthodox Jews in all matters of religious activity. Historian Haym Soloveitchik has argued that this elevation of "religious stringency," or *humra*, was due to a loss of "mimetic culture" among traditionalist Jews. Whereas in the European shtetl, and to a degree in immigrant urban neighborhoods, traditions were learned from one generation to another mimetically, or by copying, contemporary Orthodox Jews learn rituals "by the book." Because textual sources often quote multiple opinions on specific practices, Orthodox Jews will often adhere to the strictest rulings to ensure that they would not be violating the "right one" (whichever it might be). The result is a tendency toward maximum strictness in observance.[36] As it pertains to the kosher lifestyle, this is manifest in the increasing adoption of such observances as *halav yisrael* (lit., Jewish milk, refers to practice of using only milk or milk products that were produced entirely by Jews).[37] Another popular stringency is the practice of *gebrokts*, a Yiddish term referring to the practice of cooking of Passover matzo with water. (Because of the very strict prohibitions against consuming leavened products on Passover, some Orthodox Jews will not even mix already-baked matzo with water to limit any possibility of leavening.) Although the particular minutiae pertaining to *gebrokts* are not relevant in this discussion, the point is that this is an increasingly prevalent practice among Orthodox Jews who a generation or two earlier would not have worried about this. The popularity of such stringencies is such that one can find many advertisements for kosher restaurants and Passover resorts that proudly declare how they serve "only *halav yisrael*" and are entirely "*gebrokts*-free" so as to ensure that they will attract even the strictest of kosher consumers.

Not surprisingly, the merging of religious strictness with suburban consumerism led many to wonder if religious consumerism had gone too far. As early as 1961, an article in *Jewish Life* chided the Orthodox Jewish community for its commercialization of the holiday of Hanukkah, which was rapidly becoming the "Jewish Christmas." The proliferation of "numerous novelties, cards, display materials" as well as the "endless variety of *menorahs* [candelabra]— bubbling menorahs, plastic menorahs for indoor and outdoor use, decorative menorahs, musical menorahs, and so on and on" had reduced the holiday to a "businessman's dream" and denuded it of any real religious meaning.[38] Two decades later, an Orthodox Jewish rabbi questioned the value of integrating religious and modern styles when such synthesis resulted in little more than "Jewish men with yarmulkes dancing at fashionable discos."[39] In a similar vein, an article in *Tradition*, the journal of the centrist Orthodox Rabbinical Council of America, asked simply, "Is Club Med Kosher?" While it was laudable, the article's author explained, that Orthodox Jews sought to adhere strictly to the ritual laws of kashruth even when on vacation, it was less clear whether one should even take such vacations in the first place.[40]

Through the 1980s and 1990s, as the Orthodox Jewish world moved rightward, the debates over consumerism increased. In the late 1980s a controversy arose in New York City over the kashruth certification of the Glatt Yacht. Marketed as a kosher version of Manhattan dinner cruises, the Glatt Yacht offered fine dining and dancing on the Hudson River. For the Kof-K agency, the organization that supervised the Glatt Yacht, the dining was fine but the dancing was not. It threatened to withdraw the certification unless the boat ended the dancing; nothing, however, was said about the food that was served. Those who supported the boat argued that a kashruth question should be solely about the food and its permissibility. Opponents claimed that a kashruth agency's stamp of approval of a restaurant implies an endorsement of *all* activities in that restaurant, and because the Kof-K did not approve of the mixed dancing, it had every right to withdraw certification. At stake, of course, was not the particular certification of the Glatt Yacht, which went and found another agency to provide supervision, but the concept of Glatt Yachts in general. Were dinner cruises, like Club Meds, kosher? Should Orthodox Jews partake of dining and dancing overlooking the Manhattan skyline?

Even the popularity of hotels for Passover raised eyebrows, setting off a "debate about whether a ready-made Passover dilutes tradition, cheats the children, or neglects the whole notion of commemorating the holiday with personal sacrifice."[41] As one Orthodox Jewish author argued, "Rather than going off to vacationing hotels with their country club activities, one should spend these holy periods together with family, the element of which the Jewish nation is built." In short, whether on a dinner cruise or at a hotel for Passover, kashruth is a "package deal. It includes the food . . . the entertainment, and all other activities. If there is mixed dancing or any dancing that violates the *Halacho*, even though you may not participate in the activity, you cannot be a guest in such a place."[42] Such admonishments, however, were a case of too little, too late; religious consumption had become an integral part of the North American suburban Orthodox Jewish experience.

Ironically, even as debates continue within Orthodox Jewry over the limits of kosher consumerism, the secular world has come to accept and even embrace all things kosher. Today, Orthodox Jews are a minority of the more than fourteen million consumers of kosher food products in North America.[43] For non-Jewish consumers, the designation "kosher" represents "quality," "healthful," and "good-for-you." Some consumers seek out kosher food for religious reasons. Observant Muslims, for example, buy kosher certified food knowing it contains no non-*halal* ingredients. Seventh-Day Adventists rely on kosher food labeled "pareve" because they know that it contains no animal ingredients. Other nonreligious vegetarians buy kosher food for the same reasons. Lactose-intolerant consumers look for the "pareve" notation on foods because they can be assured that the food has no dairy ingredients. And millions of others simply assume that because a rabbi or organization oversees the preparation process, it must meet some level of quality or healthfulness. The reality is, of course, that kosher food in no way implies healthy food, and it is likely that Orthodox Jews become far more excited by newly certified M&M's and Milky Way bars than they do by kosher tofu or granola products.

The evolution of the kosher lifestyle, then, points to a major transformation in the suburban Orthodox Jewish experience. The geographical relocation to suburbia and the socioeconomic upward mobility that accompanied this movement turned Orthodox Jews from a minor religious community into a desirable consumerist "market." The change in kashruth supervision from small-time individual rabbis to multimillion-dollar international supervisory organizations, the emergence of kosher restaurants and vacation packages, the growth in "kosher" music and multimedia, and the widespread secular acceptance of kashruth as a marketing tool all confirm Edward Shapiro's notion that the "classical sociological relationship between Orthodoxy and social status and affluence" has been "turned on its head" in the postwar period.[44] No longer relegated to the margins of the Jewish community and the even further margins of secular society, Orthodox Jews and their religious practices have become mainstream. Even when most consumers are likely unaware of the reasons for an "OU" on a food label, the fact that a label even has such a marking in the first place proves that two-thousand-year-old religious practices could mesh quite well with material consumerism of the late twentieth century. Religious consumerism, in the Orthodox Jewish form at least, thus represents an important way in which suburban commercialism and religious traditionalism fuse into a single idea.

Notes

I would like to thank Diane Winston and John Giggie for helping to shape the ideas and structure of this essay. Thanks also go to Mary Mapes for her helpful comments and to Judith Snowbell Diamond for her support and encouragement. A version of this essay appears in my book, *And I Will Dwell in Their Midst: Orthodox Jews in Suburbia* (Chapel Hill: University of North Carolina Press, 2000).

1. Morris Freedman, "Orthodox Sweets for Heterodox New York: The Story of Barton's," *Commentary* (May 1952): 472–480.

2. Ibid., 478.

3. Two of the more famous works that adopted this position include Will Herberg, *Protestant, Catholic, Jew: An Essay in American Religious Sociology* (Garden City, N.Y.: Anchor Books, 1955); William H. Whyte, *The Organization Man* (New York: Touchstone, 1956). Whyte opined that "when a couple moved from the Ozarks, they were likely to join the Methodist church rather than the Holiness church from back home" (301). Herbert Gans's analysis of Levittown similarly dismissed traditionalist religion's presence in suburbia, even as it was clearly evident that people were joining these kinds of congregations. Herbert J. Gans, *The Levittowners: Ways of Life and Politics in a New Suburban Community* (New York: Pantheon Books, 1967).

4. See, for example, Marshall Sklare, *Conservative Judaism: An American Religious Movement* (Glencoe, Ill.: Free Press, 1955); and Nathan Glazer, *American Judaism* (Chicago: University of Chicago Press, 1957).

5. For further explanations of the laws of kashruth, see Yacov Lipschutz, *Kashruth: A Comprehensive Background and Reference Guide to the Principles of Kashruth* (New York: Mesorah, 1988).

6. For a history of kashruth supervision problems, see Harold P. Gastwirt, *Fraud, Corruption, and Holiness: The Controversy Over the Supervision of Jewish Dietary Practices in New York, 1881–1940* (Port Washington, N.Y.: National University Publications, 1974).

7. Saul Bernstein, *The Orthodox Union Story: A Centenary Portrayal* (Northvale, N.J.: Jason Aronson, 1997), 92.

8. Union of Orthodox Jewish Congregations of America, Department of Public Relations, "Heinz to Be Honored for Being First Company to Debut Kosher Symbol," press release, May 25, 1999.

9. *Jewish Standard*, May 1, 1952.

10. *Jewish Standard*, March 1, 1958; *Canadian Jewish News*, April 19, 1989 [hereafter *CJN*]. For similar stories on the development of other community kashruth programs, see Louis Engelberg, "Kashruth Is a Community Program," *Jewish Life* 16, no. 5 (June 1949): 34–37; and Arnold J. Miller, "They Did It in Worcester," *Jewish Life* 18, no. 1 (September–October 1950): 27–33.

11. *CJN*, April 28, 1961; September 28, 1962.

12. John R. Seeley, R. Alexander Sim, and E. W. Loosley, *Crestwood Heights: A Study of the Culture of Suburban Life* (New York: Basic Books, 1956), 45.

13. For a recent discussion of Orthodox Jewish women in the workforce, see Nina Siegal, "Working World Grows for Orthodox Women," *New York Times*, January 4, 2001. Even as early as the mid-1950s, Orthodox Jewish magazines recognized the trend toward women entering the workforce. See Walter Duckat, "Careers for the Sabbath Observant," *Jewish Life* 20, no. 1 (September–October 1952): 16–21.

14. Union of Orthodox Jewish Congregations of America, press release, December 1963, Yeshiva University Archives, Benjamin Koenigsberg Papers, Folder 9/5.

15. http://www.koshertodayonline.com/resourcecenter/charts/sld006.htm>; and <http://www.koshertodayonline.com/resourcecenter/charts/sld004.htm>. March 26, 2001. Data provided by www.koshertodayonline.com, a division of Integrated Marketing Communications, Inc.

16. For an extensive discussion of the Jewish affinity for spicy foods, and Chinese foods specifically, see Gaye Tuchman and Harry Gene Levine, "New York Jews and Chinese Food: The Social Construction of an Ethnic Pattern," *Journal of Contemporary Ethnography* 22, no. 3 (October 1993): 382–407.

17. For a discussion of the impact of supermarket chains on local and ethnic grocery stores in the 1920s and 1930s, see Lizabeth Cohen, *Making a New Deal: Industrial Workers in Chicago, 1919–1939* (Cambridge: Cambridge University Press, 1990), 106–120.

18. *CJN*, June 27, 1962; February 23, 1968; September 22, 1967.

19. Kashruth Council of Toronto, *Kashruth Directory* (1968), Ontario Jewish Archives.

20. James Donner, "The Food Revolution and Kashruth," *Jewish Affairs* (November 1965): 18, in Yeshiva University Archives, Benjamin Koenigsberg Papers, Folder 10/1.

21. Howard G. Goldberg, "Slaves No More to Sweet Wine," *Jerusalem Report* (April 20, 1995), 56–57; Michael Ben-Joseph, "Renaissance: The Revival of Israel's Wine Industry," *Jerusalem Report* (August 2, 1999), 27–36.

22. *CJN*, March 10, 1961; March 17, 1961; July 28, 1961.

23. *CJN*, July 11, 1975; July 18, 1975; July 25, 1975; January 24, 1980.

24. Edward S. Shapiro, *A Time for Healing: American Jewry Since World War II* (Baltimore: Johns Hopkins University Press, 1992), 182.

25. For a history of kosher resorts and summer "bungalow" colonies, see Stephan Kanfer, *A Summer World: The Attempt to Build a Jewish Eden in the Catskills, from the Days of the Ghetto to the Rise and Decline of the Borscht Belt* (New York: Farrar, Straus, and Giroux, 1989).

26. On Passover, one is forbidden to eat any form of leavened food that contains flour, grain, or grain by-product, a restriction that eliminates most foods eaten during the year. Instead, one must eat only specially supervised "Kosher for Passover" food. In addition, because one must not even see or own forbidden leavened food products during the week of Passover, traditionally observant Jews clean their entire house to remove even crumbs that are hidden from sight. Kitchens are scoured and *kashered* (made kosher) for Passover, and special Passover dishes and utensils are used during the week. With all the cleaning and other preparations that precede Passover, it is not difficult to understand the popularity of Passover hotel packages.

27. *New York Times*, April 27, 2000.

28. "Kosher Today Newsletter, 26 March 2001," <http://www.koshertodayonline.com/weeklynews.htm>. March 26, 2001.

29. See an early advertisement for a kosher vacation tour to Puerto Rico by a company called "Orthodox Tours," in *CJN*, August 5, 1966.

30. Colin Campbell, *The Romantic Ethic and the Spirit of Modern Consumerism* (London: Basil Blackwell, 1987), 37.

31. *New York Times*, April 19, 2000.

32. *Smart Shopper's Guide*, June 1996: 9; *Smart Shopper's Guide*, September–October 1996, 55.

33. *Toronto Community Directory, 5754*; *Toronto Community Directory, 5755*.

34. Duckat, "Careers for the Sabbath Observant."

35. Even in the late 1990s Sabbath-observant Jews still sometimes faced difficulties in balancing work and religion. For a personal account of this negotiation, see Alan J. Borsuk, "Old Fashioned Jew, Old Fashioned Reporter," *Nieman Reports* 51, no. 3 (fall 1997): 15–17.

36. Haym Soloveitchik, "Rupture and Reconstruction: The Transformation of Contemporary Orthodoxy," *Tradition* 28 (1994): 64–130.

37. There is a great deal of debate over the restrictions of *halav yisrael*. The main reason given for this observance is that at one time, dairy farmers would mix nonkosher milk (say, from a pig) into the cow's milk. As a result, one should only use milk that came from a reliable Jewish source. Today, many hold the opinion that because all milk produced in the United Sates is regulated by government agencies, there is no chance of nonkosher products being mixed into the cow's milk; therefore, all milk has the status of *halav yisrael*, even if it is not actually produced by Jews. Others hold a stricter opinion that even government-regulated milk is not acceptable and that one still needs to obtain the specially supervised milk.

38. Louis M. Tuchman, "Chanukah—or Jewish Christmas?" *Jewish Life* 29, no. 1 (October 1961): 47–51. For a broader critique of all branches of North American Jewry, see Harry Loewy, "The Vulgarization of the American Jewish Community," *Jewish Life* 32, no. 5 (May–June 1965): 38–41.

39. Joshua Berkowitz, "The Challenge to Modern Orthodoxy," *Tradition* 33, no. 1 (winter 1984): 101–106.

40. David Singer, "Is Club Med Kosher?" *Tradition* 21, no. 4 (fall 1985): 27–36. A response to Singer's article with a larger discussion of leisure in Orthodox Judaism is found in Shalom Carmy, "Rejoinder: Synthesis and the Unification of Human Existence," *Tradition* 21, no. 4 (fall 1985): 37–51. For two critiques of the place of moral values within the world of observant Judaism, see Justin Hofmann, "Are We Teaching Our Values?" *Jewish Life* 22, no. 4 (March–April 1955): 16–19; and Irving H. Levitz, "Crisis in Orthodoxy: The Ethical Paradox," *Jewish Life* II (new series), nos. 2–3 (fall–winter 1977): 23–28. Joseph Berger, "Holy Hypocrites," *Moment* 25, no. 1 (February 2000): 50–55, 98–99, provides more recent analysis of cases of moral corruption within Orthodoxy.

41. *New York Times*, April 27, 2000.

42. Avrohom Blumenkrantz, *The Laws of Pesach: A Digest* (Far Rockaway, N.Y.: 2000), 397.

43. <http://www.koshertodayonline.com/resourcecenter/charts/sld007.htm>. March 26, 2001. Data provided by www.koshertodayonline.com, a division of Integrated Marketing Communications, Inc

44. Shapiro, *Time for Healing*, 184–185.

Contributors

Etan Diamond is a social historian with an interest in metropolitan growth and religious change. He is author of *And I Will Dwell in Their Midst: Orthodox Jews in Suburbia* (University of North Carolina Press, 2000). Diamond lives in Toronto with his wife and children.

John M. Giggie is an assistant professor of history at the University of Texas at San Antonio. He is currently completing a book entitled *God's Long Journey: African-American Religion and Modernity in the Mississippi Delta, 1875–1915.*

Fran Grace is an assistant professor of religious studies at the University of Redlands. She is author of *Carry A. Nation: Retelling the Life* (Indiana University Press, 2001) and is coauthoring a project on religion and sexuality.

Paul E. Ivey is an associate professor of art history at the University of Arizona. He is author of *Prayers in Stone: Christian Science Architecture in the United States, 1894–1930* (University of Illinois Press, 1999).

Kathryn Jay is an assistant professor of history and director of American studies at Barnard College. She is currently working on two book projects: a study of American Catholic family life after 1945 and an examination of the impact of Title IX legislation on women's sports.

P. C. Kemeny is an assistant professor of religion and humanities at Grove City College. He is author of *Princeton in the Nation's Service: Religious Ideals and Educational Practice, 1868–1928* (Oxford University Press, 1998).

Melani McAlister is an assistant professor of American studies at George Washington University. She is author of *Epic Encounters: Culture, Media, and U.S. Interests in the Middle East, 1945–2000* (University of California Press, 2001).

David Morgan is the Phyllis and Richard Duesenberg Professor in Christianity and the Arts, Christ College, Valparaiso University. He is author of *Visual Piety: A History and Theory of Popular Religious Images* (University of California Press, 1998) and *Protestants and Pictures: Religion, Visual Culture, and the Age of American Mass Production* (Oxford University Press, 1999).

Roberto Lint Sagarena is an assistant professor of religion at the University of Southern California. He is currently working on a book about the influence of religious culture on the development of California regionalism.

J. Terry Todd is an assistant professor of American religious studies in the Theological School and the Caspersen School of Graduate Studies at Drew University. He is writing a book about exhibitions of religion at the 1939–1940 New York World's Fair.

Judith Weisenfeld is an associate professor of religion at Vassar College. She is author of *African-American Women and Christian Activism: New York Black's YWCA, 1905–1945* (Harvard University Press, 1995) and the forthcoming *Through a Glass Darkly: On Religion, Race, and Gender in American Film, 1929–1950.*

Diane Winston is a program officer in religion at the Pew Charitable Trusts. She is author of *Red-Hot and Righteous: The Urban Religion of the Salvation Army* (Harvard University Press, 1999).

Index

activism: and civil rights, 203, 207, 219; and Nation of Islam, 203; and secularism, 135, 136, 144, 146; and Supply the Demand for the Supply, 178, 184–185, 191, 194, 195n2

advertising: aimed at Jews, 238, 239; and Bruce Barton, 46, 47; and Christian Science, 109, 116; and mass-produced image, 37, 39; and Carry Nation, 71n9, 72nn15, 17; and John Roach Straton, 78; and Billy Sunday, 51; and Supply the Demand for the Supply, 179, 185, 186–187. *See also* postcards; souvenirs

Africa, 214. *See also* Egypt

African Americans, 155–173, 175n26, 199–220

agency, 152n37, 178, 184. *See also* individual; self

alcohol, 77, 83, 84. *See also* temperance

Alemany, Joseph, 93

Ali, Muhammad, 200

Altman, Rick, 170

American Civil Liberties Union (ACLU), 145

Americanization, 50, 85, 100, 101

American Mercury (magazine), 140, 142

Anglo-Aryans, 96–97, 106n20, 112

Anglo-Saxons, 69, 70, 84, 85

Anthony, Susan B., 69, 72n27

Anti-Saloon League, 58, 84, 86n13, 145

anti-Semitism, 208, 218, 219, 225n65, 239. *See also* Jews

Arabs, 204, 205, 208, 218, 219

architecture: in California, 90, 91–104; and Christian Science, 108–110, 111, 117–129; classical, 109, 117, 118, 119, 122–123, 124, 125, 126, 127, 128; colonial, 128; Italian, 102; mission, 91, 93, 94, 95, 101, 102; and Native Americans, 105n7; in Santa Barbara, 104n1; Spanish revival, 91–92, 101, 102; and John Roach Straton, 75, 80–83

Arminianism, 50, 51

art, 43–47, 45–46, 53, 57, 213, 215, 218. *See also* dance; image, visual; literature; movies; music

Arthur, Timothy Shay, *Ten Nights in a Bar-Room,* 57

Asbury, Herbert, 134

assimilation. *See* Americanization

athletes, and Christianity, 47, 51, 53, 70

audience: for Black Arts movement, 211, 212; for Carry Nation, 59, 60–61, 66, 68–69; for John Roach Straton, 80

automobile, 75, 78, 79

avant-garde, 140, 142, 148

Bader, Robert Smith, 67

Baldwin, James, 219; "Letter from a Region in My Mind," 206

Ball, Walter S., 33

Baraka, Amiri, 200–201, 203, 210, 211, 213, 214–217, 221n10; *Black Fire,* 216; *A Black Mass,* 214–216, 217, 225n65

Barton, Bruce, 46–47, 48–49, 53–54, 56n24; *The Man Nobody Knows,* 47; *A Young Man's Jesus,* 47

Barton, William, 43

Barton's Chocolates, 227–228

Beard, Frederica, *Pictures in Religious Education,* 43

beauty, 109, 118, 126, 177, 178, 179, 180, 181, 185, 186, 187, 188, 194. *See also* fashion

Portland Community College Library